IMPERIAL CLASSROOM

Imperial Classroom

*Islam, the State, and Education
in the Late Ottoman Empire*

BENJAMIN C. FORTNA

OXFORD
UNIVERSITY PRESS

OXFORD
UNIVERSITY PRESS

Great Clarendon Street, Oxford OX2 6DP

Oxford University Press is a department of the University of Oxford.
It furthers the University's objective of excellence in research, scholarship,
and education by publishing worldwide in
Oxford New York

Athens Auckland Bangkok Bogotá Buenos Aires Cape Town
Chennai Dar es Salaam Delhi Florence Hong Kong Istanbul Karachi
Kolkata Kuala Lumpur Madrid Melbourne Mexico City Mumbai Nairobi
Paris São Paulo Shanghai Singapore Taipei Tokyo Toronto Warsaw
with associated companies in Berlin Ibadan

Oxford is a registered trade mark of Oxford University Press
in the UK and in certain other countries

Published in the United States
By Oxford University Press Inc., New York

British Library Cataloguing in Publication Data
Data available

Library of Congress Cataloging in Publication Data

Fortna, Benjamin C.
Imperial classroom: Islam, the state, and education in the late Ottoman Empire/
Benjamin C. Fortna.
p. cm.
Includes bibliographical references and index.
1. Education—Turkey—History—19th century. 2. Education—Turkey—History—20th
century. 3. Islamic education—Turkey. 4. Education and state—Turkey—History—19th
century. 5. Education and state—Turkey—History—20th century. 6. Turkey—History—
Tanzimat, 1839–1876. 7. Turkey—History—1878–1909. I. Title.
LA941.7 .F67 2002   379.561—dc21   2001035853
ISBN 0-19-924840-0

1 3 5 7 9 10 8 6 4 2

Typeset in Galliard CC
by Best-set Typesetter Ltd., Hong Kong
Printed in Great Britain
on acid-free paper by
Biddles Ltd, Guildford and King's Lynn

ACKNOWLEDGEMENTS

This book was written over a number of years and in several places. It is a pleasure to acknowledge the help and encouragement generously offered by so many along the way. The idea for this book emerged as a part of my graduate training at the University of Chicago, and is a revised version of my Ph.D. dissertation, completed under the supervision of Rashid Khalidi, with strong assistance from Richard Chambers and Şükrü Hanioğlu. It is difficult to imagine a more professional and congenial committee and I thank them for their continuing interest and support. While at Chicago I also benefitted enormously from the advice of Camron Amin, Cyrus Amir-Mokri, John Craig, Robert Dankoff, Cornell Fleischer, Michael Geyer, John Meloy, Nader Sohrabi, Mark Stein, and Mehmet Ulucan.

In Istanbul, where the main research for this book was undertaken, I enjoyed the scholarly company of Selim Deringil, Tony Greenwood, Karen Kern, David Roxburgh, Akşin Somel, and, again, Nader Sohrabi and Mehmet Ulucan. A temporary teaching position at Washington University in St Louis afforded me the opportunity to learn from colleagues and students alike, including Etem Erol, Indira Falk, Ahmet Karamustafa, and Tim Parsons.

I would like to thank the staffs of a number of libraries: the Regenstein Library of the University of Chicago; the Prime Ministry Archives (Başbakanlık Osmanlı Arşivi), the Istanbul University Rare Book Library, and the American Research Institute in Turkey Library, all in Istanbul; the National Library (Millî Kütüphane) in Ankara; and the School of Oriental and African Studies Library and the British Library in London. The photographs in this book are reproduced with the kind permission of the Istanbul University Rare Book Library and the British Library.

Several institutions provided material support along the way. A Fulbright-Hays dissertation research grant supported a year's stay in Istanbul. A Spencer Foundation Dissertation Fellowship for Research Related to Education not only supported the writing of much of my dissertation, but also brought me into contact with others working in the field of education whom I would not otherwise have met. A US

Department of Education Title IX Fellowship allowed me to complete the dissertation. Throughout my doctoral work I received support from the Kingsley Trust Association of New Haven, Conn., for which I am extremely grateful. Seminars organized on successive summers in Germany and America by the German American Academic Council and funded by the Social Science Research Council, New York, and the Wissenschaftskolleg, Berlin, provided the opportunity to think about my research in a broader framework and to benefit from the ideas and camaraderie of a highly engaging group.

In London my newfound colleagues at SOAS offered a welcoming and truly collegial environment. I thank Peter Robb and Ian Brown, successive Heads of the History Department, for all of their kindness and assistance in getting me started at SOAS and for protecting me from an excessive workload during my first years at the School. Other colleagues have been generous with both time and help. Among the many here to whom I am obliged, I mention Ali Ansari (now at Durham), Daud Ali, Laila Asser, Peter Colvin, George Dedes, Frank Dikötter, Wayne Dooling, Ulrike Freitag, Bill Hale, Gez Hawting, Colin Heywood, Nick Hostetler, David Morgan (now in Madison, Wisc.), John Parker, Richard Rathbone, Bengi Rona, and Charles Tripp. Special thanks go to Joy Lewis and Carol Miles for keeping the History Department functioning—and smiling. I would also like to thank the School's Publication Committee for an award to cover the costs of obtaining permission to publish the images in this book.

I have been fortunate to have recourse to the advice and encouragement of many colleagues in the fields of Ottoman and Middle Eastern history. I thank Camron Amin, Palmira Brummett, Randi Deguilhem, Elizabeth Frierson, Dan Goffman, Hasan Kayalı, Eugene Rogan, David Roxburgh, and Christoph Schumann for offering help on a variety of matters.

Several colleagues and family members have been kind enough to read and comment on various versions of this book, in whole or in part. They are: Robert Fortna, Sarah Fortna, Ulrike Freitag, Adeeb Khalid, Şerif Mardin, Mark Stein, Charles Tripp, and Pamela Young. While I have not acted on each of their many helpful suggestions, I thank them all for the many improvements they have made. I also thank the anonymous readers chosen by Oxford University Press; their comments were exceedingly helpful in preparing the final typescript for publication. Naturally, all errors, whether of omission or commission, are my own. I thank Ruth Parr, my editor, for her thorough professionalism and kindness, and all those at Oxford University Press, including Anne Gelling and Dorothy McCarthy, who have spent time on this book.

I would like to thank my family who have tolerated much from me over the years. My parents, Evelyn Nelson Carr Fortna and Robert Tomson Fortna, lovingly introduced me to many worlds, including the world of learning. As woefully inadequate recognition for all that they have given to me, I dedicate this book to them. I thank my brother Ned and my sister Page for their unfailing affection and sense of humor. I would also like to acknowledge the often overwhelming support of my parents-in-law, Laurie Malarkey Rahr and Guido Reinhart Rahr, Jr., and the warmness with which they accepted me into their family. Final thanks are reserved for my own family, especially for Sarah whose unflagging love and support have, more than anything else, made this book possible, and also for our three boys, Will, Nick, and Benjy, each of whom in his own way provides a constant source of inspiration.

To my parents
Evelyn Nelson Carr Fortna and Robert Tomson Fortna
with love and esteem

CONTENTS

LIST OF ILLUSTRATIONS

TABLE

MAP

LIST OF ABBREVIATIONS

BOA	Başbakanlık Osmanlı Arşivi
EI2	*Encyclopaedia of Islam*, 2nd edn.
İA	*İslam Ansiklopedisi*
IJMES	*International Journal of Middle East Studies*
IU	Istanbul University Rare Book Library
JAOS	*Journal of the American Oriental Society*
LC	Library of Congress
MEJ	*Middle East Journal*

Note: Abbreviations used in references to the archival sources on deposit at the BOA, IU, and LC collections are provided in the first section of the Bibliography.

NOTE ON TRANSLITERATION

For the sake of uniformity, words in Ottoman Turkish have been rendered into Latin script according to the system employed in the *Redhouse Yeni Türkçe–İngilizce Sözlük/New Redhouse Turkish–English Dictionary*, 12th edn. (Istanbul: Redhouse Press, 1991). Arabic words have been transliterated according to the system employed by *IJMES*.

Place-names familiar to Western readers have generally been given in their Anglicized version, thus "Istanbul" (and not İstanbul), "Aleppo" (and not "Halep"), and "Salonika" (and not "Selânik"). Likewise terms of Arabic, Persian, or Turkish derivation common enough to be found in an English dictionary are introduced with italic script but are not subsequently set off from the text. For example, the term "ulama," meaning the learnèd men of Islamic theology, appears thus (and not so as to preserve its original Arabic orthography, "'ulamā'.").

PREFACE

There are few who would argue with the notion that education has played a critical role in the creation of the modern world. Indeed, some scholars have identified modern education as the defining characteristic of the age. In the Islamic world, where learning has always carried particularly lofty status, the impact of the more comprehensive forms of education envisioned in modern schooling has assumed perhaps an even more transformative nature. It is difficult to imagine the modern Middle East without the ideological and social effects that education has putatively occasioned. Yet for all the undisputed importance of education, the reasons for its arrival and the ways in which it operated are only partially understood.

One of my chief aims in writing this book has been to explore and question some of the prevailing assumptions about education and its links with modernity. One of the most problematic tendencies, in my view, has been the extent to which education has been assigned its own motive force; it has frequently been treated as an outside agent, independent from local realities, and operating with its own pre-conceived trajectory and innate *modus operandi*. Relatively little attention has been paid to the processes by which imported educational concepts and instruments were integrated into indigenous traditions. Recognizing the distinction between the ways in which education is conceived and understood and the ways in which it operates seems especially important in the case of the late Ottoman Empire given the fact that much of its educational apparatus was based on Western European models. That the Ottoman school system served as the foundation for those of the post-Ottoman states in the Middle East and the Balkans only adds to the importance of understanding its complexities and seeing it in its proper context.

Throughout this book I have emphasized the extent to which Ottoman education reflected Ottoman imperatives. I hope to have demonstrated some of the ways in which key elements of what initially was a largely exogenous educational system were altered to conform with Ottoman assessments of what the empire required in, from Istanbul's perspective, an increasingly hostile atmosphere due to the acquisitiveness of the foreign powers, the aggressiveness of their missionaries, and the restlessness of neighbors and minority groups alike. I have tried to explain why late Ottoman educational policy changed in response to these trends. I describe the ways in which the ambitious late Ottoman educational endeavor was shaped by a combination of the fears these trends provoked and the hopes engendered by the essentially forward-looking nature of education itself. I then go on to analyze how such a change manifested itself in the schools of the late Ottoman state, ranging from the intentions with which they were built, to their architecture, daily regimen, discipline, and pedagogy. Analysis of such artifacts as the maps used to impart geographical knowledge and the textbooks intended to teach an overtly Islamic morality presents opportunities to attempt the wide gulf between the relatively rich material available about the state's educational agenda and the way it is perceived by those on its receiving end.

This raises the issue of source material. It is often said that Ottoman history has been both blessed and cursed by the massive information available from the state's perspective. The existence of the records of the Ottoman central bureaucracy is praised for allowing historians access to the inner workings of a sprawling state in considerable detail. This has been handled in a variety of ways, ranging from the fascinating to the mind-numbing. But the richness of the state-based archives has also meant that researchers have perhaps been less adventurous in the use of alternative material. This study relies largely on primary material produced by Ottoman officialdom, and thus must be counted as contributing to the problem in some way. My only defense is that I hope that I have uncovered new material and interpreted that previously available in new ways. There is one further point to mention: I have insisted, perhaps stubbornly so, on grounding my argument almost entirely on primary material produced during the period considered by this study. Thus I have used such sources as memoirs only rarely and somewhat reluctantly. Such selectivity is intended to guard against the inevitable historical, ideological, and cultural biases that necessarily creep into the retelling of events that occurred in a different era and, in the case of the late Ottoman period, within radically different political borders and realities. Most memoirs covering this period were written in the post-Ottoman period. Given the extent to which the successor states of the Ottoman Empire, whether in the Balkans, Anatolia, or the Arab lands, based a consider-able part of their justification on an anti-Ottoman rhetoric, the ambient conditions obtaining at the time this autobiographical material was written were even more prone to bias than this inherently tricky material normally occasions.

I must note, finally, that the appearance of my highly valued col-league Selçuk Akşin Somel's *The Modernization of Public Education in the Ottoman Empire, 1839–1908: Islamization, Autocracy, and Discipline* (Leiden: E J Brill, 2001) at a time when this book was already at the typesetters has meant that it cannot benefit from Dr Somel's thorough and, undoubtedly, excellent study. Seeing, for example, that his book contains a chapter based largely on memoirs and that it draws on his previous research on the primary level of schooling while my own is largely informed by developments at the preparatory level, I can only hope that readers will find our approaches complementary.

BCF

London

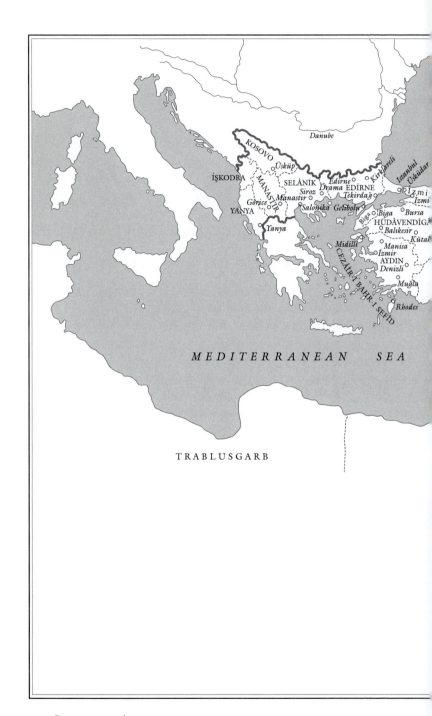

Ottoman provinces *c.* 1900

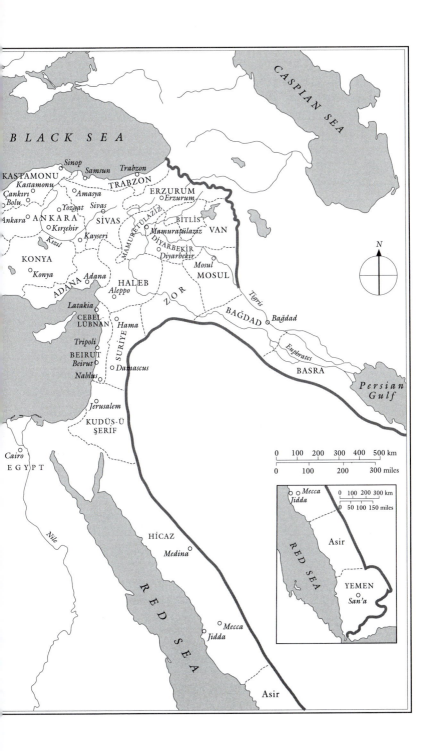

I

Education and Agency

INTRODUCTION

In recent years the conjunction of state, education, and Islam has sparked controversy. The headscarf issue has only been the most visible aspect of a broader and more trenchant disagreement about the place of religion in contemporary society. For many, both in the Islamic world and in the West, the divisive "return" of Islam to school classroom and university campus, areas assumed to be the preserve of secular progress and national homogenization, has been deeply troubling. Whether or not we agree with this reaction, the prevailing historical treatment supports such a pejorative, dismissive approach to Islam in the context of "modern" education. By turning a blind eye to the continuities in the relationship between Islam and modern learning, histories of the region have perpetuated the belief that the two are mutually exclusive. The dominant view suggests that in the transition from the Ottoman Empire to its largely secular successor states Islam was supposed to recede from the public sphere into a private and essentially vestigial position. New-style schools were meant to remove pedagogy from the religious environment, both physically and ideologically. In Turkey, heir to the core Ottoman lands and to much of its educational infrastructure, education has been vital to the modernizing agenda. The reappearance of Islam in Turkish education shocks precisely because its banishment has been central to the national project, a project informed by a strong sense of directionality. In unabashedly teleological fashion the histories of this period have traced the inexorable "processes" of Westernization, secularization, and modernization as they began in the eighteenth century, gathered strength in the nineteenth, and triumphed in the twentieth. The headscarf issue, like the rise of Islamist politics generally, is for many only an annoying sign that much of the country still lagged "behind" the progressive view. For others it offers a reminder that the prevailing historical record, not to mention the emplotment of the deeper national narrative, is gravely flawed.

The teleology inherent in late and post-Ottoman times has been supported by what one scholar has termed the "enormous condescension" of the prevailing wisdom.[1] Such patronizing has appeared in a cluster of related notions. One of the most persistent has been the view of the Ottoman Empire as the "sick man" of Europe, whose only hope for revival lay in Westernization as spelled out in the reforms of the Tanzimat period (1839–76), generally perceived as the first broad application of the Western cure outside the military sphere.[2] Particularly intriguing is the implicit assumption that, once administered, the course of the Western fix would necessarily retain its putatively constant, superior, and successful form, culminating ultimately in the secular Westernism epitomized by the Turkish Republic. Current struggles over the nature of public instruction in Turkey make it impossible for all but the most ardent secularists to ignore the fact that the dominant historical strain has failed to prepare us for today's fraught reality or, indeed, for anything other than a unidirectional understanding of modernity. As Nilüfer Göle's recent work on Turkey has revealed, Islam is equally productive of alternative modernities.[3] Closer to the topic at hand, Elisabeth Özdalga's recent research on the controversy surrounding the extension of mandatory education from five to eight years shows that, as was the case roughly a century ago, the fraught nature of Islam in Turkish education is once again at the forefront of the public

---

[1] Adeeb Khalid, personal communication, 30 June 1998. For an example of the way such condescension can be overturned in a related context, see his recently published study, *The Politics of Muslim Cultural Reform: Jadidism in Central Asia* (Berkeley: University of California Press, 1998). For the Ottoman Empire, see Selim Deringil, *The Well-Protected Domains: Ideology and the Legitimation of Power in the Ottoman Empire, 1876–1909* (London: I. B. Tauris, 1998).

[2] As the work of Butrus Abu Manneh and others has shown, the prevailing reading of the Tanzimat is itself subject to important reappraisal. See e.g. "The Islamic Roots of Gülhane," *Die Welt des Islams,* 34 (1994), 173–203.

[3] Nilüfer Göle, *The Forbidden Modern: Civilization and Veiling* (Ann Arbor: University of Michigan Press, 1997); "The Quest for the Islamic Self Within the Context of Modernity," in Sibel Bozdoğan and Reşat Kasaba (eds.), *Rethinking Modernity and National Identity in Turkey* (Seattle: University of Washington Press, 1997), 81–94.

agenda.[4] In her view, the military chose the issue of education precisely because it is considered so divisive in the current political atmosphere in Turkey.

This book elucidates the connections between the educational worlds of the late Ottoman Empire and the present day. It reveals that the contested quality of education in the late Republican period is best seen as a continuation of the battle for education—and for the direction that society should take—that began in the late Ottoman era but actually reflected long-standing Ottoman and Islamic practices, a continuity for which the prevailing historical treatment has left us ill prepared.

In the cause of fitting the ungainly body of late Ottoman history to the Procrustean bed of modernization theory, many purported anomalies have been rather elegantly amputated. This study seeks to account for some of the truncated parts of the corpus of late Ottoman history, such as the persistence of Islam in allegedly secular endeavors, the combative stance toward the empire's perceived enemies, the Western powers in particular, and the critical role of Ottoman agency in this period. Restoring the notion of agency is vital to overcoming the misperception that outside influences determined the "fate" of the late Ottoman Empire. The policies of the state were often reactive, its room for maneuver was clearly limited, and gaps existed between the ideal expectations and actual results, yet it is important to remember that Ottoman policy was committed to creating its own solutions. As the following chapters reveal, these solutions did not necessarily conform to Western models or Westernizing historical perceptions. Neither were they part of an exotic, Oriental, and ultimately Quixotic project, as has sometimes been assumed. It was informed by a very enlightenment notion of progress that relied heavily on Western European models but cut them with a strong dose of Ottoman and Islamic elements that were deemed capable of meliorating the deleterious side-effects of Western influence. The resulting fusion of influences and its experimental, transitory nature has been little appreciated because, I suggest, they have not conformed to the prevailing, directional view of

---

[4] Elisabeth Özdalga, "Education in the Name of Order and Progress: Problems Related to the Recent Eight Year Obligatory School Reform in Turkey," paper presented at the Annual Meeting of the Middle East Studies Association, 6 Dec. 1998, Chicago.

late Ottoman historiography. Recapturing the sense of Ottoman agency in the empire's educational agenda allows many of the supposed anomalies and overlooked aspects of this period to come to light.

An appreciation of Ottoman agency is key to rethinking the transition from the Ottoman to the post-Ottoman period. Once we have apprehended the fact that educational "reform" was not an external concept that inevitably "happened" to a passive Ottoman Empire, we can begin to explain many of the anomalies in the prevailing historical accounts. First, the competitive spirit of late Ottoman educational policy begins to make sense. Although initially reactive, the aggressive counterpunching that emerged in the Ottoman educational campaign reflected a vigor and a resourcefulness which has not received sufficient attention, for it failed to conform to the prevailing notions of Western influence and Eastern passivity. Meanwhile, government functionaries were busy altering both the form and function of their educational offerings so as to make them often unintelligible to those expecting vehicles for Westernization. Sometimes subtle, such as in the architectural ornament added to French-inspired school buildings, sometimes blatantly obvious, such as in the purging of "dangerous" Western content from the imperial curriculum, these changes represent, as we shall see, clear expressions of Ottoman agency.

New-style schooling provided the Ottoman state with a mission. Despite formidable financial constraints, the imperial bureaucracy mobilized a wide range of resources in order to disseminate its educational message. Together with such expected vehicles as the school, the teacher, and the textbook, the Ottoman project also mustered the Islamic men of learning—the *ulama*. They were charged with inveighing against the evils associated with competing educational institutions, with playing an important role in planning the curricula of the state schools, and with actually taking up positions in those institutions, clear evidence that the secular label the literature has routinely assigned to these schools is at best misleading.

Informing this increasingly combative notion of Ottoman educational policy was a near-utopian vision of the future that is difficult to imagine in our own day. This is especially germane in the English-speaking West where what passes for contemporary debate over the role of education in society has a tired quality that reflects the lost opportunities of countless reform initiatives. Enthusiastic claims to be the next "Education President" of the United States or to offer superior schooling to all children in Britain carry an increasingly hollow ring. Compounding the inherent pessimism about the role of Western-style education in the West, hindsight's verdict over a "doomed" Eastern empire presents a major impediment to appreciating the enthusiasm of the late Ottoman initiative. Optimism in the transformative power of new-style schooling energized the entire Ottoman political spectrum.[5] Not merely limited to the high-level state bureaucrats responsible for its implementation, it extended to petty functionaries, and opposition figures of all stripes, uniting radical positivists, conventional liberals, nationalists of all flavors, and Islamist thinkers. In spite of the empire's dire situation as the nineteenth century drew to a close (and the fourteenth Islamic century began), education in the abstract offered a semi-miraculous promise of deliverance. But if the concept of new-style education served as a shared panacea, it was the state's pragmatic fusion of the new pedagogy with Ottoman and Islamic elements that informed educational developments on the ground. The indigenous religio-cultural spirit was deemed critical to infuse the new education with an Ottomanness sufficient to keep the empire intact, indeed to help it thrive in the future. This combination of elements of "modernity" with those of "tradition" necessarily altered both as they were fused into a system that functioned across the breadth of the far-flung empire on a daily basis. In part, this book represents an attempt to understand the implications of such a fusion in spite of the theoretical and empirical barriers in the way of apprehending its complexity.

At the root of such an understanding must come the role of the individual. This should not be a radical statement, yet given the paucity of attention to the perforce various ways in which individuals respond to different materials and situations and, putting it more directly, the overemphasis on the collective, such a corrective insistence on the individual is nearly revolutionary. Part of the problem has been one of sources, including a predilection for analyzing school regulations. The easiest to obtain and read, these texts are abstract by their very nature, giving the false impression that students exist as generic vessels to be

---

[5] M. Şükrü Hanioğlu, *The Young Turks in Opposition* (New York: Oxford University Press, 1995), 12.

filled with learning, disciplined according to the rules, and moved along from one grade to the next in precise, predictable fashion. Needless to say, such sources offer little glimpse into what transpired within the actual schools. Among the most rewarding findings of the many hours I have spent in the Ottoman archives have been materials documenting disciplinary cases that reveal actual students and their superiors in historicized settings. Whereas the prescriptive texts emphasize the idealized power of the state, these real-life cases remind us of the fragility of its position as represented by individuals with their own foibles and shortcomings and as undermined by what Michel de Certeau has termed the subversion of the everyday.[6] These sources inform the discussion of school life in Chapter 4 and generally provide a much-needed corrective to the prevailing treatment of schools as vehicles of unbridled state discipline.

But that is only part of a larger problem that goes beyond the availability of source material. A particularly troublesome feature of the literature has been the tendency to emphasize the collective over the individual. This has meant that schooling is treated as a process with foregone conclusions, foremost among which is the notion that state education produced "cadres" of like-minded graduates who emerged with a similar worldview. While there is no denying that many of these young men developed common modes of thought, such as a proclivity for secularism and political activism, the extent to which these traits were universal must be seriously questioned.

The tendency to think of students as cohorts and not as individuals, however, reflects an inclination to think of education in an extremely deterministic fashion, what we might call the "mechanical engineering" approach to schooling. A constellation of factors, theoretical and logistical, has combined to shape this approach to education. First, there has been a penchant for the quantifiable, a tendency to collect data (counting schools, students, teachers, etc.)[7] and for treating the entire question of education as a problem to be solved. Open most accounts of education written in the 1960s and 1970s and you will find mechani-

---

[6] Michel de Certeau, *The Practice of Everyday Life*, trans. Steven Rendall (Berkeley: University of California Press, 1984).

[7] See e.g. Bayram Kodaman, *Abdülhamid Devri Eğitim Sistemi* (Ankara: Türk Tarih Kurumu Basımevi, 1988).

cally drawn organizational diagrams of the Ottoman and Turkish Republican school systems.[8] Such graphic representations create the impression of cohorts of pupils passing along the pyramid of education. Underlying this structural approach is an overweening privileging of the group over the individual, apparent in the wider literature on this period.[9] The broad range of potential human reactions to education rapidly becomes reduced to a dominant archetype; cohorts are treated as if they begin to act and think alike.[10] Here again, sources contribute to the problem. Quite apart from the methodological problems associated with writings produced in the dramatically altered post-Ottoman atmosphere that encouraged rejection of many things Ottoman, this collective approach has been based on an extremely small number of memoirs written by former students.[11]

By focusing on collective and individual Ottoman agency, I seek to reopen questions which have been considered closed. I argue for a nuanced rereading of the late Ottoman period, particularly as it informs our understanding of post-Ottoman history. I attempt to get beyond normative judgements and to see school life as necessarily conflicted and contested, and not as part of an inevitable process that

[8] See Andreas Kazamias, *Education and the Quest for Modernity in Turkey* (Chicago: University of Chicago Press, 1966), 268–9; Hasan Ali Koçer, *Türkiye'de Modern Eğitimin Doğuşu ve Gelişimi, 1773–1923* (Istanbul: Millî Eğitim Basımevi, 1970), 163. There is undoubtedly a connection between the elevated status of the engineer in Republican Turkey and the mechanical approach to education that has pervaded most of the writing on the subject.

[9] Şerif Mardin, "Projects as Methodology: Some Thoughts on Modern Turkish Social Science," in Sibel Bozdoğan and Reşat Kasaba (eds.), *Rethinking Modernity*, 64–80; Engin Deniz Akarlı, "Modernity and State–Society Relations in Late Ottoman History and Historiography," paper presented at the University of Chicago, May 1998.

[10] An exception to this can be found in Engin D. Akarlı, "Friction and Discord Within the Ottoman Government of Abdülhamid II (1876–1909)," *Boğaziçi Üniversitesi Dergisi— Humanities*, 7 (1979), 20.

[11] Fatma Müge Göçek, *Rise of the Bourgeoisie, Demise of Empire: Ottoman Westernization and Social Change* (New York: Oxford University Press, 1996), 74. For a discussion of a similar skewing with respect to the development of Arab nationalism, see Eugene L. Rogan, "The Political Significance of an Ottoman Education: Maktab 'Anbar Revisited," paper presented at the Syria III Conference, Bilad al-Sham: Processes of Identities and Ideologies from the 18th Century to the End of the Mandatory Period, Erlangen, 28 July–2 August 2000. My thanks to Dr Rogan for making this paper available to me prior to its publication.

itself aided and abetted the meta-narratives of Westernization, secularization, and modernization. Those concepts are far too unwieldy to be meaningful in anything more than the abstract.

This approach seems quite natural, yet it becomes critical when we recall the historical role assigned to state education in the prevailing treatment of imperial decline and national emergence. Education is invariably treated as an agent of various predetermined changes, as if schools perform a uniform and mechanical function. Yet from only the limited material available it is clear that this is a highly reductive and essentialized view of what is inevitably a complicated and varied set of interactions and reactions. Schools do not merely produce one sort of reaction among their students, who are therefore not to be thought of as cadres or cohorts, but as individuals who are as apt to respond differently as alike to the material and atmospheres to which they are introduced. The material I present in this book suggests that we need to look at a wide range of possibilities, including not only those we have been told late Ottoman schools encourage (questioning the political legitimacy of the ruler/government, inculcating a yearning for new modes of living, political thought, and socio-economic options) but also those that call into question the inevitably anti-regime tendencies assumed of student behavior. More important, we see clear signs of student assertiveness and individual agency vis-à-vis the state. This has been conspicuously missing from the prevailing top-down—and top-heavy—approach. Some rare disciplinary sources allow us to begin to appreciate a range of possibilities for which functional, mechanical models fail to allow. Individual student agency must be taken into consideration. While it is only the rare pupil who takes the extreme step of lodging a formal complaint against, not to mention discharging a loaded firearm at, his school authorities, these radical responses help us to see a range of potential reactions to school authority that must lie submerged beneath the historical record.

An appreciation of Ottoman agency is also necessary in order to make sense of an equally important yet overlooked factor: the competitive aspect of Hamidian education. Faced with an alarming array of adversaries on the educational front, the Ottomans did not roll over and accept what they considered to be a threat to the Ottoman way of life. Rather, they marshaled what resources they could to combat the proselytizing foreign missionaries, the highly motivated nationalist educators of neighboring states, and the schools of the indigenous minorities, often taking note of their competition's more effective methods in the process. The result was an Ottoman educational policy that was constantly evolving and one that frequently departed from the Tanzimat-era script. In its newly competitive mode late Ottoman educational policy relied heavily both on Ottoman and Islamic tradition and on the modernity of Western models. The process of combining these two traditions altered both of them, creating a mixture that has been but little understood. The secular curriculum was infused with large doses of religious content, while various aspects of the Islamic tradition were distilled to fit the curriculum and the regimented life of the new schools.

To recover the overlooked optimism and agency of late Ottoman history, this book re-examines a period, the reign of Sultan Abdül-hamid II (1876–1909), and an issue, the expansion of state education, both of which are critical to our grasp of late Ottoman and post-Ottoman society and, indeed, which underpinned much of the culture of nearly the whole modern Middle East. Abdülhamid II's reign was a period of tremendous expansion in the number of state schools in the empire. But in their attempt to delineate a pattern of increasing, inexorable secularization, many historians of the period have failed to appreciate the qualitative significance of the Hamidian (as this period is known) shift away from the pre-existing trends. The fact that Abdül-hamid II altered both the diagnosis and the prescribed cure seems not to have been considered especially important. In other words, during this period the way the Ottomans perceived Western influence underwent a sea change. This turn is most clearly observed in the world of education. Gone was the relatively trusting approach of the Tanzimat in which the French educational model had been imported nearly wholesale. In its stead a much more circumspect attitude held sway. A wariness of Western encroachment of all kinds translated into a more combative approach to the West in general and a more selective adaptation of its institutions.

Whereas the prevailing view has emphasized the *adoption* of Western European institutions and attitudes,[12] I concentrate on *adaptation*,

---

[12] For a refreshing and very recent exception, see Eugene L. Rogan, *Frontiers of the State in the Late Ottoman Empire: Transjordan, 1850–1921, Cambridge Middle East Studies*, no. 12 (Cambridge: Cambridge University Press, 1999), 12.

taking the field of education as my case. Focusing on adaptation allows us to see the various ways—some blatantly bold, others highly nuanced—in which the late Ottoman state modified the educational agenda of the preceding Tanzimat era. While it has been assumed that the Western provenance, logic, and outward form of educational "reform" were sufficiently powerful to withstand any amount of local meddling, the extent to which these were Ottomanized, and in some cases Islamized, has hardly been perceived. This underestimation of the educational changes effected in the Hamidian period is even more staggering when we consider that very few of the schools planned in the Tanzimat era were actually built prior to Abdülhamid's accession in 1876. The task of turning the largely paper plans of his predecessors into bricks and mortar fell to Abdülhamid II, and he assumed it with remarkable energy and purpose. When he did turn to the field of education, however, the sultan had some major changes in store. This book is the story of those changes and their important implications for understanding the emergence of the modern Middle East.

The secondary literature's insistence on the Western source and nature of educational change has been supported by remarkably pervasive assumptions of modernization theory. Until not too long ago virtually unquestioned, its most basic surmise, crudely put, held that the "rest" of the world would inevitably come to look like the West.[13] Given the inherent teleology of this assumption, it is not surprising that those aspects of late Ottoman society not deemed to fit the march to the "modern" were downplayed, even flatly ignored. One such anomaly is the role "traditional" factors, most notably Islam, played in ostensibly "modern" and "secular" education. A particularly remarkable finding of my research is the pervasiveness and importance of Ottoman and Islamic elements in informing the educational agenda of this period. Either ignored entirely or explained away as propaganda, these purportedly vestigial—but actually quite vital—links were criti-

---

[13] For critiques of modernization theory, see e.g. Reşat Kasaba, "Kemalist Certainties and Modern Ambiguities", in Bozdoğan and Kasaba (eds.), *Rethinking Modernity*, 15–36; Çağlar Keyder, "Whither the Project of Modernity?: Turkey in the 1990s," in ibid. 37–51; Akarlı, "Modernity and State–Society Relations;" Gregory Starrett, *Putting Islam to Work: Education, Politics, and Religious Transformation in Egypt* (Berkeley: University of California Press, 1998), 59–60.

cal to informing both the thinking behind the Hamidian educational campaign and the daily fabric of life in the schools it produced.

In short, this book represents an attempt to demonstrate the importance of recognizing indigenous, Ottoman agency by looking at the field of education. In that endeavor it hopes, however humbly, to complement the growing body of work that has begun to redress the imbalance or, to return to Khalid's apt metaphor, to rescue its history from the condescension of much of the earlier literature.[14]

APPROACHES

I approach this task in several ways. First, I attempt to strip away many of the assumptions about education and its largely predetermined role in such "processes" as Westernization and modernization. Secondly, I examine a wide variety of previously untapped sources, including archival materials, disciplinary reports, memoirs, and such actual teaching materials as classroom maps, atlases, and textbooks, in order to enter the heretofore inaccessible world of state education in the late Ottoman Empire. The variety of the material upon which I have been able to draw affords a multifaceted approach to late Ottoman schooling that goes well beyond the information available from the sources previously consulted, such as government regulations and yearbooks. Thirdly, I ground my approach in a comparative framework. One of the chief benefits of setting the Ottoman experience off against other contemporary educational initiatives is that it allows us to move beyond the East–West dynamic. Ottoman schools had important parallels with their counterparts in various parts of Asia, just as they did with the nations of Western Europe, but what is most telling, I think, are the similarities shared by contemporary schooling systems around the world.[15] While the usual approach has been to treat Western educational systems as static "models" to be imitated by the non-West, a comparative analysis reveals that the Western systems were themselves

---

[14] I am thinking here of such scholars as Engin Akarlı, Palmira Brummett, Selim Deringil, Elizabeth Frierson, Şükrü Hanioğlu, Hasan Kayalı, Eugene Rogan, Akşin Somel, Gregory Starrett, and Erik Zürcher.

[15] Randi Deguilhem, "State Civil Education in Late Ottoman Damascus: A Unifying or a Dividing Force?," in Thomas Philipp and Birgit Schaebler (eds.), *The Syrian Land: Processes of Integration and Fragmentation, Bilad al-Sham from the 18th to the 20th Century, Berliner Islamstudien*, 6 (Stuttgart: Franz Steiner Verlag, 1998), 224.

in flux and at the center of hotly debated controversies over which direction society should take.[16] In this regard Ottoman schools were no different. Such core commonalties offer hard evidence for the concept of a common "world time" (*Weltzeit*) for which Reinhard Schulze has so provocatively argued.[17] The comparative approach allows us to see the simultaneity of the educational experience across unexpectedly wide swaths of geography.

The main thesis of this book is that the late Ottoman state assigned education the conflicted task of attempting to ward off Western encroachment by adapting Western-style education to suit Ottoman needs. Faced with military and diplomatic pressure constricting the empire's borders and with the equally aggressive Western capitalists and missionaries operating within them, the Ottoman government felt obliged to fight back. One of the few weapons at its disposal was education. Heeding the dramatic appeals from officials across the empire, the bureaucracy in Istanbul responded with an extraordinary financial and emotional investment in education. This response can only be explained by the fact that officials at the highest level believed the very future of the empire to be at risk, that they were engaged in a battle for the hearts and minds of the young generation. But their choices for a remedy were limited by financial constraints, bureaucratic momentum, and the overwhelming belief that the Western educational model offered what one official called a "secret wisdom," factors that ensured the Western model continued to dominate Ottoman educational expansion. But Abdülhamid II, the last sultan to rule as well as reign, altered the content that this system was to deliver, in order to bring it into line with Ottoman policy and Islamic practice.

---

[16] For a recent reappraisal of the *Zeitgeist* in the West, see Ann Taylor Allen, "Feminism, Social Science, and the Meanings of Modernity: The Debate on the Origin of the Family in Europe and the United States, 1860–1914," *The American Historical Review*, 104/4 (1999), 1085–113. Taylor challenges the notion that despair and anxiety were the dominant themes of the age by revealing the optimism of the feminist movement. For the Ottomans, as we shall see, a similar mixture of possibility and fear permeated society, particularly as far as education was concerned.

[17] Reinhard Schulze, *Geschichte der Islamischen Welt im 20. Jahrhundert* (Munich: Verlag C. H. Beck, 1994), 14 ff. and "Was ist die Islamische Aufklärung?" *Die Welt des Islams*, 36/3 (1996), 317–25. For an English-language account of the debate over the question of an "Islamic Enlightenment," see Knut S. Vikør, "Muhammadan Piety and Islamic Enlightenment: Survey of a Historiographical Debate," paper presented at the ISMM, Istanbul Workshop, July 1998. I thank Ulrike Freitag for kindly bringing this to my attention.

Recognizing the Ottomanization of the pre-existing system is critical to understanding these schools not as alien imports but rather as thoroughly indigenous institutions. Paying proper attention to the frequently ignored Islamic and Ottoman influences, so integral to the schools' architecture, course content, calendar, and social intercourse, opens fresh possibilities for interpreting the way this hybrid education was received by its students. For example, it allows us to question a central tenet of social change in this period, namely, the notion that Western influence, or as some would see it, the refusal to abide by it, caused a yawning rift in the empire's social fabric. Late Ottoman society has been depicted as deeply divided by a clash of worldviews. On the one hand is the "traditional" world of the ulama, historically responsible for the majority of the empire's education. Almost always associated with an unchanging Islam, these men of religion are depicted as resistant to modernization on ideological as well as personal grounds; their jobs threatened by the new schools, their knowledge considered outmoded, their pedagogy ridiculed.[18] Ulama were, as we shall see, involved in various aspects of the new, so-called secular system, ranging from the membership of the commissions called to modify the curriculum to schoolteachers across the provinces, and even to local and itinerant preachers who were paid by the state to inveigh against the evils of sending Muslim children to foreign schools. The image of the ulama that emerges from this study contrasts sharply with that stock figure of late Ottoman history, literature, and memoir, namely the teacher in a *kuttab*, hidebound, corrupt, physically abusive, and pedagogically primitive.

On the other hand, and in marked contrast, stand the Western-influenced educators cum statesmen of the nineteenth and early twentieth centuries, men who appear valiantly intent on applying Western European ideas—and ideals—to an Ottoman Empire otherwise incapable of its own preservation. They are invariably associated with Enlightenment and Progress. The resulting chasm between these two groups, described as "cultural dualism" and "bifurcation," has

---

[18] Ongoing prosopographic research by Klaus Kreiser will add immensely to our understanding of the ulama in this period. The doctoral research of Halil İbrahim Erbay at the University of London seems likely to reveal that the ulama's views on "modernization" were hardly as monolithic as has been assumed.

dominated discussions of late Ottoman society.[19] Some have even gone so far as to suggest that the inability to reconcile these competing worldviews led to cultural schizophrenia—a "schizoid society"—in spite of numerous examples of individuals and institutions that bridged the presumed gap in productive and creative ways.

Looking at Ottoman society through the lens of educational change helps us to understand why this dichotomous view has prevailed—and why it is deeply problematic. First it suggests that this view of a split society owes much to the frequently bitter controversy between the competing religious and secular claims to contemporary culture in the post-Ottoman states. In the case of Turkey, projecting a post-Kemalist dichotomy back onto late Ottoman society is both natural—all history reflects the time in which it is written—and inevitably distorting.[20] By denying agency to its Ottoman predecessors the Kemalist historical project has sought to bolster the anti-Western credentials of the Republic in spite of, or rather because of, its own headlong Westernizing push. Situating the East–West rift in the Ottoman period serves to diminish the wrenching effects of the Kemalist Kulturkampf. This book shows that in the field of education the continuities between the Ottoman and Republican periods are stronger than usually perceived.

Secondly, a reading of Ottoman educational change alongside that of its most influential analog, France, points to another likely explanation for the inordinate attention paid to the notion of cultural dualism. As the model for Ottoman state schools and for Ottoman tastes in fashion, literature, and thought in general, France is an obvious point of comparison. As we shall soon see, Ottoman and French education shared many features, but the implicit assumption in the prevailing wisdom that the conflicts in both countries worked in the same way, or even that they represented a clash between similar sets of opponents, is not tenable.

France had long served as the focal point of Western emulators in the Ottoman Empire. Whether in the fields of literature, social and

---

[19] For the concept of cultural dualism, see Niyazi Berkes, *The Development of Secularism in Turkey* (Montreal: McGill University Press, 1964), 106 ff., esp. 109; Carter V. Findley, *Ottoman Civil Officialdom: A Social History* (Princeton: Princeton University Press, 1989), 35–9, 135 ff.

[20] Elisabeth B. Frierson, "Unimagined Communities: Women and Education in the Late-Ottoman Empire, 1876–1908," *Critical Matrix*, 9/2 (1995), 55–90.

political thought, or fashion, Ottomans turned to Paris for models. As one Young Ottoman journal expressed this relationship: "Our position in comparison with France is like that of an uneducated child beside an accomplished scholar."[21] In the field of education we shall see that, although Ottoman educators frequently exhibited a willingness to alter or depart from the content supplied by this "accomplished scholar," it was nevertheless the French model with which they started. We must proceed from a deceptively simple fact, namely, that the French system was the one on which the Ottomans patterned their own school-building program. We know that the French Ministry of Education, under Victor Duruy, drafted the report upon which the Ottoman Education Regulation of 1869 was based.[22] Although Abdülhamid II's educational strategy drastically altered the schools' content and overall *raison d'être*, the 1869 plan continued to serve as the touchstone for their formal articulation well into the twentieth century. Indeed, the centralized, systemic quality of the French-to-Ottoman transfer has stood out as its chief characteristic. This has reinforced the notion that the late Ottoman state was attempting to impose a highly uniform pedagogical and disciplinary regime, the better to control its disparate regions and ethnic groups. Centralizing logic featured prominently in late Ottoman policy, to be sure, but I argue that relying too heavily on the more than slightly sinister image of the state as a ruthlessly standardizing and homogenizing force hides many of the subtleties, contradictions, and complexities of late Ottoman education. In any case, such a powerful stereotype cannot stand the test of scrutiny, either in the Ottoman Empire or in France. The frequently cited image of the French minister of education proudly looking at his watch and claiming to the Emperor "that he could state what, at that precise moment, all the children in France were studying" gave rise to a powerful myth that obscured the persistence of non-conformity and the wild fluctuations that continued to characterize public education in France for generations.[23]

---

[21] This and other similar observations appeared in the journal *İbret* during the early 1870s. As cited in Hanioğlu, *Young Turks*, 14.

[22] Berkes, *Development*, 179–80.

[23] Robert Gildea, *Education in Provincial France, 1800–1914* (Oxford: Clarendon Press, 1983), 1, 50; Theodore Zeldin, *France 1848–1945*, Vol. II, *Intellect, Taste, and Anxiety* (Oxford: Clarendon Press, 1977), 180.

Let us briefly consider the historiography of the French case, where the lines were long assumed to have been sharply drawn between Republicans and Catholics. Durkheim, asked at the end of the nineteenth century how the problem of France's seemingly endless government crises could be solved, answered that there was no easy answer, because her political troubles were the result of "genuine and fundamental disagreements." "'Christian or republican,' said Proudhon, 'that is the dilemma.'"[24] Yet under the scrutiny of such historians as Theodore Zeldin, François Furet and Jacques Ozouf, and Mona Ozouf even the rigidity of the French divisions has had to yield to more nuanced and subtle interpretations.[25] That being the case, it should be quite plausible to cast doubt upon the certainty of the Ottoman bifurcation. In fact, it is not difficult at all. Any Ottoman counterpart to Durkheim or Proudhon who had declared society to be fundamentally split would have been considered mad. Even the radical proponent of Darwinist positivism Ahmed Rıza Bey—he went so far as to date his correspondence according to the Positivist calendar—was always careful to hide his outlying atheism behind a smokescreen of Islamic rhetoric for popular consumption.[26] In the late Ottoman Empire he was truly on the far fringes of political thought.

The third and most deeply embedded reason underlying the presumed cultural cleavage stems from the predominantly positivist reading of history, a reading that manages to make a radical figure like Ahmed Rıza Bey appear to have been a natural development in a larger progression. Supporting both the presentist projection and the influence of the highly dichotomous French model is a much broader set of assumptions about the directionality of historical change. Reduced to its bare essentials, the chronological element in this cluster of assumptions presupposes a distinction between early and late that is freighted with normative meaning, as Gregory Starrett has recently

[24] Theodore Zeldin, "Introduction: Were there Two Frances?" in Zeldin (ed.), *Conflicts in French Society: Anticlericalism, Education and Morals in the Nineteenth Century* (London: Allen & Unwin, 1970), 9.

[25] Zeldin, *France 1848–1945*; François Furet and Jacques Ozouf, *Reading and Writing: Literacy in France from Calvin to Jules Ferry* (Cambridge: Cambridge University Press, 1982); Mona Ozouf, *L'École, l'église et la république, 1871–1914* (Paris: Editions Cana, 1982).

[26] On Ahmed Rıza Bey, see Hanioğlu, *Young Turks, passim.*

observed.[27] Early/traditional yields to late/modern, as bad gives way to good. Starrett goes on to say that the divide between the religious and the secular is another in a string of "false typological opposites" that engender historical misreading. Starrett is concerned in the first instance with Egypt, with all of the complications of British colonial rule, but what he has to say about the way the directional aspect has distorted the role of Islam has tremendous resonance for the Ottoman case. Add to this teleological obsession with progress the widespread dismissiveness of the explanatory value of religion prevalent in the social sciences, and the possibilities for misapprehension of Islam's role in education become even clearer.

The insularity of Ottoman historiography is also doubtless part of the problem. Until recently much of Ottoman and Middle Eastern history has been written as if it belonged to a closed universe, unsusceptible to broader trends, both global and interregional. The need to situate the Ottoman experience in a broader historical frame, always desirable, is even more critical in later centuries, given the relative increase in communication and institutional borrowing over time. The educational angle on this historiography reveals a cautionary tale, and thus offers a correcting perspective.

The Ottoman case has therefore found itself the unwitting object of temporal, comparative, and normative influences that do not necessarily accord with the historical record. This and subsequent chapters will show that the religious/secular divide is particularly unsuited to the Ottoman educational system, with its strong doses of Islamic content, its mix of religious and civil employees, the Islamic dimension to its yearly calendar and daily routine, and perhaps most important of all, as we shall soon see, the religio-cultural justification for its construction in the first place.

A more nuanced approach is needed, one open to the possibilities of synthesis in the place of absolute and dichotomous antagonisms. For synthesis was in many respects the operative condition for most of those involved in some way with the late Ottoman state. To take only one example, Paul Dumont has shown, through his reconstruction of the life of a mid-ranking government clerk, that even someone

---

[27] Starrett, *Putting Islam to Work*, 15 ff.

extremely well versed in the literature of France and attached to his carriage, symbol of late Ottoman chic, was at bottom a man of synthesis.[28] His Said Bey may appear almost stereotypically Westernized in
some of his tastes, but remains attached to unquestionably indigenous
cultural interests and pleasures. He is as much at home with a French
novel as with the Turkish shadow puppet tradition, with Parisian
fashion as with drinking *rakı*. The secular/religious opposition is too
simplistic, too influenced by divisions of the present day. Secular
education is invariably fingered as responsible for effecting "cultural
dualism," but my work challenges the "secular" label and the notion of
bifurcation. I suggest that this construct has been created by a small
number of memoirs and a later historiographical tendency to project
an "inevitable" secularism back into the late Ottoman period when, as
the assimilation in the schools emphasizes, it was only one of several
potential paths to modernity.

Due to its inherently temporal project—to shape the future by
working in the present, while being strongly influenced by the experience of the past—education is critical to interpreting any society's historical self-conception. In the late Ottoman case, education carried the
added burden of negotiating several broad transformations of enormous import for the Ottoman Middle East and the Balkans. Although
not acting alone, the Ottoman educational project was nevertheless
freighted with a number of weighty obligations. Among the most
salient were: (1) redefining the empire's historical trajectory, seen from
one perspective as plotting a course between tradition and modernity;
(2) redrawing the boundary between Western and indigenous, most
notably Ottoman and Islamic, influence; (3) rearticulating the role of
the state in society, and thereby initiating a new relationship between
the authorities and their subjects—a relationship that would be increasingly critical to the pre-eminence of the nation state in the twentieth
century.

These propositions juxtaposed historically broad trends with specific
agendas. In them we can see signs of the Hamidian instinct to step
back and re-examine the certainties of the preceding Tanzimat period.

---

[28] Paul Dumont, "Said Bey—The Everyday Life of an Istanbul Townsman at the Beginning of the Twentieth Century," in Albert Hourani, Philip S. Khoury, and Mary C. Wilson
(eds.), *The Modern Middle East: A Reader* (Berkeley: University of California Press, 1993),
271–87.

As the relationship with the Western powers grew increasingly strained due to the further reduction of the Ottoman borders, the increasing financial, cultural, and missionary penetration inside them, and the unmistakable sense that the powers were less and less interested in the preservation of the empire itself, Ottoman policy changed. Although acting within severe limitations, Abdülhamid II and his officials found room in which to maneuver. Education was one area among many that offered attractive options for the young sultan. This study explains educational policy in light of the Hamidian penchant for questioning and then reformulating the basic assumptions of the Tanzimat era. It documents the increasingly jaundiced, ultimately combative Ottoman stance toward the educational competition provided by foreign missionaries, neighboring states, and the local minority communities, and demonstrates the practical steps the state took as a result. By analyzing the specifics of the state's efforts to modify the curriculum, commission textbooks, redraw classroom maps, and monitor religio-moral conduct within the school system, we can observe the interplay between broad historical shifts and the more pressing demands of the day.

All three transformations identified had momentous consequences for the individual and his or her place in society. Redefining the empire's historical trajectory had clear implications for the ways in which Ottoman subjects of all stripes perceived themselves, their place in the world, and their relationship with their state and their respective religious communities, and increasingly, with political attempts to redraw some of the pre-existing affiliations, nationalism being only the most obvious example. While I do not attempt to address in detail all of the apposite ramifications in this study, I do try to demonstrate the centrality of the state's schooling project to each of them. For example, the state's attempt to include Islam in its agenda of creating an imperial loyalty has implications for later manifestations of Islamic nationalism. More important in a general sense is the theoretical task of opening up the possibilities, heretofore only rarely apprehended, of imagining an array of potential "outcomes" over which education was well positioned to exert critical influence.

One implication of the radically increased role of the state in the field of education is the increase in the numbers of students being exposed to state-sanctioned, "official" history, the legacy of which has often been rudely apparent in the former Ottoman lands to this day. Because this subject has been conscientiously examined by others,[29] I do not attempt to duplicate but only to complement their fine work.

Here I am more interested in how state education shaped the way young Ottoman subjects thought about their empire, and specifically how it affected their conceptions of their own period within and against the long duration of its history. But official schools were also critical in getting their pupils to think about the Ottoman Empire in relation to other contemporary states. Selim Deringil's recent book on the Abdülhamid II era makes excellent use of such a comparative outlook to place state ideology and legitimization in a global perspective. Here it is important to remember that just as Ottoman officialdom went to great lengths to present the empire as a world power—students were taught to think of their empire as on a par with the Habsburgs and Romanovs of the world—with all of the appropriate trappings of rule, so also did the less spectacular pedagogical manifestations of state authority work their way into the young consciousness of its students. The books and maps they studied, the authority structure of their schools, their daily schedule, and even the food they were given to eat all produced a much wider range of reactions and impressions than we have been led to believe. This naturally had tremendous implications for the ways these students thought of their own position vis-à-vis their sultan and the rest of the world, a consideration I address in the final two chapters. Here again, I hold out for a range of possibilities such teaching may have engendered in the students subjected to it, an impossibility when they are approached as unified cohorts.

The second major transformation, that of redrawing the boundary between Western and indigenous influence, is likewise critical to our understanding of socio-cultural change in the nineteenth and twentieth centuries. Here the attempt is to problematize the notion of cultural influence. Much has been made of the impact of Western modes of learning and organizing knowledge in the non-Western world. In

[29] Here I am thinking of such scholars as Claudia Kleinert, Christoph Herzog, and Christoph Neumann. For a treatment that takes this trend into the post-Ottoman Arab world, see Ulrike Freitag, *Geschichtsschreibung in Syrien 1920–1990: zwischen Wissenschaft und Ideologie* (Hamburg: Deutsches Orient-Institut, 1991). The ongoing project investigating school texts in contemporary Turkey and Greece and headed by Dr Yasemin Soysal at the University of Essex promises to update this line of enquiry.

this study I emphasize the constructive and not the genealogical approach. I am more interested in the ways in which the late Ottoman state combined various aspects of the exogenous and the indigenous traditions (for example, the positivist and the Islamic, the Ottoman and the Western European) to form a blend that it considered particularly suited to its educational mission. It is the resourceful, adaptive, and combined qualities of the late Ottoman educational project that need to be emphasized if we wish to form a more nuanced view of its possible effects. I argue that the combination of influences, Eastern as well as Western, demands a range of possible reactions. We cannot assume that late Ottoman schools necessarily "produced" Westernized graduates bent on building a secular future. Certainly some of the graduates of these schools went on to play active roles in radically different post-Ottoman societies. Yet we cannot take the handful of memoirs written by men such as these to represent the rest of their former schoolmates. Ultimately we can never know the full range of reactions elicited by these schools, but by thinking of their students as inhabiting a spectrum we can begin to appreciate the register of responses. By insisting that individuals must have reacted in many different ways to a "process" that was itself quite variegated, I hold out for a variety of responses and against any predetermined readings of a period so crucial to comprehending its twentieth-century legacies.

State schooling was critical to a third development, namely that of rearticulating the state's role in society. Public education initiated a new relationship between the authorities and their subjects—a relationship increasingly critical to the pre-eminence of the nation state in the twentieth century. My analysis of this transformation takes issue with what I consider the overemphasis on state power in much of the relevant literature. While it is clear that the Ottoman educational agenda was part of a larger project of state aggrandizement, and that the state was entering into manifold new relationships with its subjects and proto-citizens, I think it necessary to avoid being carried away with the raw power of the state. While many have chosen to depict the state as assuming a quasi-monstrous and mechanistic role, particularly where, given the influence of Michel Foucault, some would see schools and think of them as prisons, others, such as Pierre Bourdieu, see education as domination which involves complicity between those who possess and those who submit to the various forms of power, resulting in the effacement of the individual in the institution.[30] Such a totalizing, top-down approach may make sense for an analysis of post-1968 France, but it hinders our appreciation of the evolving and often quite fragile educational apparatus of the late Ottoman state. In this more precarious and essentially experimental setting, I think it important to appreciate the limits and vulnerabilities associated with state education. Drawing on Michel de Certeau's notion of the resistance of the everyday and Mikhail Bakhtin's concept of answerability, I analyze school disciplinary cases to reveal the ways in which state power dissipated in a local context. Here I seek to redress what I perceive to be a serious imbalance in much of the existing relevant literature on the Middle East by drawing on recent literature that calls into question the all-powerful depiction of the "state." Gregory Starrett's recent work on Egypt is especially helpful here, not least because his critique of Timothy Mitchell's *Colonising Egypt* opens up space for fruitful discussion of the limits of state control in education.[31] The more nuanced approach to state schooling that emerges is, moreover, supported by contemporary developments which suggest that schooling may be less important in human development than we have been led to believe. Scaling back expectations for what was achieved within the four walls of a school is not something that comes naturally, particularly for those of us who seem to spend an inordinate amount of our lives studying and working in educational institutions, but it may nevertheless be necessary to avoid some of the pitfalls that stem from overstating their effects.

While the state has clearly been overstated in the literature, Islam has not. Under-represented, explained away, and even flatly ignored, Islam was nevertheless critical to late Ottoman education despite the state's arrogation of many of the prerogatives of the religious establishment, schooling included. A major element in the modified curriculum, Islamic content was central to the state's educational message, a topic explored in Chapter 3. As with Khalid's Jadidists of Central Asia,[32] their Russian rulers, or for that matter with most "secular" education in the

---

[30] Pierre Bourdieu, *The State Nobility: Elite Schools in the Field of Power*, trans. Lauretta C. Clough (Cambridge: Polity Press, 1996), 3 ff.

[31] Starrett, *Putting Islam to Work*; Timothy Mitchell, *Colonising Egypt* (Cambridge: Cambridge University Press, 1988; Berkeley: University of California Press, 1991).

[32] Khalid, *Politics*, 12.

nineteenth-century West, there was no contradiction for Ottoman educators in combining religious with worldly knowledge in the pursuit of a modern educational system. That later writers should see a contradiction in such a pairing reflects the prevailing thinking about modernization and secularization, as well as a general prejudice against the explanatory value of religion in the social sciences.

Islam was also critical to the state's extra-curricular profile. The new schools created new environments for living as well as learning, as I observe in Chapter 4. Officially sanctioned Islam gave rhythm to daily life in the schools in the form of prayers, holiday observances, and vacations. Students were monitored in terms of their religio-moral conduct as well as academically, and members of the ulama were a constant feature on the school scene. Stepping back from the local reality of the schools, we see that Islam colored the spirit in which they were imagined, built, and staffed. It was not mere semantic convenience that prompted Ottoman officials to refer to their nominally interdenominational institutions as "Muslim" schools.

The Islamic emphasis can in part be explained by an attempt to assert an aspect of Ottoman life that had previously needed little accent. As we see in Chapter 6, for example, the previously unstated (because implicitly understood) Islamic elements of Tanzimat-era moral instruction gave way to a clearly voiced Islamic emphasis in the Hamidian period. This can perhaps be explained as a precursor of what Dale Eickelman has termed the "objectification" of Islam.[33] By concentrating on textual production, by consciously marking as Islamic those texts used to impart moral information, the Islamic aspects of which had previously been taken for granted, and by systematizing Islamic knowledge generally, the late Ottoman educational project produced many manifestations that recent scholarship has associated with "modern" Islam.

Exploring the diachronic links between the late nineteenth- and late twentieth-century Islamic Middle East forces us to historicize the relationship between Islam and social, cultural, and political change, and therefore to re-examine the concept of modernity in this changing context. It also challenges us to question and to rethink the

---

[33] Dale F. Eickelman and James Piscatori, *Muslim Politics* (Princeton: Princeton University Press, 1996), 37 ff.

assumptions surrounding such topics as Islamic "revival" and "resurgence." Given the centrality of official Islam in the late imperial attempt to revivify Ottoman cultural and political life, it is perhaps more appropriate to identify secularism—and not religion—as the anomalous construct most requiring explanation.

When understood on its own terms and not as part of a later agenda to fit it into a broadly normative meta-narrative, the late Ottoman project serves as a highly informative road only partially taken. The radical Republican break with so many substantive and symbolic aspects of indigenous tradition—and the "natural" assumptions inherent in the Westernization and nationalist theory that undergirded it—consigned the late Ottoman approach to appear a forlorn, outmoded option while, however, the new system still benefited freely from all of its infrastructural and organizational headway. Belated recognition of the rift in the social, historical fabric that Kemalism begot—and here we have the source of bona fide bifurcation—prompts a closer look at the late Ottoman alternative. This is not to suggest, as some would naively like to believe, that Hamidian policy contains a solution for the current impasse. But as an attempt to navigate the changing dispensation of the late nineteenth century, the unhesitating fusion of the Western with the indigenous inherent in the Ottoman project holds important lessons for the early twenty-first.

This book restores Islam and the context of religio-cultural competition to their rightful and perversely downplayed roles in the late Ottoman endeavor. This is only a natural restitution of the pragmatism that has historically been the hallmark of Ottoman policy and administration.

One danger to be avoided is the tendency to essentialize Islam, to treat "it" as unchanging and undifferentiated. By virtue of its mobilization of Islamic content and symbol in this new pedagogical endeavor, the Ottoman state necessarily altered Islamic "reality" in ways not always readily apparent. Exploring the resulting relationship between Islam, state, and individual shows that this new dispensation, in turn, was susceptible to interpretation depending on context and mindset, both of which were themselves subject to vacillation and re-interpretation. Although many social scientists, not to mention avowed secularists, are loath to grant salience to religion other than as propaganda or as a mask for other explanatory factors, religion nevertheless retains a vitality despite, or rather because of, modernity.[34] In the Ottoman and post-Ottoman case, discounting Islam, however constituted, is folly. This is as true now in the case of post-Erbakan Turkey as it has been since the late Ottoman era and the early years of the Republic.

All three of the book's broader themes—rewriting history, redrawing the balance of Western and indigenous influences, and rearticulating the state's role in society—share a common element, that of redirecting society through a sort of triangulation. Reckoning so as to sight indigenous and exogenous influence on a more nearly equal footing, the Hamidian state sought to rechart its course to the future. Restoring Ottoman and Islamic influence to the educational system was key to the new project of societal triangulation, offsetting the heavy pull of Westernization with an Ottoman and Islamic emphasis. Although the Turkish Republic again adjusted the trajectory in an attempt to supplant the Islamic religion, it nevertheless has been and continues to be critical to the task of navigating such a path. Writing Islam back into the history of the late Ottoman period allows us to apprehend the possibilities as well as the pitfalls for the contemporary and future relationship between Islam and state. The history of education, situated at the juncture of social, institutional, intellectual, political, and economic history, affords a unique vantage point from which to observe this interplay.

At the crux of educational change rests the question of identity. The Ottoman project yields a remarkably precise reading of the state's attempt to influence identity formation among its young subjects. The paperwork left in the trail of the Ottoman educational project offers specific information about what the state hoped to accomplish through education. Some of these findings are what we have come to expect: an emphasis on "producing" loyal students capable of assuming posts in the burgeoning state bureaucracy. Others are more novel, including the state's emphasis on Islam as a major component of nascent student identity, both in the classroom and in extracurricular life. Less precise, but immeasurably suggestive, is what we can glean from the other side

---

[34] For an intriguing discussion of the possibilities for a "new Islamic synthesis," see Richard W. Bulliet, *Islam: The View from the Edge* (New York: Columbia University Press, 1994), in particular ch. 11.

of the educational equation, namely, from the "reality" that forms the
rejoinder to the state's intentions. Previously untapped school disciplinary records, the only sources available that allow the contemporary
student voice to be heard unmediated by the altered atmosphere of
post-Ottoman society, force us to rethink many of the assumptions
assigned to the students themselves. Whereas most approaches have
assumed a common student identity, here we see the necessity of allowing a range of emerging identities. These proto-citizens were clearly
capable of resisting the state's attempts at identity formation, but often
in ways that the prevailing literature has not prepared us to expect. By
analyzing disciplinary cases, I demonstrate that students were as liable
to incorporate as to reject the state's Islamic rhetoric, depending on the
context and the individuals involved. To be able to allow for such a
range of identities means abandoning the heavily bounded notion of
the group mindset that runs through the understanding of education
bequeathed to us by modernization theory and its advocates.

   For all of its promise, the field of education also carries with it a
hidden danger, namely, the tendency to read our own deeply rooted
educational preconceptions and experiences into the subject. Many of
us have spent a very high proportion of our lives in educational institutions, and we therefore think we know what education is and what
it does in most times and places. As Theodore Zeldin has pointed out,
it is impossible to find "independent, outside observers" of education
the way one might for, say, coal-mining.[35] There is a further, related
problem: the propensity to overestimate the causative, transformative
role of formal education. This view persists in spite of strong evidence
to the contrary in our own classrooms and in broader terms in the societies in which we live.

COMPARISONS

It is helpful to identify two broad and inherently interrelated features
that the Ottoman schooling initiative shared with its international
analogs. These are the temporal and what I shall call the attitudinal,
reflecting the substantive and psychological expectations from and the
investment in educational change. I begin with a brief critique of some

[35] Zeldin, *France 1848–1945*, 139.

of the assumptions made about the role of late Ottoman education. Instead of presenting an exhaustive literature review,[36] I seek to set the stage for the discussions of the temporal and attitudinal comparisons and of the specificities of the Ottoman case which follow.

It is important to see the Ottoman case as forming part of a much broader phenomenon that was nothing less than the worldwide expansion of state education of the nineteenth and twentieth centuries. Awareness of this temporal development reminds us that the Ottoman case, for all of its particularities, formed part of a truly global trend. To comprehend this is to go beyond the usual exoticism offered in treatments of the late Ottoman Empire.[37] The Ottoman educational endeavor very much belongs to what Theodore Zeldin dubbed the "Age of Education." Zeldin was writing about France, but his temporal assessment fits the Ottoman case quite well. Like numerous governments all over the world, the Ottoman state was standardizing, centralizing, and modifying an educational plan that had developed through fits and starts earlier in the century. The Ottoman effort shared many attributes of this global pattern. One of the most striking is the chronological correspondence with educational developments in countries whose historical trajectories are not normally considered synchronous with the Ottoman Empire. While it would be foolish to attach too much importance to what may appear to be chronological coincidences, it is nevertheless instructive that the year 1869 marked not only the promulgation of the chief Ottoman plan for state education (the Education Regulation produced with considerable input from the French Ministry of Education), but also the appearance of a key program in Russia, following on trips of two key Russian educationalists to Prussia and France (where similar plans had been put forward by Victor Duruy only two years before).[38] The following year marked the appearance in Japan of the "first comprehensive plan for

---

[36] For a more thorough literature review, see my "Education for the Empire: Ottoman State Secondary Schools during the Reign of Sultan Abdülhamid II (1876–1909)," Ph.D. diss., University of Chicago (1997), 7–17.

[37] Selim Deringil's recent monograph, cited above, ably delineates—and goes a long way toward rebutting—the exoticizing tendency affecting our comprehension of the late Ottoman period.

[38] Eugen Weber, *Peasants into Frenchmen: The Modernization of Rural France, 1870–1914* (Stanford: Stanford University Press, 1976), 306.

all levels of education."[39] In all cases the legislation called for a high degree of centralization and preceded a strong push in the crucial area of secondary education,[40] among other similarities to be noted below. Even in France, the source of some of the Russian and much of the Ottoman initiatives, there was a surprising degree of chronological convergence. After the defeat of 1870, the French Ministry of Education of the Third Republic became a strong agent of change; the ensuing, famous reforms of Jules Ferry during the 1880s turn out to be highly analogous to their Ottoman counterparts.[41] It is therefore possible to detect remarkably similar patterns in national/imperial educational development between a country like France on the one hand and the Russian, Japanese, and Ottoman empires on the other. In spite of major differences in such critical areas as literacy, industrialization, and class consciousness,[42] striking similarities in governmental approach to creating a national system of schooling emerge from comparing the model and its distant emulations. The time-lag that one might expect given the emphasis on the impact of the West in the secondary literature is barely apparent; clearly there is more at work than mere cultural adoption.[43]

More important than the precise years in which laws were passed or reports submitted was a more widely shared phenomenon: the period centering on the 1880s was a time of momentous change. Eugen Weber notes a "profound sea change" in France, a point echoed by Furet and Ozouf.[44] In Germany Detlef Müller observes this decade as marking a

[39] Byron K. Marshall, *Learning to be Modern: Japanese Political Discourse on Education* (Boulder, Col.: Westview Press, 1994), 26.

[40] Patrick L. Alston, *Education and the State in Tsarist Russia* (Stanford: Stanford University Press, 1969), 86 ff.

[41] Fritz Ringer, "On Segmentation in Modern European Educational Systems: The Case of French Secondary Education, 1865–1920," in Detlef K. Müller, Fritz Ringer, and Brian Simon (eds.), *The Rise of the Modern Educational System: Structural Change and Social Reproduction, 1870–1920* (Cambridge: Cambridge University Press, 1987), 53–87; Weber, *Peasants into Frenchmen*, 308–9.

[42] To take only one example, Furet and Ozouf say that by the time the educational laws of the 1880s were passed the battle against illiteracy in France was "pretty well won." Furet and Ozouf, *Reading and Writing*, 45. This could be said for neither the Russian nor the Ottoman case.

[43] See my "Islamic Morality in Ottoman 'Secular' Schools," *IJMES*, 32/3 (August 2000), 369–93.

[44] Weber, *Peasants into Frenchmen*, p. ix; Furet and Ozouf, *Reading and Writing*, 45.

chronological break between the "emergence" and the "constitution of a school system".[45] In Russia, Alston considers 1881 to be a turning point; after the assassination of the Tsar, education was to be deployed to inoculate against the noxious effects of anarchy. Russian education increasingly reflected the desire to strengthen moral values and to move away from European cultural models.[46] Japanese educational trends during the last two decades of the nineteenth century shared much with what was happening elsewhere. An increasingly centralized and rationalized educational system exhibited an emphasis on Confucian morality, the role of the emperor, and anti-foreign sentiment.[47]

As we shall see in the next chapter, the 1880s in the Ottoman Empire were a period of remarkable activity on the education front, particularly at the secondary level. After the tumultuous years of 1876–8, which included the year of three sultans, the negotiations over the constitution, a disastrous war with Russia, and the establishment of the foreign-controlled Public Debt Administration, the Ottoman government was finally able to devote considerable attention to implementing educational plans that had been on the books since 1869. Yet, as we shall see, the guiding principles of Ottoman education had been considerably altered in the intervening period. The details and implications of realizing a fully articulated state-run system will emerge in the next chapter. For the time being it suffices to underscore the temporal and thematic connections with a number of other contemporary systems.

Whatever the particulars of the individual countries observed, the broad commonalities are striking, as we shall see when looking at the concern with moral schooling shared by such diverse countries as China, France, the United States, and Russia. It is tempting to invoke the notion of a "world time" at work, given the common anxieties over the "demands of the present," the perception that the pace of time was accelerating,[48] and frequent recourse to "traditional" religio-moral constructs, however reworked in the process.

---

[45] Detlef Müller, "The Process of Systematization: The Case of German Secondary Education," in Müller *et al.* (eds.), *Rise*, 15–52.

[46] Alston, *Education and the State*, 114–15.

[47] Roberta Wollons, "The Black Forest in a Bamboo Garden: Missionary Kindergartens in Japan, 1868–1912," *History of Education Quarterly*, 33/1 (Spring 1993), 11–12.

[48] Selim Deringil, "The Invention of Tradition," 3.

The common temporal frame to educational expansion also helps us to recover the optimistic spirit with which "modern style" education was so enthusiastically greeted around the world. It is this universal hopefulness that comprises its chief attitudinal feature, one that is frequently difficult to imagine fully in our own era, in which the ratio of rhetoric to funding seems perpetually to favor the former, a problem that continues to plague current governments in both Britain and the United States. In the Ottoman Empire, on the other hand, education was an issue which inspired confidence across all shades of the politically active spectrum. Here again, the parallels between the Ottoman and other cases, both near and far, are particularly strong. Like their counterparts elsewhere, Ottoman educators believed that public education would solve a host of problems, ranging from those of economic and military competitiveness, to those relating to manpower, social control, cultural identification, and political loyalty.

In France, education provided a shared source of optimism for conservatives and republicans alike. An optimistic faith in the "incomparable power" of the school pervaded both sides of the often intense debates over education that took place in the Third Republic.[49] The educational panacea was sufficiently widespread so as to turn the idea of modern instruction into an indispensable commodity.[50] The solution to all problems was seen to lie in the spread of education, now considered second in importance only to earning a living.[51] In Germany, education was seen as being crucial to the direction society was taking. State schooling was perceived as part of the increasing rationalization of life associated with a decrease in confessional religious belief.[52] Yet, as elsewhere, the new educational dispensation inherited much from what had gone before in the way of schools, ideas,

---

[49] Mona Ozouf, *L'École, l'église et la République*, 225–26.

[50] Patrick J. Harrigan, *Mobility, Elites and Education in French Society of the Second Empire* (Waterloo, Canada, 1980), 119; Zeldin, *France, 1848–1945*, 139.

[51] Zeldin, *France, 1848–1945*, 139.

[52] James C. Albisetti, *Secondary School Reform in Imperial Germany* (Princeton: Princeton University Press), p. i.

[53] Detlef K. Müller, "The Process of Systematisation: The Case of German Secondary Education" (Fritz Ringer, trans.), in Detlef K. Müller *et al.* (eds.), *Rise*, 16–17.

and individuals.[53] As Zeldin has written of this persistence in France, "Men did not break away from their past so easily."[54]

It is more apposite to look elsewhere for parallels with the Ottoman case. In Russia, China, and Japan, as in the Ottoman Empire, religiously informed expectations and content were integral to state education in this period. National and imperial education was shaped by an even more powerful impulse, namely, the belief that education was critical to safeguarding the empire's future. In all cases, this cause assumed political, religious, and cultural dimensions. In Russia, the new education was considered one of the empire's two top priorities in the last quarter of the nineteenth century; the other was the railroad, that parallel symbol of progress and agent of centralization. Key educational reformers of the nineteenth century such as Dimitri Tolstoy and Mikhail Katkov saw themselves in the role of "saviors of the fatherland," campaigning against ignorance and backwardness in the face of advances in Western Europe, and the lack of a coherent educational system in Russia; as Pushkin wrote in *Eugene Onegin*, "We all pick up our education in bits and pieces."[55] As in the Ottoman case, the campaign for Russian education amounted to nothing less than a crusade intended to preserve the holy empire, both from Western influence and from itself.

In neighboring Iran, where the trajectory of educational change was clearly influenced by the Ottoman efforts, modern education was similarly invested with weighty expectations. As in the Ottoman Empire, widespread enthusiasm for education in Iran stemmed from a combination of factors, both indigenous and exogenous. Menashri cites Zoroastrian, Islamic, and Western European influences as contributing to the optimism for education in late nineteenth-century Iran.[56] This optimism was not confined to the state alone. Just as missionary education was expanding in the Ottoman lands, so too was it increasingly evident in Iran throughout this period.[57] Both missionary and state

---

[54] Zeldin, "Were there two Frances?," in Zeldin (ed.), *Conflicts in French Society*, 9–10.

[55] Alston, *Education and the State*, 66.

[56] David Menashri, *Education and the Making of Modern Iran* (Ithaca, NY: Cornell University Press, 1992), 13 ff.

[57] Michael P. Zirinsky, "A Panacea for the Ills of the Country: American Presbyterian Education in Inter-War Iran," *Iranian Studies*, 26/1–2 (1993[–4]), 119–37.

efforts acted on and reinforced the notion of education as the "secret" of positive development. As Bernard Lewis has written, many in the East sought "to discover and apply the illusive secret of its [i.e., the West's] greatness and strength."[58]

In Iran, this approach has been described as "the ambivalent approach of simultaneously wishing to adopt and reject the ways of the strong—but infidel—West."[59] This might as easily describe the late Ottoman dilemma. As we shall soon see, the concept of education as a Western "secret" appears verbatim in the Ottoman context. Much of the rest of this book is dedicated to showing the way this secret was applied. As we shall see, the Ottoman application of the Western model was in large part carried out in order to thwart the influence of the very same West.

In China, the "self-strengthening" movement was largely informed by the need to fend off the intrusions of Western missionaries. Japanese reform efforts were partly concocted to thwart foreign influence. Western missionaries were viewed both as the bearers of useful expertise and as foreign threats.[60] In the Ottoman Empire, as we shall shortly see, the twin nature of new-style education, as hope and as menace, was abundantly apparent.

Yet the Ottoman predicament was heightened, nearly to the point of desperation, by another factor, namely, the perceived failings of the Muslim community to provide education that satisfied the "demands of the present." There were important indigenous attempts at providing a form of education that would satisfy "modern" concerns while remaining faithful to Islamic pedagogical tradition, but their results were geographically scattered and numerically meager.[61] Important Ottoman officials considered them to be deplorably wanting on an imperial scale, and not without justification. Unlike France, where the state could draw upon the educational inheritance of the

---

[58] As cited in Menashri, *Education*, 25.   [59] Ibid.

[60] Wollons, "The Black Forest," 10–11.

[61] For an overview of the situation in one province, see Martin Strohmeier, "Muslim Education in the Vilayet of Beirut, 1880–1918," in Cesar E. Farah (ed.), *Decision Making and Change in the Ottoman Empire* (Kirksville, Miss.: Thomas Jefferson University Press, 1993), 215–41. For the reform-minded Midhat's views on the situation in Syria, see Ezel Kural Shaw, "Midhat Pasha, Reformer or Revolutionary; His Administrative Career and Contributions to the Constitution of 1876," Ph.D. diss., Harvard University (1975).

church, and even unlike Russia, with which the Ottoman Empire shared the need not merely to tinker with an already existing school system, as the states of Western Europe were seen to do, but rather to create one,[62] Ottoman educational planners had little to build on. Overhauling the madrasa system seems never to have been contemplated.[63] The Ottoman state thus saw itself as single-handedly responsible for remedying the considerable educational shortcomings of the empire. Or rather of its Muslim majority, for in spite of its *de facto* openness to all subjects, the state schools were largely conceived of as Muslim schools.

Thus, in the Ottoman Empire the educational endeavor was informed by a profound sense of contestation, even confrontation. It was not, as in France, primarily between two conflicting factions within society, but rather a battle between the Ottoman Muslim majority and a phalanx of combatants. This sense of besiegement, almost universally overlooked, is critical to understanding the Ottoman predicament— and therefore key to much of what follows in subsequent chapters. It clarifies the conflicted Ottoman attitudes toward the need for education, seen primarily as a beacon of hope but also as a fearful menace when deployed by an array of hostile parties. It also explains the Ottoman commitment to fighting back, to adopting an unmistakably combative stance in one of the few arenas where the Ottomans had room to maneuver. Beyond such largely strategic concerns, this embattled stance helps us to understand the Ottoman impulse and commitment to reworking the fledgling state schooling system, the subject of the next chapter. By ordering daily school life according to a consciously Islamic sense of propriety, by incorporating religious content into the previously more nearly secular curriculum, and by emphasizing the unity of Ottoman territory on school maps and texts, late Ottoman statesmen sought to create a system that would staunch the loss of the Ottoman way of life among the majority of the empire's population.

All of this points to the conflicted quality of the Ottoman effort, caught between seemingly boundless optimism for its power to effect

---

[62] Alston, *Education and the State*, 66.

[63] For the history of an interesting World War I effort in the direction of uniting madrasa and civil education, see Martin Strohmeier, *Al-Kullīya As-Salāhīyya in Jerusalem* (Stuttgart: Franz Steiner, 1991).

positive change and profound anxiety over its already visible negative consequences. The notion of education as hope was tempered by the specter of education as menace when deployed by less-than-friendly actors, foreign, neighboring, or internal. This Janus-faced quality finds parallels in many contemporaneous cases. Much of the flurry of educational activity in Western European countries in this period is linked to (not unfounded) fears of being overtaken by their neighbors, not just in a military sense but in a technological and cultural one as well. Thus, the legacy of 1870 animated educational expansion in France, where it was thought that German victory was due in large part to superior Prussian education, while Germanophobia and Germanophilia alternately affected the shape of Russian educational developments.[64] We have already seen that the presence of Western missionary schooling in China and Japan influenced educational policy in those countries. But it was not merely cross-border influence that affected educational change in this period. Frequently internal divisions spurred action. For example, the Catholic–Protestant rivalry affected some regions of France. Catholics reacted to Protestant activity with a heightened sense of purpose that one scholar has likened to that of missionaries.[65] As recent research on nineteenth-century France reveals, the Catholic church was engaged in what was tantamount to a battle to maintain its grip on education that in many ways resembles the Ottoman effort. By creating and staffing its own schools in response to a number of threats—Republican, Protestant, and fiscal—the Catholic church fought back with congregational schools at the local level.[66]

Thus the "demands of the present" generated both optimism and anxiety that seemed to accelerate with the pace of historical change in this period. Both the hope and the fear were equally founded on the principle that education was inherently a powerful commodity, able to transform society either for good or bad, depending on whose education was being provided. It was precisely this question that occupied the minds of Ottoman officials. Examining Ottoman perceptions of the competition at the local and imperial level will show that the empire

[64] Zeldin, *France 1848–1945*, 151; Alston, *Education and the State*.

[65] Harrigan, *Mobility*, 117.

[66] Sarah A. Curtis, "Supply and Demand: Religious Schooling in Nineteenth-Century France," *History of Education Quarterly*, 39/1 (1999), 71.

was, like its contemporaries elsewhere, engaged in an extremely pressing educational struggle.

EMPHASIZING MORALITY

A comparative perspective is extremely helpful for placing the Ottoman case in its contemporary context. While it cannot supply the objectivity of Zeldin's hypothetical external observer, it can nevertheless help us to see that the Ottoman case was in many senses not unique. This account will be quite selective, for reasons of time and space, focusing on the common moral component in late nineteenth-century education in a handful of countries.

The Ottoman attempt to integrate the Western system with moral content appropriate to the Islamic and Ottoman context shared much in common with contemporary approaches to state education elsewhere. A moral agenda of one sort or another lay at the heart of state educational projects unfolding in disparate parts of the late nineteenth-century globe. In the United States, an ethical ethos sufficiently permeated public high schools that one historian has described it as "the moral world of the high school," into which students passed in seamless fashion from their "God-fearing Protestant homes."[67] In Russia, the Ottomans' acquisitive neighbor to the north, a variety of educational offerings served the state's campaign, or even its "crusade," to reform society from above,[68] but religio-moral teaching coupled with loyalty to the holy person of the Tsar featured prominently in all of them. Rules for "secular" schools expressed the common consideration that religion was "the foundation of the Russian state system."[69] As in the Ottoman Empire, the expansion of public education in Russia proper was symptomatic of the secularizing logic of the state and of the severing of the monopoly of the religious establishment over the written word. But it also meant that the state increasingly relied on the co-operation of the religious authorities and on the lesson content they supplied.

[67] William J. Reese, *The Origins of the American High School* (New Haven: Yale University Press, 1995), 162.

[68] Alston, *Education and the State*.

[69] Jeffrey Brooks, *When Russia Learned to Read: Literacy and Popular Literature, 1861–1917* (Princeton: Princeton University Press, 1985), 47.

In Central Asia, moral education was critical to educational change, both that offered by the Tsarist government and the emerging Jadid movement. Adeeb Khalid's fine study of the Jadids places education at the center of cultural and social change in Central Asia.[70] The shared features with the Ottoman Empire are many, so close were the educational agenda of the Jadids and the Ottomans. They include: a profound faith in learning that Khalid calls the "cult of knowledge;" an overarching confidence in the corrective and transformative power of that knowledge, when applied through the form of standardized education, to "awaken" the slumbering people from the inertia of ignorance; the necessity of the new pedagogy to prepare young students to face the "needs of the age;" the creation of new schools, classroom furniture, textbooks, and wall maps in order to carry out this modernizing mission; and the penchant for combining new techniques of learning (the Jadids' "new style" schools derived their name from a phonetic approach to literacy that contrasts with the syllabic approach taught in the maktabs, i.e. Qur'an schools) with religio-moral content distilled from the maktab and madrasa curriculum. As in the Ottoman case, religious knowledge was desacralized, transforming the notion of what constituted "Islam" just as, conversely, the "secular" nature of modern schooling was itself altered as it became a vehicle for religious education. Many of Khalid's Jadids were in contact with the Ottoman Empire, among other parts of the world, through travel, correspondence, or periodical subscription. While there was naturally some mutual influence as a result, Khalid emphasizes that Jadidism was first and foremost an indigenous phenomenon, further supporting the notion that the nexus of regional permutations of a modern, moralistic pedagogy was a world phenomenon, and not one merely reliant upon Western European influence.

In China, the parallels with the Ottoman case are remarkable. An equally proud imperial tradition increasingly felt itself under attack both from the outside world and from internal opposition. Missionary education affected the government's own efforts, although probably in a less overt manner than those of their Ottoman counterparts. As in the Ottoman case, military defeat concentrated educational thinking. In the wake of defeat by Japan in the late nineteenth century and

---

[70] Khalid, *Politics*.

the suppression of the Boxer rebellion in 1900, moral instruction was emphasized as a critical component of the "self-strengthening" movement. The new schools that emerged as a result bowed to the need to emulate foreign education (both European and Japanese), but they based their curriculum on the Confucian classics.[71] Moral training textbooks—a new method of inculcating the morality of the old examination system—were employed to meet the "educational aims" issued by the Board of Education in 1906. As in the Ottoman Empire, Chinese educators sought to instill in the students of the new schools a cluster of ideals that included loyalty to the emperor, practical study, and indigenous (i.e. Confucian) morality.[72]

Egypt provides some important parallels with the Ottoman case, but with some crucial differences given the complications of colonial rule. Still technically under Ottoman suzerainty but under *de facto* British control since 1882, Egypt saw her educational development seriously affected by colonial desiderata. Starrett shows us the importance of the moral in British policy; both in England and in Egypt the Victorian ethos permeated the educational mindset, ensuring that moral considerations received top priority. British administrators in Egypt came up against what they perceived to be the backwardness of "traditional" education in the maktabs, where learning took the form of "literal incorporation of the text of the Qur'an."[73] Starrett contrasts the Egyptian impetus for a "ritual" memorization of the sacred scripture through oral recitation with the British desire to distil the "moral" message of the Bible via absorption of the printed word. He demonstrates that with time indigenous educators continued the British penchant for extracting religio-moral "lessons" from the Qur'an. "The traditional study of the Qur'an . . . now became the study of Islam as a moral system, a study removed from its living context and placed on the same

---

[71] Paul Bailey, *Reform the People: Changing Attitudes Towards Popular Education in Early 20th Century China* (Edinburgh: Edinburgh University Press, 1990), 26–7. I thank my colleague Frank Dikötter for this and other helpful references. For a synopsis of the situation in Japan, where a similar movement away from the Western model was exhibited and where moral instruction was also critical in this period, see Wollons, "The Black Forest."

[72] Paul Bailey, "Translator's Introduction," in Marianne Bastid, *Educational Reform in Early Twentieth-Century China* (Ann Arbor: Center for Chinese Studies, University of Michigan, 1988), pp. vii–xi.

[73] Ibid. 37.

level as other secular categories of knowledge."[74] Interestingly, the Ottoman state schools we shall encounter shortly incorporated elements of both approaches: such ritual aspects of the "traditional," oral approach as memorizing texts and attending prayers as a student congregation coexisted alongside the "moral" approach as represented in the pedagogical style of distilling moral instruction from texts for courses in religion that shared curricular space with worldly topics.

This string of countries could be extended in a number of geographical directions, but it is perhaps more apposite to revisit the subject of moral instruction in France. As we have already seen, the historiography of French education in the nineteenth century provides a suggestive if cautionary tale for parallel developments in the Ottoman Empire. The history of education in France now sees continuities where previously sharp breaks dominated the view. Emphasizing the give-and-take in the French educational context affords the possibility of accommodating the persistence of traditional (particularly religious) modes alongside, or perhaps underneath the surface of, the new modus operandi.

The French case is most instructive in pointing toward a realization that the sharp lines and trajectories that have characterized the history of education have yielded to a considerably more nuanced depiction. This is particularly apparent with respect to the role of religion and morality. As in the Ottoman Empire, religious schools in France were easily targeted for their pedagogical backwardness and slavish devotion to teaching religious texts in an atmosphere where memorization far exceeded understanding.[75] The state schools were often deemed little better. Eugen Weber describes early provincial state schools as adjuncts of the religious establishment. The teachers were frequently treated as "acolytes" of the local priests until liberated by the advent of the Third Republic.[76] But even then the similarities between the old and new pedagogy did not miraculously disappear. The republican schools were greatly indebted to their religious precursors, and in many ways can be seen to have taken up the church's mission.[77] As the state prised open

---

[74] Bastid, *Educational Reform*, 71.

[75] Weber, *Peasants into Frenchmen*, 306; Zeldin, *France 1848–1945*, 148.

[76] Weber, *Peasants into Frenchmen*, 316.

[77] For a recent rethinking of the historical role of Catholic education in France during the July Monarchy, see Curtis, "Supply and Demand."

the ecclesiastical grip on teaching, it simultaneously came to rely more and more on religiously informed attitudes on education. The focus on morality was only the most visible aspect of this complex inter-twining of the secular and the religious in France.

As we have seen, one only needs to scratch the surface of state-supplied "modern" education around the globe to reveal the centrality of the religio-moral element. Although often occluded by moderniza-tion theory-driven historiography, the religious dimension persisted in state efforts long thought to have been overwhelmingly secular in nature. We have seen that the unstated but powerfully prevailing analogy, French republicanism is to French Catholicism as Ottoman secularization is to Islam, can be wildly misleading where education is concerned. Unless itself problematized, the French case is unhelpful in that it prevents us from seeing the connections between the men of religion and the state's new agenda. The deeply contested nature of public education in France, the persistence of elements of non-confor-mity, the wide swings of the educational pendulum between a Catholic and a laic agenda, and the emphasis on moral instruction across the educational divide,[78] all suggest a level of complexity that we would do well to remember in attempting to trace the various interwoven strands of the Ottoman case.

Two main lessons emerge from this comparative geographical per-spective. First, despite the geographical and historical range separating these cases, the similarities stand out over against the more expected differences. Commonalties in the educational systems, the debates sur-rounding their *raison d'être*, their sources of inspiration, the details of their articulation, their social effects, among other areas, suggest not just that we rethink the notion of Western influence and Eastern adop-tion but also that we therefore imagine a more truly global history, not one that merely relies on the "diffusion" of ideas stemming from an inevitably Western European source. Shared patterns in the timing of educational change alone demand that attention be drawn to the rela-tive simultaneity of educational change. This synchronic element needs emphasizing because of the prevailing assumption that the East lagged

---

[78] On the French efforts to inculcate a "secular" notion of morality, see Phyllis Stock-Morton, *Moral Education for a Secular Society: The Development of* Morale Laïque *in Nine-teenth Century France* (Albany, NY: State University of New York Press, 1988).

well behind its Western exemplars, chronologically and in qualitative and quantitative terms. By contrast, common aspirations across the divides of East and West, North and South, developed and developing, Christian and Muslim, suggest examining educational change on a global scale. The synchronic commonalties have been raised in the field of education by Zeldin, who has termed this period the "Age of Education."[79] More broadly, as we have seen, Reinhard Schulze has argued against the essentialism of the East in part by referring to a common "world time" in which like concerns among diverse states set an agenda more shared than divisive. Approaching the Ottoman case from a global perspective supports the applicability of Schulze's "world time" to the question of educational expansion. Educational change does not necessarily result from a borrowing from the West by the East. Such simultaneity suggests that there was a common world-time reaction to the perceived speeding up of time,[80] to concerns about keeping abreast with the "demands of the present," and to the feeling that flight from the "traditional" theological understandings of the way in which the world worked was accelerating, leading to moral decay. The Ottoman Empire shared with France, and with Russia, China, and countless other lands, an extraordinary optimism that looked beyond a myriad of pressing ideological and infrastructural problems. New-style education appeared as a seemingly universal beacon of hope, particularly when it was meant to convey a reworked but "traditionally" inspired notion of morality. It is, however, this moral dimension which is frequently overlooked in assessing educational change.

Here we come to the second broad comparative finding: the common twists and turns that emerge in the way the history of education has been written. In the historiographic rendering of education—what is retained from the vastness of human experience at school—in each of these three cases there are apprehensions and misapprehensions that prove cautionary for our own case. The subjective quality of "recognizing" what education is and does, combined with the meliorative agenda built into the pedagogical, results in histories which are invariably linked to the broader paths of national "emer-

[79] Zeldin, *France 1848–1945*, 139.
[80] A point Deringil makes effectively with respect to the Eurasian empires: "Invention of Tradition," 3. Expanding the basis of comparison to include China and the United States only underscores its salience.

gence" cum modernization, Westernization and secularization. These strong, near totalizing, projects have imposed themselves upon the histories of this period in ways that are only slowly becoming clear. By restoring the importance of the moral agenda to the late Ottoman state project, this book opens one way to rethink a critical aspect of this region's history.

CHAPTER OVERVIEW

After introducing the subject by placing late Ottoman education in historiographical perspective, Chapter 2 turns to the situation in the Ottoman Empire in more detail. Here I present education as an attempt at assimilating competing worldviews, namely, the Western and what we may term the "Ottoman/Islamic," in order to compete with Western encroachment on a number of levels. This chapter demonstrates that the state's educational campaign was a direct response to the challenges brought by foreign missionaries, neighboring states, and the empire's indigenous minority groups. Dispatches sent to Istanbul from provinces ranging from the Balkans to Baghdad, and preserved in the Ottoman archives, reveal the extent to which these rival educational advances provoked Ottoman officialdom to fear for the very future of the empire. This competition explains both the belated urgency of the state's campaign to build its own schools and its simultaneous and systematic program to alter the content of what was to be taught inside them.

Chapter 3 traces Ottoman educational expansion, as plans on paper were converted into bricks and mortar throughout the empire's provinces. This chapter explains the importance of the secondary level of education as a bridge between the early attempts at reforming primary schools and the spate of higher institutions being built in the capital. It begins by reassessing the institution in Istanbul that served as the model for the secondary schools, the lycée of Galatasaray. Important signs of Ottomanization and Islamization in this experimental establishment that are usually dismissed as incongruous actually prefigured the way the secondary schools were refitted to conform to the state's agenda.

Subsequent chapters concentrate on the actual buildings this effort produced, and on what transpired within their walls. Chapter 4 addresses the schools' urban context, the role of their architecture in shaping new patterns of activity, and their use of ornament to differentiate themselves from both the competition and the traditional loci of Islamic learning. Set apart physically and architecturally, the new schools were marked as part of a novel endeavor, closer in style to other government structures than to the maktab or the madrasa of classical Islam. Yet their beaux arts façades concealed the fact that these buildings actually incorporated mosques within. Their new architecture, modified versions of French school buildings, demanded new patterns of learning, living, and ceremony. Disciplinary cases reveal both the advantages and the disadvantages inherent in the Ottoman attempt to regulate these everyday patterns according to Islamic morality. Instances of actual human interaction, these cases afford a rare opportunity to get beyond the prevailing tendency to treat the schools as abstract, statistical entities.

Both Chapters 5 and 6 analyze the material consequences of the state's effort to refit classroom content so as to protect its young subjects from the corruptive influences of the competition. Chapter 5 documents a key shift in the way the empire was represented in the classroom. Abandoning the inherited European cartographic practice of framing the Ottoman domains continent-by-continent, the state consciously began to create school maps that displayed its territory in a single frame, in a belated effort to foster patriotic affiliation with the empire and, by extension, the Ottoman dynasty. Chapter 6 turns to examine the prominent role that a distinctly Islamic morality played in the Ottoman educational endeavor. Focusing on moral pedagogy and practice reveals the Islamic nature of supposedly secular schooling, and therefore calls into question some of the most basic assumptions concerning the directionality and boundedness of social change. It concludes the volume by plumbing the state's optimistic attempt to inculcate the discipline and morals it deemed necessary to control student behavior and thought, and thereby safeguard the empire's future.

2

Hope Against Fear

INTRODUCTION

The late Ottoman educational endeavor, like its counterparts around the world in the nineteenth century, was fueled by both hope and fear. It shared with school-building drives around the world an extraordinary optimism in modern-style pedagogy as a panacea for a wide variety of ailments and shortcomings, both real and perceived. In Western Europe, where the new education had developed, this "amazing optimism" was sufficiently widespread for one historian to term this period "the Age of Education." In many non-Western locales, faith in new-style education was redoubled by the sense that the by-now undeniable advantage of the Western powers derived in large part from a secret: superior education. The "secret wisdom" of the West was especially appealing because it appeared so easy to apply, particularly in the many cultures, such as those of East Asia and the Islamic world, where an abiding, deeply held respect for learning held sway.

If the widespread hope that schooling inspired may not always have been founded in reality, the fears that prompted educational change were more immediate, more specific. True, there were general fears about the rush of the modern; for example, the notion that the pace of change was accelerating too rapidly, that moral strengthening was needed in the wake of social disruption,[1] or that inaction would afford an irretrievable advantage to the frequently invoked perils of ignorance. But it was more pragmatic fears that provided the specific goad to educational expansion, East and West. Schools were pawns in larger battles

---

[1] On the connection between societal disruption, moralizing, and fear, see Marshall, *Learning to be Modern*, 31–2.

between various sets of adversaries in various locales: for example, church and state in France; traditionalists and progressives in the United States; aristocrats and levelers in Tsarist Russia; classicists and modernizers in Wilhelmine Germany; and nativists and Westernizers in Meiji Japan. Each contest provoked particular fears that manifested themselves at the local level. There was apprehension, if not terror, at the prospect of the adversary's advance, whether in the form of a changed curriculum or the disappearance of prevailing privileges. Such dread was not only confined to the internal dynamics being worked out on the national scale; cross-border fear was a frequent motivation. For example, the Prussian model loomed large, not only in France but also in Russia. The fear that one's neighbors were getting the jump on one's own country—militarily, economically, even culturally—was linked to educational failure. Expanding and revamping the nation's school system seemed to provide the opportunity to catch up. Falling behind on the national level was often attributed to the failure of traditional institutions, such as the family and the church. The state saw fit to intervene into their preserves, and the school was the natural instrument for intercession. Behind all of the hopes and fears lay a concern for the fate of broad, often inchoate notions like "civilization" and "culture," which were threatened by change. Whether in France of the Third Republic or Japan of the Meiji Restoration, the struggle over education was frequently trenchant precisely because all parties, however far apart, shared the belief that education was crucial to charting the way forward; the conflict turned on whose education would prevail.

The Ottoman case shared the broad apprehensions over a threatened culture and a vanishing way of life, as we shall soon see. It also shared the tension between the pull of optimism and the push of fear. But compared with most of its contemporaries, the Ottoman plight appeared much more dire. The threats were more immediate, appearing inside the imperial borders, in the form of foreign bankers, battleship commanders, diplomats, archeologists, and even indigenous separatist revolutionaries. Even if we focus only on those in the field of education, there are still a variety of actors to consider. Adversaries for all practical purposes, they took the form of Western missionaries, neighboring propagandists, and indigenous minority activists. From the perspective of the Ottoman state, they were all well entrenched, better organized, well funded, and, possessing a superior product, more successful. The besieged quality of the Ottoman educational predicament has rarely been understood. Neither, therefore, has the dual nature of the imperial response. The spread of new-style education in the empire has to be seen both as something borrowed from the West in the hope of conjuring its power, and as something which, once brought in line with indigenous exigencies, would ward off Western encroachment. What is often neglected is the fact that Ottoman education, for all its foreign influence, was mainly an indigenous phenomenon, implemented for indigenous reasons. Hence the importance of recapturing Ottoman agency in educational change.

This chapter begins the process of restoring Ottoman agency by briefly situating the empire's educational campaign in the context of both global trends and indigenous requirements. In the last chapter I argued that the expansion of Ottoman education must be seen as part of a global phenomenon of educational expansion of the nineteenth and twentieth centuries. In its timing, its optimistic spirit, its state-driven agenda, and its concern with creating a new citizen/subject, the Ottoman case shared much with its global contemporaries. Even the historiographical profile of Ottoman education reflects many of the same dynamics—and problems—of its contemporaries elsewhere. Yet the story of Ottoman educational change is in many ways unique. Under intense pressure from an array of forces both foreign and domestic, the late Ottoman state summoned its historically sanctioned Ottoman and Islamic sources of inspiration, and adapted them to fitting its contemporary needs. For a variety of reasons discussed in the last chapter, the resulting mixture of "old" and "new," "traditional" and "modern", has been little understood. This chapter demonstrates that far from being the result of the inchoate, disembodied processes of "modernization," "secularization," and "Westernization," Ottoman education was a conscious response to the situation on the ground in Ottoman provinces that appeared increasingly vulnerable to encroachment from a variety of actors: missionaries, neighboring propagandists, and the empire's own minority groups. Responding to alarms sounded by officials across the far-flung provinces, the central government set out to rework its educational strategy. The result was, as we shall see, a fusion of the exogenous and the indigenous that reflected both the global trends and the particular dynamic inherent in the Ottoman predicament.

The global expansion of public education in the nineteenth century reflected an unprecedented level of state involvement in the lives of its subjects. The first point of contact between the state and many of its people, the new schools were invariably critical to mediating this changing relationship. Given the range and depth of the issues raised by this new dispensation, it is impossible to provide more than a survey at this point in the discussion. Many such issues will be addressed in detail in subsequent chapters. The point of departure for all of them was the fact that it was the state that acted as the primary purveyor of education, one of many attributes of the state's new-found role as engine of change in the late nineteenth century. States around the globe shared similar agendas: they were in the business of centralization, standardization, and homogenization, yet regionalism, variation, and anomaly persisted, resisting the dominant trend with often surprising tenacity. An economic program buttressed the obvious political and military implications of the state's agenda; competitiveness was the byword of an increasingly Darwinian recasting of an earlier mercantilism. Education was seen as an economic imperative, as a means of assuring the competitiveness of a given nation vis-à-vis its rivals and neighbors. But beyond purely practical and strategic concerns, civilizations and cultures, variously understood, were considered threatened by upheaval. In turn-of-the-century Europe there was much wringing of hands over the fate of French "culture génerale," German "Bildung," and the Anglo-American "liberal education." In many places there was near obsession with the social effects of expanding education. The debate over the social consequences of rapidly increasing educational options—"practical" versus "literary"—consumed many countries in the West. But elsewhere, as in Russia and the Ottoman Empire, the chief aim was to create, not refine, a national educational system.

The rise of the national systems of schooling had clear implications for women and the family. By taking more of their citizens or subjects (both male and to a lesser extent female) into their buildings for more of the time, the states were inevitably assuming parental responsibilities. In other words, the vertical expansion of the centralizing state from the center out was paralleled by a horizontal movement from the top down. In many cases this was a conscious effort, aimed at removing the young generation from what paternalistic statesmen deemed to be an unhealthy or unfortunate domestic environment. The family, said Émile Durkheim, was a failure; the schools must replace it.[2] In the Ottoman Empire, as elsewhere, this new dispensation had far-reaching implications—ranging from its role in shaping collective social consciousness to the construction of the individual as the social unit over which the state attempted to hold sway. Yet the assumption that the state's new stance inevitably resulted in Western-style modernization is clearly problematic. Elizabeth Frierson's work has shown that women's periodical press and consumption patterns paralleled the highly selective, highly critical stance toward Western ideas, products, fashions, and mores adopted by the late Ottoman state.[3]

The Ottoman schooling effort was strongly influenced by a sense that the empire was under siege from a host of threats to its increasingly vulnerable position. In the field of education these threats came in the form of an array of educational competitors operating within the empire's borders: foreign missionaries, neighboring states, and indigenous minority groups. Unlike the countries of the West, where educational energies were concentrated on regional homogenization and nation building, the Ottoman Empire, owing to its weakened position, had to fight a double battle. On the one hand it wanted to keep up with the "demands of the modern age" just as much as its contemporaries did.[4] On the other hand, the Ottomans had to fend off a number of challenges—military, diplomatic, economic, ideological, and cultural—that most of its contemporaries did not face. As one British missionary observed, the reverse situation sounded most absurd: "Let us imagine a Mahometan Potentate sending missionaries to England,

---

[2] Zeldin, *France 1848–1945*, 157.

[3] Elizabeth Brown Frierson, "Mirrors Out, Mirrors In: Domestication and Rejection of the Foreign in Late-Ottoman Women's Magazines (1875–1908)," in D. Fairchild Ruggles (ed.), *Women, Patronage, and Self-Representation in Islamic Societies* (Albany, NY: State University of New York Press, 2000), 177–204; and "Cheap and Easy: The Creation of Consumer Culture in Late Ottoman Society," in Donald Quataert (ed.), *Consumption Studies and the History of the Ottoman Empire, 1550–1922: An Introduction* (Albany, NY: State University of New York Press, 2000), 243–60. My thanks to Elizabeth for making these studies available to me.

[4] Variations on this phrase crop up repeatedly in the writings of a number of high-ranking Ottoman officials. It bears striking resemblance to the "demands of the present," so important in the context of contemporaneous educational debates in Europe. For the example of Wilhelmine Germany, see Albisetti, *Secondary School Reform*.

and opening schools denouncing Christianity in London: I doubt if we should bear it silently."[5] The Ottomans bore the burden of a proud empire trying to maintain its dignity in frequently undignified circumstances. Unlike still other countries that had succumbed to European imperialism, the Ottoman Empire had to organize—and pay for—its own educational attempt. It did so with enthusiasm and remarkable optimism, believing that the secret of the West's success could be easily applied to Ottoman circumstances. The key was thought to lie in adapting Western methods, but selectively and with the best interests of the Ottomans in mind.

In order to make sense of this effort—its urgency, the sacrifices it required, its agency, its use of indigenous characteristics, and its recourse to Islamic morality—it is first necessary to comprehend the palpable sense of competition that shaped it. The competitive context helps explain the frequently de-emphasized and misunderstood aspects of the Ottoman endeavor. The complicated relationship with the West, both a major source of emulation for the Ottoman educational system and a threat to the very existence of the empire, can only be appreciated in light of the competitive milieu. Likewise, the Ottoman emphasis on Islam and an Islamically informed morality only makes sense as an attempt to inoculate the empire's young subjects against what its officials considered the contagion of cultural encroachment.

PLEAS FROM THE PROVINCES

The writings of the Ottoman officials directly involved with education in the provinces offer the most accessible gauge of the milieu in which the new state schools were built.[6] Their perception of the competition is critical to understanding the formation of Ottoman educational policy in this period. Furthermore, the concerns they express in the context of reporting the local situation elucidate their general conception of education. The hopes and fears expressed in their tales from the

---

[5] As quoted in Rogan, *Frontiers*, 146.

[6] The number of documents relating to education in this period is remarkably large; in what follows I sample this documentary evidence to give a sense of its regional and thematic range.

front of the schooling battle offer insights into the tremendous potential, both positive and negative, they associate with education.

The descriptions of the local situation provided by Ottoman officials on the spot are remarkable for their palpable sense of competition with other sources of education. In the eyes of the Ottoman officials zealously manning their imperial posts, the competitors generally take one of the following forms. The most obvious educational competitors are the Western missionaries. They are rarely described specifically but remain an ominous presence, seemingly able to command vast financial, cultural, and political resources. Next in line come the members of the local minority communities, who are often described as impressively diligent, both in their devotion to the concept of education and in the practical undertakings necessary to ensure their success. The minority groups are often viewed as political clients of the foreign powers, if not their outright agents. Last are the competitors that the Ottomans faced from neighboring lands, such as Iran, Greece, and Bulgaria. The challenges these represented tended to be localized, affecting the border provinces, and were thus not as critical as those posed by the above-mentioned adversaries, who were capable of mounting a sustained effort throughout various Ottoman provinces. However, the fact that no frontier seemed to be free of competition must have exacerbated the Ottoman sense of siege. As we will see, the Ottoman officials take a mixed view of the educational accomplishments of these three forms of competition. Often vilified for the havoc they wrought in Ottoman lands, the various competitors' commitment to the ideal of education and its practical success are nevertheless frequently held up as examples to be emulated.

Provincial officials almost universally described the situation in their provinces as bleak. Descriptions assumed the tone of laments, and recommendations often took the form of desperate pleas for help. Naturally one has to discount some degree of exaggeration in petitions that had to compete with similar entreaties for the inherently limited supply of attention and funding that the center could spare in this period.[7] Nevertheless, the despair contained in the dispatches is palpable and contrasts poignantly with the simultaneously manifested faith in education's potential to reverse the lamented "decline." It is necessary here

---

[7] For a description of the pressures facing the Hamidian state, see Akarlı, "Problems."

to underscore the magnitude of the optimism that modern education inspired in the late Ottoman period because it was so crucial to the entire educational effort of the state. In the late Ottoman period the disparity between the pessimism over present circumstances and the optimism for the future speaks to the tremendous hope that state officials placed on education. There is an almost magical, esoteric quality ascribed to education which, if properly conjured, would somehow suffice to right the numerous wrongs detailed in the memoranda sent to Istanbul.

WESTERN MISSIONARIES

Of all the competition faced by the Ottomans, that provided by Western missionaries was the most alarming. Foreign schools were the first "modern" schools in these provinces, and therefore set the standard for all subsequent institutions. The demonstration effect of the foreign schools was first felt by the local minority groups and later on by the nascent Muslim benevolent societies.[8] These Muslim societies were generally only able to found a modest number of schools; those that were established were the exceptions that proved the rule of relative Muslim educational inactivity. Thus the responsibility for providing the bulk of its population with education fell to the state—a massive burden but one it accepted as part of a general program to arrogate more power and areas of control to an increasingly rationalized central government. The biggest inducement for the state to act was the aggressive and directly felt presence of foreign missionary schools. Not only was the existence of foreign schools painful as a matter of principle, but their growing numbers in the 1880s and 1890s made Ottoman officials fear for the very future of the state. Realists among them could perhaps accept their presence, given the military and political pressures being exerted on the empire by the Great Powers. However, it was the perceived success these foreign-run

---

[8] Donald J. Cioeta, "Islamic Benevolent Societies and Public Education in Ottoman Syria, 1875–1882" *The Islamic Quarterly*, 26/1 (1982), 41. Cioeta discusses the situation in Syria, but his analysis can be extended to the areas having a high percentage of Armenian inhabitants which also became the focus of intensive foreign missionary activity. For an account of missionary activity among the Armenian population, see Jeremy Salt, *Imperialism, Evangelism and the Ottoman Armenians, 1878–1896* (London: Frank Cass, 1993).

schools enjoyed in attracting the children of Ottoman subjects into their classrooms that made them increasingly difficult to ignore.

One case illustrates the Ottoman preoccupation with missionary education. The newly created province of Beirut, consisting not only of the area around the city of Beirut but also the non-contiguous areas of Latakia, Tripoli, Acre, and Nablus,[9] had been the focus of considerable foreign activity. In fact, one of the main reasons for establishing this new province, which was now administered from Beirut, was that the government could maintain closer scrutiny of foreign—especially French—interests along the coast.[10] It is clear that one such foreign interest was education. Early after the establishment of the new province in 1888, its governor wrote to the capital expressing his concerns over the damages (mazarrât) that foreign schools have inflicted in the province.[11] In order to combat them, he proposed prohibiting children from entering these foreign schools and to enroll them in equivalents provided by the state. In order to do so, it would be necessary to carry out an immediate plan, including the reopening of the *mekteb-i sultanî*[12] in Beirut. It is important to note that both the

---

[9] The State Yearbook (Devlet Salnamesi) for 1308 [1890–1] lists the *sancak*s included in the vilayet of Beirut as: Beyrut, Akka, Trablusşam (Tripoli), Lazkiye (Latakia), and Bilka (Nablus). Saida, Sur (Tyre), etc. are listed as *kaza*s. This arrangement was new, these areas having been detached from the province of Damascus (Şam) in 1888. The rest of the area of Lebanon was administratively organized as a special governorate, the *mutasarrıflık* (Ar. *mutaṣarrifiyya*) of Mount Lebanon (Cebel-i Lübnan), created in 1861 to replace the double *kaimmakamlık* (Ar. *qāʾimmaqāmiyya*) instituted in 1842 after Egyptian control over the area was ended. For the history of Lebanon in this period see Akarlı, *The Long Peace: Ottoman Lebanon, 1861–1920* (Berkeley: University of California Press, 1993).

[10] A. L. Tibawi, *A Modern History of Syria, Including Lebanon and Palestine* (London: Macmillan, 1969), 181.

[11] BOA, Y Mtv. 32/45, # 1, 19 Şaban 1305 (1 May 1888). NB: In dating the archival sources to be used throughout this work, I provide in the first reference to the document the Hicrî date (i.e. that derived from the Muslim calendar) and then the Gregorian equivalent in parentheses. Ottoman fiscal (Malî) dates, also provided in some documents, are generally ignored unless they provide the only means of dating the source.

[12] For opposing claims over who actually founded this school, see Martin Strohmeier, "Muslim Education in the Vilayet of Beirut, 1880–1918," in Farah (ed.), *Decision Making and Change*, 215, n. Strohmeier concludes that the original impetus for the school came from the Islamic Benevolent Society (known in abbreviated form as the *Maqāṣid*) and not from the central government. This seems clear both from Strohmeier's sources and from the mere fact that it was originally called the Medrese-i Sultaniye (*Madrasa sulṭānīyya*). It seems that its name was changed to "mekteb" when it was incorporated into the state system in 1887.

Muslim benevolent societies and the central government viewed the Beirut sultanî as important for the role it could play against the encroachments of Christian schools. The important reformist Egyptian thinker Muhammad 'Abduh had urged Istanbul to found a higher school in Beirut in order to counter the effects of Christian education.[13] His views and the way he presented them are strikingly similar to those found in numerous official dispatches from the provinces to the capital.

The connection drawn between the existence of the competition and the need to build Ottoman schools is clear. For the governor in Beirut the presence of the foreign schools is automatically interpreted as a goad to building Ottoman analogs which are to act as counterweights to the harmful effects of the foreign institutions. His thinking is representative of that of the majority of Ottoman officials concerned with educational policy in this period, at least those whose views have been preserved for posterity. This thinking followed a logic strikingly similar to the process known in the economics of our day as import substitution, whereby a state attempts to reduce or eliminate its subjects' consumption of a certain imported product by offering a domestically produced alternative. In carrying out such a policy the state frequently offers incentives to the domestic concern and introduces disincentives to the foreign competitor. This policy naturally presupposes both the existence and reasonable similarity of a domestically produced alternative. This last point explains, in part, the urgency with which state administrators expressed the need to create schools that would offer an Ottoman version of education—a version which, to their way of thinking, would reduce the demand for the competing foreign schools, if not obviate it entirely. It would, ideally, also allow the state to dictate the lesson content and extra-curricular life that its young subjects would follow.

The reality of the situation in the province of Beirut in 1888 was dire. According to the governor there were five French and four British schools in Beirut proper, in which roughly 4,400 students were enrolled.[14] Apart from these, there were also a good number of schools run by American missionaries and by the Italian and German

---

[13] Strohmeier, "Muslim Education," 216. For an example of an Ottoman document referring to the Beirut sultanî in the context of confronting foreign schools, see Y Mtv. 11/1. 1 Cemaziyelahır 1300 (9 Apr. 1883).   [14] Y Mtv. 32/45, # 2, 1.

governments. Their schools had approximately 500 students above and beyond those in schools administered by the Maronite, Greek Catholic, and Greek Orthodox communities. Therefore, there were more than 5,000 students, male and female, attending foreign schools in Beirut, 90 per cent of whom are estimated to be the children of Ottoman subjects.

That these figures have evidently been rounded off suggests that they may be more useful as a gauge of the governor's perception of the extent of foreign missionary activity in his province than as representing a statistical absolute. Although the precise figures that would allow us to corroborate the governor's numbers do not exist—and this despite a near obsession with statistics pervading the educational history of this period—we can use figures provided in the official Ottoman education yearbook to gain a general sense of the ratio between Ottoman state and foreign schools in the province of Beirut. A sign of the increased state attention devoted to education, the first yearbook to focus specifically on that topic appeared in 1898.[15] It lists the numbers of students attending schools of *rüşdiye* (advanced primary) level and higher for all provinces of the empire. According to the information it provides for the province of Beirut, there were 672 male students attending state-run civil schools at the rüşdiye (advanced primary) and idadî (secondary) level. This compares with 832 students attending millet-run schools and 1,307 attending foreign schools.[16] Thus, even by 1898—fifteen years after the Education Surtax of 1883 had opened the way for an energetic spurt of Ottoman school construction—the number of students that the government schools could accommodate was outnumbered by a ratio of two-to-one by foreign schools and of three-to-one by millet and foreign institutions combined.

This estimate uses the most conservative figures available; a calculation using the figures presented in a report submitted to the sultan by a young official named Mihran Boyaciyan in 1891 yields considerably more lopsided results.[17] While the yearbook has 1,307 students

---

[15] *Salname-i Nezaret-i Maarif-i Umumiye*, 1316 [AH].   [16] Ibid. 976–90.

[17] This report is summarized and presented in transliteration in Atillâ Çetin, "II. Abdülhamid'e Sunulmuş Beyrut Vilâyetindeki Yabancı Okullara dâir bir Rapor," *Türk Kültürü*, 253 (1984), 316–24. Çetin (p. 318) believes that Boyaciyan's figures compare favorably with those presented in the salnâme produced in 1898.

attending foreign schools in Beirut province in 1898, Boyaciyan lists 4,197 students attending French schools alone, and a total of 7,430 students attending foreign-run schools in 1891.[18]

To make matters worse, these foreign schools were exceedingly well financed. For example, the governor reported that the French government had recently more than quadrupled its educational subvention for Beirut. [19] We know that the total annual funding available to the Ottoman government for educational activity in the province of Beirut in the year 1888 was 1,200,000 kuruş. In accordance with the terms of the Education Surtax of 1883, half of this sum was sent to the capital to support the construction of state schools there, a source of frequent complaint from provincial administrators. Therefore, the actual amount available for use in Beirut province was 600,000 kuruş.[20] (These figures were not particularly high; consider that the cost of building a combined mosque and school in a neighboring province in this period was 300,000 kuruş.[21]) This means that the amount of money being spent on education in Beirut and its environs in the year 1888 by

[18] Atillâ Çetin, "Beyrut Vilâyetindeki Yabancı Okullara," 322. This figure is obtained by subtracting the students attending schools that Boyaciyan labels "private" (*husûsî*) and "Jewish" (*Yahudi*), because it is not clear whether or not such schools are supported from abroad. Even though such an exclusion reduces Boyaciyan's figure substantially (from 11,914 to 7,430), the reduced total still dwarfs the numbers of students attending state schools. The ratio would be greater than 10 : 1.

[19] The yearly level of support had been FF24,000 but had increased to FF104,000 per annum, or 461,760 kuruş. The latter figure more or less agrees with the sum of 116,200 francs corresponding to the French government's figure for the subvention for both the vilayet of Beirut and the Mountain in the same year (1888), assuming that the vast majority would have been spent in Beirut proper. For this and other relevant material from the French Foreign Ministry archives, see J. P. Spagnolo, "French Influence in Syria Prior to World War I: The Functional Weakness of Imperialism," *MEJ* 23 (1969), 58, n. Boyaciyan places French support at the FF140,000 level in 1891. Taking the more conservative figure of FF104,000 would, according to the currency equivalencies employed by Roger Owen and Charles Issawi (i.e. 1 pound sterling = 25 French Francs and 1 Turkish pound = 0.9 pounds sterling), equal 461,760 kuruş. Charles Issawi, *The Economic History of the Middle East, 1800–1914: A Book of Readings* (Chicago: University of Chicago Press, 1966), 522; Roger Owen, *The Middle East in the World Economy, 1800–1914* (London: Methuen, 1981), 161.

[20] İrade MM 4222. 3 Zilhicce 1305 (11 Aug. 1888). The second enclosure included with this İrade is the petition of the minister of education, Münif Paşa, requesting permission to spend 250,000 of the 600,000 kuruş derived from the local share of the education income on converting the former Medrese-i Sultanî in Beirut to the status of an idadî, "like all the other provinces have."   [21] Rogan, *Frontiers*, 152.

just one foreign government was equal to more than three quarters of the annual education funds available from the Ottoman government for the entire province of Beirut. Furthermore, foreign assistance of FF600,000 per annum was being spent in the province of Beirut, or more than four times what the Ottoman government was able to spend there. Still worse, the French government had secretly been providing additional funds for education in Beirut and in Mount Lebanon, monies that are not included in the levels of foreign assistance stated above.[22]

Foreign spending produced results that were more alarming than the catalogue of sums, buildings and enrollment figures, daunting though these undoubtedly were. The governor of Beirut complained that, aided by such increasing support, foreign schools were able to offer financial incentives to attract students, either by reducing fees or waiving them altogether. Furthermore, foreign trade schools were also reported to be attracting many students, with the result that the Muslim children are described as coming away "denuded of Islamic customs." As for the non-Muslim children, they are described as not merely bereft of an Ottoman upbringing, but also naturally inclined toward the state from whose schools they have emerged.[23]

Here we come to the crux of the issue: the struggle over whose education would prevail. The battlefront was much wider, encompassing ways of life, thought, and identification. Education was not an abstract or a statistical issue but rather one which was seen to have an enormous impact on society as a whole, and as we shall see subsequently, on the individuals that comprise it. As the governor writing from Beirut makes clear, the cultural element represented in the loss of "Islamic customs" was in many ways the most alarming, if statistically elusive, aspect of the many changes affecting the late Ottoman Empire.

Reversing these changes meant competing with the educational alternatives. Given the lopsided financial and organizational playing field, for the Ottomans competing meant recourse to a variety of methods and resources. In Beirut, the governor argued that steps had to be taken to prevent Muslim children from attending the foreign schools. At this he makes a logical leap that helps us to understand the thinking that underpins the typical Ottoman response to foreign

---

[22] Çetin, "Beyrut Vilâyetindeki Yabancı Okullara," 319.   [23] Y Mtv. 32/45.

educational encroachment. This thinking follows the assumption, natural enough for any trusting Ottoman functionary, that offering state alternatives will suffice to put an end to the unwanted attendance of foreign schools by Ottoman subjects. The document continues, stating that following the sultan's decree two rüşdiye, or advanced primary, schools and six "new-style" *ibtidaî*, or elementary, schools were built, two of which were for girls. Four or five "old style" neighborhood Qur'an schools had also been built. In other words, things were moving in the right direction.

The benefits of such school construction did not, however, extend to the rural areas of the province. There, the governor explained, the Ottoman state has not been able to put up much of a fight in the cultural war:

Coming to the districts appended to Beirut, there are many foreign schools in the Nusayri areas to the north of Latakia and Tripoli and in other provinces. Many students are being educated in them and since there are no [Ottoman state] schools in those areas apart from the rüşdiye and ibtidaî schools in the aforementioned places, the children of these areas are all growing up with foreign education and, consequently, foreign influence is easily increasing day by day.[24]

Ali Paşa warned that if this situation persists and Muslim children continue to be given over to the foreign schools, the Christian subjects will continue to acquire sciences and education while the Muslims remain entirely in the "darkness of ignorance."

The Ottoman state, as depicted in this and many similar documents, was faced with a situation in which well-financed foreign governments and missionaries had opened an alarming number of schools in the province. Given the paucity of state-run alternatives, the children of the province were left with the option of attending schools run by either the local religious institutions, depending on the confessional affiliation of the children, or by foreigners. While neither alternative was optimal to the governor, the latter was clearly the more feared; the growing numbers of students in the foreign schools has occasioned the "harmful effects" that prompted the dispatch to the capital in the first place. Since the memorandum held the education of children to be the prime political objective of the province, it was clear to its author that

[24] Y Mtv. 32/45, # 2, 1.

it was necessary to adopt a sound plan of action.[25] Denying the children an education, even a tainted foreign one, was not an option, given the pervasive belief that education was of vital importance to the empire's future.

The Beirut governor's plan called for action on all levels of the envisioned school system. While in the next chapter I address the specific role of the idadî, or secondary, schools within the context of the larger system envisioned for the empire, it is important here to note the conception of the idadî as a missing link in the chain that is to become the fully articulated Ottoman state educational system—a system intended in large part to ward off the encroachments of foreign influence.

It is also important to remember that provincial self-interest was a factor in demands for the building of schools; few provinces seem to have wanted to be passed over when it came to educational construction. The Syrian governor reported that no schools had been built on the secondary (idadî) level or higher in the province of Beirut. As a result, Muslim children, like their Christian counterparts, had not been spared the fate of attending the foreign schools. In order to avoid this unfortunate eventuality, he proposed that idadî schools be built during the ensuing year in each of the province's four districts, not including Beirut.[26] There, the *mekteb-i sultanî*, which had been founded in 1883 but apparently allowed to fall into disuse, was to be resurrected to accommodate up to 200 students. This school was to be reclassified as an idadî and to follow that curriculum until the other idadîs were completed. In order to compete with the foreign schools, the governor proposed the urgent acceptance of 200 students even though technically they would not all be qualified to enter an idadî school, since they would not have passed the necessary exam upon completion of a rüşdiye curriculum or its equivalent. The urgency was due to the current local situation, namely, the inroads made by and influence attributed to the foreign schools in the province. The proposed plan was to offer scholarships to fifty Muslim orphans and to accept 100 students from all communities of Ottoman subjects at fees that would vary with their age in accordance with those collected by the foreign schools. These 150 students would board at the school, while another fifty would be accepted as day-students who would pay only a

moderate tuition. Whatever its sources of motivation, Ali Paşa's proposal therefore envisioned the rapid matriculation of 200 students
in a preparatory school that would be administered by the Ottoman
government and would dovetail with the overarching plan to create
an integrated system of schools in the province and across the empire.

I return to the state's response to requests like this in the next chapter
in greater detail. Here it is important to note the degree to which the
Ottoman school was intended to be a counterpart to and a defense
against foreign competition. Not only was the request for such a school
broached in the context of the alarmingly advanced state of foreign
pedagogy in the area, but also many details associated with its existence
(e.g. its size and tuition-fee structure) appear to have been conscious
responses to foreign competition.

It bears repeating that this provincial Ottoman official—and his
example is fairly typical in this regard—felt himself engaged in an uphill
struggle. Indeed, the numbers involved indicate the overwhelming
nature of the contest with foreign schools alone. Yet, in spite of the
daunting task the Ottoman state was facing, its bureaucrats never questioned the rules of the competition. The perceived way to fend off the
incursion of the foreign educational offensive on Ottoman soil was, as
we shall see, an Ottoman response. But it was one that did not attempt
to alter the ground rules that had been set by Westerners. The object
was to beat the foreigners at their own game of school building, in
spite of their clear head start.

The situation in the province of Syria at the same period further
elucidates the competitive pattern of the Ottoman response.[27] When
the governor Râşid Nâşid Paşa wrote to the palace in late 1887, his
principal concern was educational funding.[28] He complained that
school construction in Syria had suffered because locally derived
revenues earmarked for local education had been diverted to Istanbul.
The resulting lack of state schools had produced "negative effects." His
correspondence makes clear the nature of the negative consequences to
which the governor refers in his cover letter. The absence of Ottoman

---

[27] For an excellent account of the Ottoman response to missionary activity in the
Transjordanian regions of this province in this period, see Rogan, *Frontiers*, ch. 5.

[28] Y Mtv. 29/48, # 1, 29 Rebiülevvel 1305 (15 Dec. 1887). I here acknowledge the kind
assistance of Dr Akşin Somel of Bilkent University, Ankara, for calling my attention to
this and other useful sources.

schools in Syria had allowed foreign missionaries the unchallenged opportunity to influence the population:

American and English missionaries, Jesuit and Lazarist [i.e., Vincentian] priests (who obtain the practical protection and financial support of the French state), and many Italian and Russian individuals—by establishing very large and exalted schools in nearly every subdistrict in Syria in the service of the political aims of the states with which they are affiliated—are educating Muslim and Christian children gratis and seducing and convincing the children of those who do not send their children to their schools by any means available and are corrupting the subjects' upbringing. In spite of this, so far no schools have been built by the [Ottoman] state as is necessary to be beneficial and to compete with them.[29]

The only exception to this situation on the preparatory level—the governor's concern in this document—was the idadî in Damascus. Since we learn from the dispatch that the construction of this school, known in the Syrian context as Maktab 'Anbar,[30] was at least partially funded by the sultan's privy purse, there had been no normal idadî school construction in the province. In universal bureaucratic fashion, the governor placed the blame for this situation on his predecessor, Hamdi Paşa, for not implementing the education finance reforms instituted in 1884–5.[31] Whatever the reason, the absence of the Ottoman schools was galling because of the noxious presence of the "seducing" and "corrupting" foreign competition.

As we shall see in the next chapter, the problems posed by missionary education were sufficiently dire as to prompt the state to depart from the script established by the Education Regulation of 1869. Apart from accelerating the pace of school construction, the central government approved an unorthodox approach: sending itinerant Muslim clerics into the countryside during the holy month of Ramadan to inveigh against the missionary schools. This short-term remedy, which also was invoked in Anatolia, Iraq, and the Aegean, will be analyzed in more detail in the discussion concerning Ottoman responses to the various forms of educational competition that appears in Chapter 3. In

---

[29] Y Mtv. 29/48, # 2, 2.

[30] On this school, see Randi Deguilhem-Schoem, "Idées françaises et enseignement ottoman: l'école secondaire Maktab 'Anbar à Damas," *Revue du monde musulman et de la Méditerranée*, 52–3 (1989), 198–206.   [31] Ibid. 1.

the present context, it suffices to note that this action was a clear departure from the Tanzimat educational blueprint. It thus underscores the
extent to which Ottoman bureaucrats were forced to react to the
increasing foreign competition they encountered in the provinces of
the empire.

Now, let us expand the geographical parameters of our discussion to
include educational competition in other parts of the empire, and of
other kinds. Each province, having its own ethnic and religious composition, naturally had its peculiar configuration of educational competition. The vast majority of provincial pleas for schools to ward off
the noxious effects of the missionaries comes from the eastern parts of
the empire, in particular, eastern Anatolia, and Syria-Palestine. Western
missionaries targeted these areas because of the high percentage of
"heathen" living there, because these areas held biblical significance,
and because of geo-political ambitions. There was Western missionary
activity in the European provinces, but it does not seem to have been
so threatening to the official Ottoman psyche as it did in regions of
the predominantly Muslim East, such as Syria, where the inroads of
Western influence were more alarming. Nevertheless, the following
synoptic sampling reveals that Ottoman officials were on guard against
educational competition, regardless of its source.

NEIGHBORS

Neighboring states redoubled the Ottoman anxieties generated by
foreign missionary activity. The threat supplied by neighboring, if
not neighborly, countries—many of which had only recently wrested
their independence from Istanbul, and then often with the assistance
of the Western powers—was in some ways even more daunting. While
the Western missionaries came from far away and often arrived
knowing little about their target populations, the activists from border
countries knew the local languages and the way society functioned. In
fact they were in many cases part of that society. Given the dispersed
demographic pattern of its various regions, the empire shared any
number of like populations with its neighbors. In this respect the cross-
border educational dynamic was quite unlike contemporary examples;
the demographic profile was very different from the other cases avail-

able for comparison. Thus there was often no difference between, say, Greeks living on either side of the Ottoman–Greek border, Armenians separated by the Ottoman–Russian border, or Serbs straddling the Ottoman–Serbian boundary. This situation was by itself not particularly dangerous; the various groups within the empire had long coexisted on more or less civil terms. But by the late nineteenth century the growth of nationalist sentiment began to alter the equation radically. The vigorous nationalism adopted in various parts of the region proved alarming for the authorities. Now territorial ambitions combined with history and myth to form a particular potent combination. The struggles that ensued took many forms, ranging from physical violence to less flagrant means of persuasion. Education was a critical component, as neighboring states vied with each other for the allegiance of the population. Establishing schools in Ottoman territory or attracting Ottoman subjects to study outside the empire were both means employed by nationalist agents. Turning to a few regional examples, we can see that the issue of educational competition—and confrontation—was rarely far from the agenda.

The island of Crete provides an interesting case in this regard, as its large Christian population and physical proximity to Greece made for a troubled situation. By the late 1880s the situation on the island was increasingly tense. In 1889 Abdülhamid II had suspended the Organic Regulation of 1868 and the pact worked out in 1878 between Karatodori Paşa and consular representatives of the Western powers. This suspension was brought about by continued attacks on Ottoman officials carried out by Greek bands. With the old arrangements in abeyance, Muslim governors administered the island, replacing the Christians who had been ruling as a result of the previous arrangement.[32] It was against this tense background that the island's governor wrote to Istanbul seeking help related to the question of education. His appeal provides us with an example of the local Ottoman response to the perceived interference of a neighboring state.[33] The underlying aim of this correspondence was to secure funding for a preparatory school to be built in Hanya. This request was based on two concerns. The first,

---

[32] Stanford J. Shaw and Ezel Kural Shaw, *History of the Ottoman Empire and Modern Turkey*, Vol. 2, *Reform, Revolution, and Republic: The Rise of Modern Turkey, 1808–1975* (Cambridge: Cambridge University Press, 1977), 206–7.

[33] YEE 18/420-18. 16 Eylül 1306 (28 Sept. 1890).

that such an undertaking would be consonant with the Education
Regulation of 1869, is one that the central government could easily
appreciate. The second reflects the local situation and evokes the spirit
of cultural erosion witnessed above. Echoing the sentiments of his
counterpart in Syria, the governor of Crete proclaims the expansion of
education to be one of the most important issues in provincial policy.
The memorandum states that, due to the lack of Ottoman educational
alternatives on the island, Christian children had no recourse but to
enroll in schools in Athens (at both the rüşdiye and higher levels). Their
minds were thus implanted with "Greek thoughts" which would eventually afflict the island "like vermin and locusts."[34] The governor argued
that the sole remedy available to the Ottoman government to combat
the incentives and encouragement offered by the Greek government to
these Ottoman subjects was the establishment of a local Ottoman
educational alternative. Clearly this Ottoman official considered educational expansion necessary because and not in spite of religio-ethnic
friction.

In the provinces of Ottoman Iraq the rivalry between Shiite and
Sunni reveals that the competitive context was not limited to a
Muslim–Christian dynamic. Education provided by the Ottoman state
was one of the chief countermeasures proposed to combat the influence
of Shiite propaganda coming across the border from another neighbor, Iran. While the rivalry with the Qajar dynasty of Iran was undoubtedly less important in geopolitical terms to the Ottomans than was
their relationship with the Christian powers, the Sunni Ottomans
and their Shiite neighbors to the East shared a long tradition of antag-
onism and distrust. This history of suspicion ensured Ottoman
vigilance against proselytizing in the provinces that bordered on
Qajar territory.

In the early years of Abdülhamid's reign, there seems to have been
little concern about the situation in Iraq. By about 1885, however, the
situation had changed, and the Porte and palace were receiving numerous reports about the growing threat of Shiism in the provinces of
Iraq.[35] These reports blamed a mixture of Ottoman neglect and Iranian

---

[34] YEE 18/420-18. 16 Eylül 1306 (28 Sept. 1890).
[35] The best account of Iraq in the Hamidian period is Gökhan Çetinsaya, "Ottoman
Administration of Iraq, 1890–1908," Ph.D. diss., University of Manchester (1994). For his

interference for the ascendance of Shiism there. In general, these reports recommend two strategies to remedy the problems they described: education and religious counter-propaganda.

One such report sheds light on educational competition in these easternmost provinces of the empire. Süleyman Hüsnü, a well-known military officer who was sent into internal exile in Baghdad by Abdülhamid II in 1878, wrote a report entitled: "Concerning the Reforms of the Region of Iraq."[36] The report, impressive by virtue of its heft and scope, offers a taxonomy of the situation in "Irak" (which he describes as consisting of the *vilayet*s of Bağdad, Basra, and Mosul) and proposes measures to correct the many problems that he sees there.

The petitioner's chief concern quickly becomes apparent. In his view, most of Iraq is territory that is hostile to the Ottoman cause. By his calculation, these three provinces contain eight ethnic groups (*cinsiyet*), twenty confessional groups (*mezheb*), and five language groups, all of which he enumerates:[37]

This distribution shows that the part of the group (*firka*) that is attached to the state's official mezheb and language is in the minority while those opposed are in the majority. Even though the success enjoyed by the Europeans in following the political course of unifying their language, ethnicity, and religious school is not an impossibility [for us], the time and situation

discussion of the Ottoman response to "The Shi'i Problem," see ch. 5. Çetinsaya describes a number of reports concerning the situation in Iraq during the 1880s and 1890s, (p. 229 ff.). As Çetinsaya provides summary information about all the relevant reports, this section will analyze only one of them, but in greater detail.

[36] YEE 14/1188. 9 Ramazan 1309 (7 Apr. 1892). On the career of Süleyman Hüsnü Paşa, see: İbrahim Alâettin Gövsa, *Türk Meşhurları Ansiklopedisi: Edibiyatta, Sanatta, İlimde, Harpte, Politikada ve her sahada şöhret kazanmış olan Türklerin Hayatları Eserleri* ([Istanbul]: Yedigün, n.d.]), 360; Deringil, "Invention of Tradition," 19–20; Deringil, "Struggle against Shiism," 53; and Çetinsaya, "Ottoman Administration, " 242–3.

[37] The term "mezheb" (Ar. *madhhab*, lit. "going," "way," or "road"), often translated as "school" or "rite," can in its more restricted sense denote one of the canonical systems in Islam. The four Sunni schools—Hanafi, Hanbali, Maliki, and Shafi'i—reflect the names of their eponymous founders. The official mezheb of the Ottoman state was Hanafi. In its less restricted sense, the term is used to connote general confessional affiliation. This would appear to be the sense intended by Süleyman Hüsnü, as evidenced by his counting twenty different mezhebs in Iraq. When, as in Süleyman Paşa's report, the question of language and legal school arises, it becomes clear that the portion of the population that shared linguistic and canonical allegiance with the capital was probably quite small in number.

are not propitious to undertake the complete, serious plan that this would entail, let alone to solve the question of its theological permissibility.[38]

The allusion to Europe is instructive. Although the chief enemy in Süleyman Hüsnü's eyes are the Shiites of Iraq, the example to which he immediately turns is that of Western Europe. So pervasive is the influence of the perceived success of the Western model that it is the first exemplar to occur to a senior paşa contemplating ways to reduce Shiite influence in Iraq. Although he acknowledges the impossibility of a drastic overhaul of the province, he does propose very specific remedies for the lamentable conditions enumerated in the report. It is not difficult to see the influence of the Western model in many of the reforms advocated by Süleyman Paşa.

However, it would be a mistake to assume that the European model he had in mind is a secular one. On the contrary, the religious component was critical to the overarching theme of his agenda, that is, the need to combat organized Shiism in Iraq. Education, in both its clerical and civil forms, is the chief force he intends to harness in this endeavor. The first practical step he urges to be taken is the founding of a group to be called the Society of Religious Learning.[39] This organization would be charged with gathering information on the various sectarian groups in Iraq, with special emphasis on their doctrinal principles (*akaid*). This information would aid the society's compilation of a book intended to refute the teachings of the various heretical groups. His second and related suggestion is the formation of a corps of missionaries. He gives both the Arabic and the phoneticized rendering of the French versions of the title by which they are to be known (*dāʿī ilā al-ḥaqq—misyoner*).[40] He stipulates that they: (a) receive the authorization of the aforementioned book of guidance; (b) be trained for two to three years in the rational and natural sciences; (c) speak Turkish and Arabic or Kurdish; and (d) be among the God-fearing and zealous

---

[38] YEE 14/1188, 1.

[39] This proposal has been discussed by Deringil, "Invention of Tradition," 19–20, in the context of Ottoman attempts to reconstitute official Sunni orthodoxy. The element of this document to be insisted upon here is the proposed use of both clergy *and* state schools in the battle against Shiism. I return to the subject of Ottoman missionaries in the next chapter.

[40] YEE 14/1188, 3. For another instance of an Ottoman official using the term "misyoner," see Rogan, *Frontiers*, 158.

*efendi*s. This last term indicates that these proselytizers are meant to be taken from among the ranks of the ulama.

Although Süleyman Paşa represents just one voice, his approach to redressing the situation in Iraq contains two constructs that are critical to understanding the Hamidian educational effort. The first is the combination of both civil and clerical forces. This is an example of an area where the historiography of this period can be misleading. The attempts to seek out the antecedents of the secular state of the twentieth century leave us with a hard distinction between what is considered "religious" and what "secular." Civil servants in the Hamidian period knew no such hard and fast categorization, but rather, it needs to be argued, a considerably more fluid range of meanings. What mattered to them was to defend the empire by marshaling any forces that they could to repel the attacks they perceived to be directed against it. Thus it was natural for a veteran military man such as Süleyman Paşa, and countless others like him, to envision using both state schools and ulama to defend the Ottoman state. Furthermore, this points us toward the notion, to be illustrated in detail over the course of subsequent chapters, that the state schools were much less "secular" than some of the secondary literature has led us to believe.

The second construct embedded in Süleyman Paşa's report is the importance of education and literacy to the service of the state. Like his contemporaries engaged in educational expansion around the globe, this senior Ottoman official was confident that increasing literacy was key to the state's agenda. The attention he devotes to stipulating the right type of people to train as missionaries emphasizes his concern with controlling the educational agenda. Just as he assumes that the missionaries who come from outside the areas of Iraq will be free of the, to his mind, corrupting influence of Shiite propaganda, he also assumes that expanding the limited network of state schools will automatically further the aims of the state:

If the state establishes a teacher-training school in Baghdad right away, and later builds an ibtidaî and a large rüşdiye in every town, village, and tax farming district according to their populations, and thereafter establishes idadî schools in the cities of Mosul, Kerkuk, Baghdad, and Basra, then the people educated there, being brought under the aegis of proper upbringing and education, will be in a position to benefit the state, and it will be able to be said of them that "we have people who can distinguish between good and evil." If not, they will be of no possible benefit to the state. On the one hand, they will remain shrouded by the nightmare of ignorance and, on the other, they will continue to be corrupted by the false principles of their spiritual leaders.[41]

In other words, with sufficient controls in place to ensure that the Ottoman "brand" of education is to be practised, educating the people is tantamount to turning out loyal soldiers in the war against the enemies of the state.

In this respect, the appalling illiteracy of Iraq afforded an attractive opportunity. If the Ottoman state could organize itself quickly enough to provide schooling for the people, it would ensure that its brand of education—and therefore its way of thinking—would obtain there. The connection between literacy and loyalty is clear:

> The expansion of education will confirm their affinity to religion, fatherland (*vatan*), and patriotism (*milliyet*), and render sincere the bonds to our highness the Caliph of the Muslims. But if ignorance continues, it will intensify and aggravate the splitting apart and disintegration [of the aforementioned affinity and bonds]. Furthermore, it is necessary [a] to establish a serious regard for the importance of increasing education in Iraq and [b] to print, publish, and send a drawing of the plan (*resim-i musattahi*) and the teaching regulation for each of the ibtidaî and rüşdiye schools to be built, since what is meant by [the terms] "school" and "level of excellence" are riddles that are unknown to the people, and [c] that the texts of reading primers for the first year of the ibtidaîs be written in Arabic or Kurdish and Turkish, and that the second-year texts be written in Turkish with the Arabic or Kurdish translations given below.[42]

Controlling literacy through selecting both the texts and the language in which they are written is held up as the key to cultivating political and confessional loyalty and, therefore, to combat the effects of Iranian propaganda on a population perceived in large measure to be hostile to the Ottoman cause in the first place.[43] The influence of linguisti-

---

[41] YEE 14/1188, 4.   [42] Ibid.

[43] The state's desire to expand educational offerings in Iraq complements its program to recruit the sons of tribal leaders through the creation of the tribal school (*Aşiret Mektebi*) in Istanbul in 1892, the year of Süleyman Paşa's memorandum. This institution was intended to act as a combined rüşdiye and idadî school in order to recruit the sons of prominent tribal shaykhs into the Ottoman bureaucratic system. For a history of this school, see Eugene L. Rogan, "Aşiret Mektebi: Abdülhamid's School for Tribes (1892–1907)," *IJMES* 28/1 (1996), 83–107.

cally—and culturally—based notions of nationhood, so important in other, better-known Ottoman thinkers such as Sāti' al-Husrī and Ziya Gökalp, is clear.[44]

Educational competition in Ottoman Asia was by no means limited to the Arab provinces. In Anatolia the impact of educational competition was readily apparent, even though numerically less significant than it was farther east. The reports of Ahmed Şâkir Paşa, Abdülhamid II's inspector-general for the Provinces of Anatolia from 1895 to 1900, reveal the extent to which the necessity of countering the educational competition was paramount in Ottoman reform calculations.[45] Şâkir Paşa's position afforded him ample opportunity to see at first hand the situation in Anatolia and the need for reform there. On the subject of education, Şâkir Paşa was struck by the contrasting opportunities that existed for the non-Muslim and Muslim populations. A witness to the various foreign-run schools in operation throughout Anatolia, he concluded that, due to the education being provided by these schools, the country's commerce and wealth was passing into the hands of the non-Muslims day by day.[46] Şâkir Paşa thought that it would be best to close these schools but knew such a rash action would incur the wrath of the

---

[44] Sāti' al-Husrı (1880–1968) was a late Ottoman educationalist who converted to Arab nationalism after World War I. A graduate of the Mülkiye Mektebi, he began his career as a schoolteacher in the Balkans, later becoming an Ottoman official in the provinces of Kosovo and Manastır. He returned to Istanbul to serve as the director of the Darülmuallimin (Teacher Training College) from 1902 to 1912, and founded and edited a journal devoted to elementary education. After the war he worked for Faisal's government in Damascus before moving on to Iraq where he worked for twenty years, becoming a chief exponent of the nationalist cause. For his life, see William L. Cleveland, *The Making of an Arab Nationalist* (Princeton: Princeton University Press, 1971).

Ziya Gökalp, born Mehmed Ziya (1876–1924), is regarded as the main theoretician of Turkish nationalism. He was educated at the rüşdiye and idadî schools in his native Diyarbekir where he was influenced by the radical ideas of Dr Abdullah Cevdet. He gravitated to Istanbul where he studied at the Imperial Veterinary School and joined the Committee of Union and Progress. His revolutionary connections were discovered and he was imprisoned in 1897. Upon release he returned to Diyarbekir and engaged in local ethnographic research and a study of Durkheimian sociology. After the revolution of 1908 he founded a local chapter of the CUP and published a number of periodicals. He later became a professor at Istanbul University. During the war he was arrested by the British and sent to Malta. He is remembered as perhaps the most influential Turkish thinker of the twentieth century. For his life and work, see Uriel Heyd, *Foundations of Turkish Nationalism: The Life and Teachings of Ziya Gökalp* (London: Luzac, 1950), and Taha Parla, *The Social and Political Thought of Ziya Gökalp, 1876–1924* (Leiden: E. J. Brill, 1985).

[45] Ali Karaca, *Anadolu Islahâtı ve Ahmet Şakir Paşa (1838–1899)* (Istanbul: Eren, 1993), 182–90. [46] Ibid. 183.

Western powers.[47] His more realistic recommendations concerning education were spurred by twin considerations. On the one hand, he concluded that expanding education was a prerequisite for the development and civilization of the Muslim population in Anatolia. On the other, he saw the need to build Ottoman schools as a conscious answer to the foreign alternatives that only served to underscore the deficiency of the state's offerings to date.[48]

Even in a province such as Konya, where hardly any foreign schools existed, the impact of foreign and neighboring competition was nevertheless still palpable. In 1901 the governor of Konya, Mehmed Ferid, who a year later was to become the grand vizier, complained that the existing idadî school in Konya was overcrowded, like its counterparts in the capital.[49] He requested the necessary permission and funding to build two more idadîs, one each in Niğde and Hamidabad (modernday Isparta) to ameliorate the situation. In the meantime many applicants had to be turned away due to the limited number of places available at the school. Some of those not gaining entrance to the schools, the non-Muslim ones in particular, opted to enroll in similar schools in "Athens and Europe." This state of affairs, the governor continued, carried attendant political damage. Those students would not come away with the desired loyalty to the Ottoman state. In this case, the competition was at considerable physical distance from the place of writing. Nevertheless, the insufficiency of the Ottoman system left the empire vulnerable to this competition—even if far away—and, ultimately, to the long-term political repercussions associated with losing control over the process of education.

Turning to the European provinces of the Ottoman Empire, that is, Rumelia, we see an analogous situation to that of Crete. Neighboring Christian states, and not foreign missionaries, presented the main threat to the government's plans to offer a distinctly Ottoman brand of schooling in provinces such as Salonika and Manastır. A report by the minister of education Zühdü Paşa concerning foreign educational intervention in the Ottoman Empire reveals the pressures that were being exerted by the Bulgarian, Greek, and Serbian governments as they maneuvered against one another for influence in

---

[47] Ali Karaca, *Anadolu Islahâtı*, 182–90.
[48] Ibid.   [49] Y Mtv. 221/114. 20 Cemaziyelahır 1319 (4 Oct. 1901).

Macedonia.[50] This struggle for influence was largely waged through schools, the pace of whose construction was rapidly increasing in the later decades of the nineteenth century, as the battle for Macedonia intensified.[51]

While the numbers of the new schools must have concerned Ottoman officials, they were perhaps more alarmed by the increasingly blatant national propaganda these institutions were disseminating. One example of Ottoman concern centered around the staffing of the Bulgarian school in Salonika. This school was important because, as Zühdü Paşa notes, it served as a model for all of the non-Muslim people of the province of Salonika.[52] As one scholar has put it, this "institution controlled Bulgarian education throughout the whole of Macedonia."[53] And the Bulgarian government had been sending prominent officials to serve in the school. For example, the colorful character Boris Sarafoff, the former Bulgarian education minister, an advocate—and later a practitioner—of armed revolution, and the future leader of the Supreme Macedonian Committee, was appointed director of the Bulgarian Secondary School in Salonika. Moreover, a former Bulgarian schools inspector named Tashod was appointed to its faculty.[54] Zühdü's analysis of these personnel moves is unequivocal:

Entirely with a view to spreading the Bulgarian political agenda and cause in Salonika, the aforementioned men were sent to these posts which had nothing to do with their previous appointments, and favorable letters of

[50] Atillâ Çetin, "Maarif Nâzırı Ahmed Zühdü Paşa'nın Osmanlı İmparatorluğundaki Yabancı Okullar Hakkında Raporu," *Güney-doğu Avrupa Araştırmaları Dergisi*, 10–11 (1981–1982), 189–219. Çetin estimates this report to have been written in 1894. Unlike the reports to which we have been referring thus far, this document was written by a cabinet level official. It is not, therefore, an indication of the position of provincially based Ottoman officials. However, the relatively late date of this document reflects the increasing awareness by the center of the types of problems that the provinces had been reporting for some time.

[51] Dakin gives the following statistics for the numbers of schools in Macedonia in 1901 and 1902: Greek: 1,000 schools with 70,000 pupils; Bulgarian: 592 schools with 30,000 pupils; and Serbian: 233 with an unknown number of students. Douglas Dakin, *The Greek Struggle in Macedonia, 1897–1913* (Thessaloniki: Museum of the Macedonian Struggle, 1993), 18–20.

[52] Çetin, "Osmanlı İmparatorluğundaki Yabancı Okullar," 197.

[53] Dakin, *Greek Struggle*, 53.

[54] Çetin, "Osmanlı İmparatorluğundaki Yabancı Okullar," 198.

recommendation concerning Sarahof's [*sic*] good conduct were sent to the vilayet of Salonika from the Exarchate, clear signs of the deceptions they have launched through the schools.[55]

In fact, a remarkable number of the Bulgarians who played leading roles in spreading nationalist propaganda served as schoolmasters or school inspectors at some point in their careers.

Written when the struggle for Macedonia was intensifying, Zühdü Paşa's report reflects Ottoman awareness of the increasing use of education in the service of competing national agendas; one study refers to Macedonia in this period as veritable dueling field.[56] Zühdü's report dates from 1894, the same year that Bulgaria abandoned its policy of "peaceful penetration of Macedonia" that had been engineered since the Congress of Berlin by its premier Stambulov.[57] His fall in 1894 led to the adoption of a much more aggressive policy vis-à-vis Macedonia. Moreover, the stepped-up Bulgarian policy in turn elicited a similarly offensive strategy on the part of Serbia, a relative latecomer to the Macedonian rivalry.[58]

The Serbian strategy did not elude Zühdü Paşa, who was also concerned with an analogous situation in the neighboring province of Manastır. There the expansionist intentions of Serbia were foremost in the statesman's apprehensions. Zühdü's ire was piqued by the fact that the Serbian government had established numerous consulates in Manastır province, institutions that had produced a voluminous correspondence aimed at establishing Serbian schools in a province which had no Serbian speakers at all, in order to spread its influence over the Orthodox population whose "national" identities were still only coa-

---

[55] Çetin, "Osmanlı İmparatorluğundaki Yabancı Okullar," 198. The Exarchate was the administrative head of the Bulgarian Orthodox church, which had been independent of the Greek Patriarchate in Istanbul since 1870. The details of the process by which the Bulgarian church broke away from Constantinople and the larger importance of this schism in Balkan politics can be found in Charles and Barbara Jelavich, *The Establishment of the Balkan National States*, Vol. 8, *1804–1920: A History of East Central Europe* (Seattle: University of Washington Press, 1977), 128–35.

[56] Bernard Lory and Alexandre Popovic, "Au carrefour des Balkans, Bitola 1816–1918," in Paul Dumont and François Georgeon (eds.), *Villes Ottomanes à la fin de l'Empire* (Paris: L'Harmattan, 1992), 86.

[57] L. S. Stavrianos, *The Balkans Since 1453* (New York: Holt, Rinehart, and Winston, 1965), 519.   [58] Ibid. 520.

lescing.[59] In Macedonia the choice of a school for one's children could determine their "nationality."[60] The fact that this report was written by the minister of education indicates that provincial pleas such as those to which we have been referring were making their impact in Istanbul. As the Macedonian context illustrates, the Ottoman state was acutely aware of the growing role that education was playing in the increasingly strident national movements. Moreover, as the following chapter demonstrates, this awareness informed the official Ottoman conception of the potential of state-supported education. The negative examples provided by the competition alerted Hamidian statesmen to the tremendous positive potential an organized educational system offered in the way of political mobilization.

DOMESTIC COMPETITION

The foregoing sampling of Ottoman perceptions of foreign-inspired education in various provinces can be summarized as follows: missionary institutions appeared to be ubiquitous, well financed, intent on undermining the authority of the state and the allegiance of its subjects, and, worst of all, successful. In many provinces where missionaries were less active, it was the covetous designs of nationalist-minded neighboring states that caused the authorities to worry—and to build schools of their own. Yet Western Europe and neighboring states were not the only source of competition for Ottoman education. A third source of educational rivalry, that of the indigenous minority groups, also provided Ottoman statesmen with ample material for comparison, most of it unfavorable, with the empire's Muslim schools. The existence of minority-run educational institutions was, of course, not alarming in and of itself. Unlike foreign-run schools, whose presence in the empire in any great numbers was a recent phenomenon, minority schools enjoyed a tradition that dated to the earliest centuries of the empire. Indeed, the Ottoman Empire was famous for its *millet*, or communal, system, the loose set of arrangements by which the central government allowed each recognized religious community to

---

[59] Çetin, "Osmanlı İmparatorluğundaki Yabancı Okullar," 198–9.
[60] Lorry and Popovic, "Au carrefour," 87.

manage its own affairs through its own hierarchy whose chief was answerable to the Porte.[61] Thus left alone, the millets were free to educate their own as they saw fit. Each of the educational systems was, therefore, analogous to that of the Muslim establishment in that it was a system in which the civil bureaucracy rarely interfered.

When, in the nineteenth century, the state began to involve itself directly in the process of public education, it was natural that its officials took a more lively interest in the millet schools. They did not always like the implications of what they saw. By the Hamidian period, Ottoman civil officialdom perceived the minority schools to have achieved superiority vis-à-vis the Muslim schools. Part of the problem, as the officials saw it, was the failure of Muslim notables to produce a "modern" educational network across the empire. There were some local efforts in this direction, for example, Midhat Paşa's attempts to inspire Muslim education in Syria, but they were deemed too sporadic and thin on the ground to warrant altering the state's totalizing program. As a result, the onus of providing the empire's Muslim youth with an education that would answer the "demands of the age" fell to the state. As in France of the Third Republic, where state schools were considered necessary to fulfill a variety of tasks formerly performed by the Catholic church, this was not an altogether unpleasant prospect for the central government in that it permitted the state to pursue its own agenda.

The scale of the task the state faced, however, was daunting. The state was, in effect, attempting to duplicate the existing network of Muslim schools from scratch. Instead of building on or adapting the existing Muslim schools, the state sought to construct a parallel system. This has universally been interpreted as an attempt to marginalize them, thereby reducing the traditional purview of the ulama. Their resistance to state education, often described as overtly secular, is a familiar trope

---

[61] A large literature exists concerning the millet system, e.g. M. O. H. Ursinus, "Millet" in EI2, vii. 61–4; Benjamin Braude and Bernard Lewis (eds.), *Christians and Jews in the Ottoman Empire: The Functioning of a Plural Society* (New York: Holmes & Meier, 1982); Bernard Lewis, *The Political Language of Islam* (Chicago, 1988), 38–9, 41–2, etc. For the semantic problems associated with the term "millet," see Benjamin Braude, "Foundation Myths of the Millet System," in *Christians and Jews*. After the Tanzimat period (1839–76), the term was generally used to denote a religious community, usually a minority community but occasionally the community of Muslims as well.

in the history of this period. We will see in subsequent chapters, however, the various ways in which the ulama were involved in the new system. Nevertheless, the perception that schools run by the religious establishment—as they currently stood—were unequal to the task of meeting the "demands of the present" was accepted. Indeed, the state's educational policy was based on that premise. It is therefore important to note the way in which Mehmed Kâmil Paşa, a central figure in the history of state education in the Hamidian period, used the lack of a quality Muslim counterpart to the millet school systems to support the state's endeavor. He blamed Muslim notables throughout the empire for failing to "properly appreciate the essence of science and education and its necessity for our time."[62] He lamented the passing of former times in which the madrasas built and endowed by private initiative formed the backbone of the learning network, while those supported by the sultans played an important but minority role. This not so subtle dig at the empire's Muslim notables was part of the rationalization that underpins the state's overall educational effort.

The perceived superiority of millet schools affected the way in which Ottoman statesmen looked upon their Muslim counterparts, but the official reaction to the millet schools was markedly different from that prompted by the foreign schools. Whereas the existence and perceived success of the missionary schools provoked universal alarm among state officials, millet schools engendered responses that were considerably more measured. None of the suspicions they harbored toward the subversive agenda behind the missionary schools appear in their reports concerning millet equivalents. On the contrary, state bureaucrats frequently hold up their example as a source for emulation, if not outright praise.

What impressed Ottoman observers of minority-run education was both its prevalence and its high degree of advancement. Minority communities such as the Greeks and Armenians were perceived to have

---

[62] MKP 86/1-55. It is important to note the terms Kâmil uses here. As Niyazi Berkes has pointed out, there was a critical distinction to be made between religious knowledge, *ilm*, and the modern notion of *maarif*, the "knowledge of useful things." The later term is what undergirded the entire notion of the state's educational agenda. The term maarif, translated here as "education," is in fact the term employed by the late Ottoman Ministry of Education. The term ulum is used by Kâmil Paşa to refer to what is generally translated as "science(s)."

schools and churches of enviable size, organization, and fiscal health even in the smallest of villages.[63] Given the long tradition of independence in communal affairs, this situation was not inherently threatening. In fact, the Islahat Fermanı of 1856 had authorized "every community . . . to establish public schools of science, art, and industry. Only the method of instructions and the choice of professors in the schools of this class shall be under the control of a mixed council of public instruction, the members of which shall be named by my sovereign command."[64] Civil servants argued that the successes these schools had enjoyed in strengthening the moral qualities of their minority students provided examples that the state would do well to emulate.[65] Most officials who addressed the issue of the millet schools acknowledged the soundness of the methods their competitors used, for example, community dedication, financial sacrifice, and, significantly, a strong clerical role.[66] They were convinced of the successes to come once the Ottoman state began to apply them in a concerted manner.

Thus, while they did not provoke the panic that the foreign schools did, the millet schools did prompt comparison with the Muslim schools—comparison that was cause for consternation. Generally described as dilapidated, retarded, and underfunded, the Muslim community schools were no match for their non-Muslim counterparts. The contrast grew more galling for official Ottomans when the minority accomplishments were considered on a per capita basis.[67] Although perhaps slower to be appreciated as threatening, mounting evidence of the superiority of millet education contained worrying long-term ramifications.

---

[63] See e.g. YEE ıı/1419.

[64] English translation in J. C. Hurewitz (ed.), *The Middle East and North Africa in World Politics*, Vol. 1, *European Expansion, 1535–1914* (New Haven: Yale University Press, 1975), 317.

[65] e.g. İrade Dah. 80409.

[66] It is worth remembering that the Ottoman state's own reforms during the Tanzimat had played no small role in reviving minority education, the effects of which were so manifest in the Hamidian period. The reorganization of the non-Muslim millets of the 1860s enhanced the relative power of secular forces within the various millets at the expense of their clergy, thereby unwittingly encouraging minority politics to assume a more nationalist flavor. Roderic H. Davison, *Reform in the Ottoman Empire, 1856–1876* (Princeton: Princeton University Press, 1963), 114 ff.

[67] YEE ıı/1419.

Like accounts of missionary school success, appraisals of the superiority of millet educational offerings also prompted calls for action. Officials frequently argued for increases in the number and quality of Muslim schools by comparing them with the minority schools. Officials invoked examples of millet success to advocate a wide variety of initiatives, ranging from the routine to the sweeping. One official writing from the Anatolian province of Kastamonu used a general comparison of non-Muslim and Muslim schools to advocate a specific request, the hiring of school inspectors in that province.[68] Other officials contrasted the two sets of schools in order to push for extensive changes in educational policy, such as reforming the curriculum in all state schools.[69] Of particular interest is an imperial decree from 1887 establishing a commission to revamp the instruction in all state-run schools in order to improve moral instruction.[70] Calling attention to signs of weakness in the moral principles of the state school graduates, the decree specifically refers to the positive aspects of moral instruction in the non-Muslim schools. Moreover, it dictates that changes be made so as to reform the Muslim schools to correct the glaring contrast between the two pedagogical systems. The frequent recourse to such contrasts underscores the powerful role that the example of the millet schools played in conceptualizing late Ottoman education policy.

Because the millets were part of the empire, their example cut two ways. On the one hand, acknowledging minority success begged the question of why the Muslims were deemed to have fallen behind. On the other hand, the example of the millets offered hope; state officials praised their organization and their ability to inculcate moral education as models the state should emulate. Perhaps most important, the millet schools buoyed the Ottoman hope that proper dedication and organization were possible without the *deus ex machina* of foreign initiative and capital.

THE VIEW FROM THE CAPITAL

Not surprisingly, the view of senior officials in Istanbul reflected the impact of the provincial voices. Like their provincial colleagues, these

[68] YA Res. 107/50. 9 Safer 1318 (8 June 1900).
[69] YA Res. 100/13. 6 Muharrem 1317 (17 May 1899).
[70] İrade Dah. 80409. 4 Cemaziyelevvel 1304 (29 Jan. 1887).

policy-makers often sounded an initially pessimistic note when taking stock of the situation in the empire as a whole. They registered increasing alarm at the inroads the foreign missionaries had made. Since their perspective encompassed the whole empire, the cumulative effect was even more devastating.

The sheer volume of their collective writings on the empire's educational plight indicates that the dispatches from the provinces were making an impact. Since such documents are many and tend to reflect the same concerns found in the memoranda produced in the provinces, they will not be analyzed in detail here.[71] Rather, two techniques can represent the view from the center in complementary fashion. The first approach takes advantage of the economy of statistics. In the Hamidian period the state began to compile inventories of the various non-Muslim schools in the empire. These catalogues graphically illustrate both the problem the state faced in the form of educational competition and the state's growing awareness of that problem. The second approach is to focus on the correspondence of one senior Ottoman statesman, Mehmed Kâmil Paşa, whose voice on the subject of education reflected the concerns of the central government. Kâmil Paşa had a timely perspective that was simultaneously unique and typical of the official outlook. Each in its own way, these two sets of documents— one statistical and the other prose—illustrate the full extent and implications of the state's educational competition.

So far we have been considering the competitive context of educational expansion by sampling memoranda written by Ottoman bureaucrats in various provinces and in the capital. In order to appreciate the cumulative pressure that this competition placed on Ottoman educational policy, it is sufficient to glance at a few of the various state-compiled inventories of foreign and minority schools in the empire. These inventories represent the symbolic aggregate produced by the totality of the provincial pleas we have examined so far. The existence of these inventories, not to mention their sheer length and the result-

---

[71] The following documents contain descriptions of educational competition from the imperial, as opposed to the provincial, perspective, either in whole or in part: MKP 86/1-55; MKP 86/1-60; İrade Dah. 80409; Y Mtv. 37/56; YEE 35/232; YEE 14/1535; YEE 31/1899; YA Res. 71/10; YA Res. 100/13; YA Res. 101/39; YEE 11/1765; Y Mtv. 221/114; YEE 11/1419; YA Res. 112/59; YA Res. 122/88; MKP 86/22-2136; YEE 5/109; YA Res. 137/8; MKP 86/32-3194.

ing heft of the registers in which they were presented, immediately suggests both the scope of the problem the Ottomans were facing and their awareness of it.

The existence of these inventories raises a troublesome issue: finding accurate figures for the number of foreign schools in the empire. One Ottoman inventory from 1894 lists 427 foreign schools in the empire. This figure appears small compared to İlber Ortaylı's claim that the number of American schools alone was close to 400 by 1886.[72] Yet when compared with the 1903 tally of a US consular official in Beirut, Ortaylı's estimate appears quite plausible. The official, one Franklin E. Hopkins, lists sixty American schools in just one vilayet, that of Beirut, twenty-one of which are declared to be temporarily closed.[73] However, the aim here is not to ascertain an exact count of missionary schools. It is the perception of foreign educational encroachment that is important for understanding the state's reaction to the alarming array of foreign institutions. Gathering information about its competitors was a natural prelude to the state's taking action. Inventories compiled by the state in the 1890s and 1900s represent graphic evidence of official Ottoman interest in keeping tabs on the competition.

One such tally, dated August 1893, consists of a twenty-eight-page register listing Protestant and American schools in the empire.[74] Entries are organized by province and offer information, when available, about the schools' location, date of founding, and curriculum, provided by various provincial education directors (*maarif müdürleri*).[75] According to this register, there were 392 Protestant and American schools currently in the empire, including boys and girls, boarding and day. Of those, 284 were founded prior to Abdülhamid's accession and 108 were founded since. Notable is the attention paid to whether the schools were opened with or without official permission. According to the statistics presented in this inventory, thirty-three of the foreign schools were permitted by sultanic decree, seven by orders of the grand vizier,

---

[72] İlber Ortaylı, "Some Observations on American Schools in the Ottoman Empire," *Turkish Public Administration Annual*, 8 (1981), 95.

[73] YA Res. 122/88, # 10. 7 Cemaziyelahır 1321 (31 Aug. 1903).

[74] YEE 35/232. 19 Muharrem 1311 (2 Aug. 1893).

[75] Zühdü Paşa served as education minister for more than eleven years, from 15 Zilhicce 1302 (25 Sept. 1885) until 7 Rebiülevvel 1304 (4 Dec. 1886) and again from 29 Muharrem 1309 (4 Sept. 1891) to 4 Cemaziyelahır 1319 (18 Sept. 1901).

and eleven by patents issued by the minister of education in accordance with the procedures laid down in the Education Regulation of 1869. The remaining 341 are listed as having no permission at all. The education minister Zühdü Paşa blames the "connivance" of provincial officials for this situation.[76] The attention paid to accountability in this document is indicative of the belated Ottoman attempt to rein in the educational competition.

Another inventory, reproduced in transliterated form by Çetin who dates the report to 1894, corroborates the information gathered in the previous tally.[77] No longer limited to American and Protestant institutions, this compilation lists 427 foreign schools in the Ottoman Empire. This listing is likewise accompanied by a report from Zühdü Paşa that reflects an increased vigilance in ensuring that foreign schools abide by the rules of the Education Regulation. Zühdü stresses the importance of the foreign schools' meeting certain requirements (for example, obtaining certificates for their teachers, gaining approval for the lesson plans and books to be used, and submitting to government inspection) as prerequisites for obtaining permission to operate. The purpose here is to prevent lessons "contrary to customs and state policies and ideology" (*adab ve politikaya mugâyir*) from being taught in the schools.[78]

Yet another holding is a large file containing fourteen items of official correspondence concerning American schools in the empire.[79] Two inventories, one regarding Lebanon and one concerned with the empire as a whole, demonstrate the difficulties Ottoman officials encountered in obtaining reliable statistical information about educational institutions. This file also reflects the extent to which all levels of the civil administration (e.g. the Grand Vizierate, the Council of Ministers, individual governors, and the Ministry of Education) were involved in the attempt to monitor the competition.

Still another roster, dated July 1904, is a list of American schools in

---

[76] YEE 35/232, # 1.

[77] A romanized version of a report on the subject of foreign schools in the empire, together with an inventory of the schools, is reproduced in Çetin, "Osmanlı İmparatorluğundaki Yabancı Okullar," 189–219. Curiously, the author of this article does not provide information concerning the document's location in the Ottoman archives.

[78] Çetin, "Osmanlı İmparatorluğundaki Yabancı Okullar," 195.

[79] YA Res. 122/88. The latest item is dated 7 Cemaziyelevvel 1321 (1 Aug. 1903).

the empire.[80] Also organized by province, this list provides the location, name, and date permission was granted. The inclusion of this last piece of data together with the name of the minister or governor who granted the permission reflects increased Ottoman vigilance in monitoring foreign educational activity throughout the empire.

The fact that Ottoman bureaucrats were gathering information on the foreign schools in the empire and compiling those data into inventories suggests several important developments. First, the number of these schools had become sufficiently large—particularly in some of the more politically sensitive provinces—to warrant the concerted attention of the central government. No longer do we find individual bureaucrats raising the alarm from various locations throughout the empire. The government was now engaged in tracking this development in an active and centralized manner. Secondly, just as the individual petitioners were quick to associate the foreign institutions with political and moral damage, so also did the central government assume the worst intentions of the missionary activity. The fact that Protestant, especially American, schools were singled out reflects the fact that the North American revivalism had hit Ottoman lands in full zeal and fiscal strength. This also explains the state's desire to monitor it more closely. Thirdly, as the next chapter will demonstrate, the state's increased awareness of the extent of foreign educational penetration—and suspicion of the motives behind it—was a prelude to the government's taking active measures against the foreign schools.

The broad view of a seasoned observer and participant provides a counterpoint to the concision of statistics. The influential Ottoman statesman Mehmed Kâmil Paşa saw the struggle over education as part of the larger rivalry with the West. In many ways Kâmil's thinking on education and its inherent connection with geopolitical rivalry recalls the "national realism" of the Russian educationalists after Dimitri Tolstoy. By the 1880s major voices in both the Russian and Ottoman empires opposed the massive borrowing from the West. In Russia such figures as Ushinsky were advocating that the way forward lay in an educational agenda that suited domestic considerations.[81] Kâmil Paşa, seeing the linkages between and among the educational, the economic,

---

[80] YEE 5/109. 13 Cemaziyelevvel 1322 (26 July 1904).

[81] Alston, *Education and the State*, 89–93.

and the military spheres, represents the late Ottoman reappraisal of the prevailing Europhilia of the Tanzimat. Like Ushinsky, Kâmil believed that his empire needed to be more selective in adapting European models. Kâmil Paşa was part of a broader trend in Ottoman education that calls to mind the Russian reassessment of the European influence exercised in the era of Tolstoy's reforms. Although he held the Education portfolio only relatively briefly, his voice was particularly important on the subject, not least because he served as grand vizier three times, thereby ensuring that his views be heard.[82] His opinions on education are important both because of his considerable role in affecting—and effecting—educational policy and because they set the Ottoman effort in a broader perspective.

After a period in Egypt where, among other things, he learned English and French, Kâmil Paşa began his career as an Ottoman official on the island of Cyprus, his place of birth. Subsequent postings in Sidon, Beirut, Tripoli (in Syria), Aleppo, Filibe, Jerusalem, Herzegovina, and Istanbul, where he served as minister of education, pious endowments, and justice, and ultimately rose to be grand vizier, afforded him ample opportunity to observe at first hand the situation in the empire.[83] While governor of Aleppo, his second posting there, he is reported to have run afoul of British intentions and to have been removed due to the pressure exerted in Istanbul by that power.[84] This and other experiences in his early career doubtless colored his perception of the Ottoman struggle with the West.

Kâmil Paşa's concerns regarding education reveal the strong degree to which the spirit of competition flavored his thinking. In a memorandum probably written in 1881 while he was minister of education, and thus important as one of the first central government documents to lay out a practical plan to implement the Education Regulation of 1869, competition in the educational field is an obvious theme.[85] He

---

[82] Kâmil Paşa's first and longest term as grand vizier lasted from 25 Sept. 1885 to 4 Sept. 1891. He returned briefly to the position in 1895 and in 1908–9, after the Young Turk Revolution.

[83] İbnülemin Mahmud Kemal İnal, *Osmanlı Devrinde Son Sadrıazamlar* (Istanbul: Maarif Baımevi, 1955), iii. 1347–51.

[84] Ibid. 1349.

[85] MKP 86/1-55. This document is not dated but internal evidence suggests that it was written while Kâmil Paşa had the Education portfolio, i.e. between 7 Şevval 1297 (12 Sept. 1880) and 14 Muharrem 1299 (6 Dec. 1881). These dates are taken from Mahmud Cevad

begins by drawing a very unfavorable comparison between the Muslim and non-Muslim schools. He describes the existing Muslim schools as being insufficient. Those that do exist, he asserts, lag far behind their competitors. He claims the Muslim schools are not teaching the right subjects, only offering a little reading, writing, and arithmetic. Another of Kâmil's comparisons denigrates the schools in favor of their predecessors in the glory days of Islamic culture. He calls for a large effort to correct this unfortunate situation. Such an effort will need to be supported by the donations of the general population, due to the lack of assistance available from the central government. We will return to the important problem of financing the expansion of state schooling and Kâmil's contribution to solving it in Chapter 3. Here we must note the clear connection Kâmil Paşa draws between the East–West rivalry and the necessity of education in national, or in this case imperial, achievement. For Kâmil, state schools are valued not only as a means of restoring the past glories of Islam but also as a measure to counter the very present encroachments of the West.

Before examining Kâmil's interest in using the schools in the rivalry with the West, it is first necessary to plumb his overall conception of the uses of education. Kâmil Paşa, like most Ottoman policy-makers in the Hamidian period and his contemporaries in numerous countries around the world, appreciated the potential of state-run schooling to accomplish a variety of governmental objectives. Ideally, a fully articulated Ottoman educational system would produce a steady supply of right-minded subjects who would be trained to staff the increasingly large and complex bureaucracy. "In short, the freedom of the sublime state from internal and external anxieties depends upon causing Ottoman subjects to follow a career which is propitious for the benefits

ibn el-Şeyh Nâfi', 200 and 212. İnal corroborates the latter date but gives the beginning of his term as education minister as Şevval of 1297 (i.e. Sept./Oct. of 1879), *Son Sadrıazamlar*, 1351. Unat provides a third starting date for Kâmil's ministry, 12 Nov. 1880, a date which contradicts his calculation of the time elapsed during his tenure (1 year, 2 months, and 19 days.) Faik Reşit Unat, *Türkiye Eğitim Sisteminin Gelişmesine Tarihî Bir Bakış* (Ankara: Millî Eğitim Baımevi, 1964), 123. The reverse of the document shows the date 5. 5. 1298 (= 3 Apr. 1881). An unknown hand has written the following note in roman script at the top of the document: "İmza ve târih yok. Fakat üslûp ve fikirler tamamen Kâmil Paşanın. Nefis bir maarif programı. Kendisi Maarif Nâzırı iken yazılmış olacaktır" ("Unsigned and undated but the style and ideas are Kâmil Paşa's exactly. An excellent education program. It must have been written while he was Education Minister").

of the state."[86] This desideratum combined the theoretical wish to inculcate political loyalty in the minds of faceless servants of the state with the practical need to fill specific governmental positions. A properly designed school network would also have the favorable result, ideally speaking, of obviating the need for foreign schools in the empire or, perhaps more realistically, of offering them some stiff competition.

Such thinking is predicated on the begrudging acknowledgement of the accomplishments of the foreign schools. "However disagreeable this may seem at first glance, it is evident that the foreigners, through various means and expense, have organized to the point where they are able by seduction to divert the people of the empire onto a path which serves their [i.e. the foreigners'] aims."[87] That education can be harnessed to serve the needs of the state is beyond question. The real issue is whose version of education is to prevail.

For Kâmil Paşa the rivalry being fought out over education was part of a larger struggle. We have alluded above to his comparison between the Ottoman domains and the countries of Europe. In Kâmil's mind, the relationship between East and West was not limited to the trappings of cultural attainment. For him such achievements were made possible only by the underlying economic situation:

Furthermore, the people of Europe were previously in the state that we are in now with respect to wealth. As for education, when we had more of it than they, we subsisted on our own agricultural production and, adding to our national wealth by selling them the yearly excess, our national honor and might attained a lofty degree. Subsequently aware of the secret and wisdom (*sır ü hikmet*) of science and education, the Europeans, [using] schools in their own countries, spread the science and education that they gleaned by translating from and experimenting with Eastern books.[88]

This passage contains two critical notions that recur frequently as underpinning for Hamidian education policy. The first is the belief, noted above, that science and education contain an inner secret that affords progress and prosperity to those who discover and employ it. This semi-mystical element can perhaps best be explained by the perceived need to catch up with the formerly inferior West. If the nations

---

[86] MKP 86/1-60, # 1, 7. 27 Ramazan 1298 (23 Aug. 1881).
[87] Ibid.   [88] MKP 86/1-55.

of Western Europe have been able to advance so rapidly from their previously undistinguished position by latching onto this secret wisdom, so can the Ottoman Empire. The second is the mix of influences that inspire the school program—the glories of the Ottoman past and the might of the Western European present:

[While they were] progressing by dint of all sorts of sacrifices, it became necessary for us, due to the suspension and obsolescence of our national trades and manufactures, to purchase all of our clothing and furniture [from abroad]. In this way the need to purchase many other things, arms and necessities from Europe became greater than we could afford. Not only did selling our harvests to Europe squander their value, but the price they fetched was insufficient; both the imperial government and the people of the empire became afflicted with debts. In short, for us to save ourselves from this completely disastrous situation, it is necessary to inculcate the benefits of increasing our national wealth as of old by producing in our own country better products instead of sacrificing what we have for European manufactures that are merely eye-catching.[89]

No sooner does Kâmil finish expounding his economic agenda than he turns to his education plan, so closely are they linked in his thinking. He continues:

And an education council is to be established in every city and town in the provinces. In this way all of the primary schools are to be reformed. By hastening to establish public schools in these cities and towns, first idadî, agricultural, and trade schools and subsequently a teachers' college is to be founded in each of the major cities which serve as provincial capitals. It is necessary that the sciences and education and the types of trades and skills to be taught therein are to be established and organized to the degree that, even if only basic at first, their future progress will suffice for the demands of the age.[90]

For Kâmil Paşa, education is inextricably bound to economic production and the balance of trade between the empire and Western Europe. Moreover, implementing the Ottoman school system represents his immediate program to redress the imbalance with the West that he holds to be responsible for so many Ottoman ills.

---

[89] Ibid.   [90] Ibid.

CONCLUSION

Ottoman educational expansion did not occur in a vacuum. Contrary to the impression produced by one historiographical tradition which sees schooling as a natural and inherently modernizing trend (e.g. Andreas Kazamias) and another that sees the state as bent on prosecuting its policy of institutional and mental "enframing,"[91] (e.g. Timothy Mitchell), there were other, more immediate concerns involved. Ottoman education policy was informed by the spirit of competition—with the West, with neighboring states, and with the various minority groups. Contending with such an array of adversaries and potential sources of emulation was nothing new for the Ottoman state. What had altered the situation dramatically by the late nineteenth century, however, was the relative ease with which the competition could now operate inside Ottoman territory. The empire's enemies were no longer anticipated only on its borders. Given the changed balance of power in the late nineteenth and early twentieth centuries, these adversaries were now increasingly able to operate from within. What was once a traditional military confrontation fought along a more or less distinct frontier was emerging in the modern era as a battle being waged internally for the hearts and minds of the population. The massive underlying economic imbalance ensured that this battle favored those who could marshal the various manifestations of technology (steamships, printing presses, etc.) to their own advantage. In retrospect and writ large, this is one manifestation of the struggle that led to the dismantling of the Ottoman Empire. For all of the parallels between the Ottoman predicament and its contemporary analogs, Western penetration on a number of fronts marks the Ottoman experience as distinct. Russia was at times driven by anti-Western nationalism, but this was the result of an essentially internal dynamic. China and Japan shared the problem of missionary encroachment, but were not faced with neighboring and internal threats on the same scale as those faced by the Ottoman state. The Ottoman struggle stands out as unusually difficult by comparison.

That the West would "win" the battle was perhaps "inevitable," given

[91] There is a wide array of works in the former category. Of those in English, perhaps that of Andreas Kazamias is the best-known. The second group is much smaller, but has been highly influential. Timothy Mitchell's *Colonising Egypt* is the main example here.

the fact that the Ottoman state had adopted its model of education as the dominant paradigm. It is significant that, despite its increased reliance on the Islamic common denominator and the refitting of curriculum in accordance with an increasingly jaundiced perception of Western intentions, the state chose not to continue to base its education effort on the Islamic model. The acceptance of the Western model as the formal basis for the Ottoman educational initiative can be explained partly by inertia—this model had been on the books for many years before Abdülhamid II took power. Yet, there is a more profound explanation. Like many segments of late Ottoman society, state officials deeply believed that positive, rational science would provide a solution for the empire's problems. In their eyes, and somewhat paradoxically, modern education contained the secret which, if discovered and applied on a uniform basis, would allow the empire to overcome its unfavorable position. Yet equally important, as we shall soon see, was the notion that this foreign system could, indeed should, be indigenized to fit with the particular historical trajectory and current demands of the Ottoman Empire. The Ottomanization of this borrowed system was, as in the case of the "self-strengthening" movement in China, a fascinating case of cultural adaptation.

The optimism that fired this project of assimilation is, as I have suggested, particularly difficult to fathom in the context of the early twenty-first century when what passes for a debate on education has descended into pessimism brought about by so many failed schemes. In the late Ottoman context, however, the notion of education was fresh and quasi-magical, implying the ability to right all of society's wrongs. So strong was this faith in education's power—and the need to act and act quickly to counter the competition—that state officials seemed relatively undaunted by the overwhelming odds they faced in the form of foreign and domestic pedagogical competition. If only the new-style schools can be built, their petitions hopefully suggest, the empire will be able to overcome its imbalance vis-à-vis the West. Indeed, the vitality ascribed to education is clear from the metaphors used by the authors of the foregoing provincial pleas. In the hands of the competition, education is depicted as biologically menacing. Foreign schools are described as a "contagion" and as "vermin." The competition is said to be "afflicting," "threatening," and in danger of "spreading" to other areas of the empire. Interestingly, despite abandoning the Islamic model of instruction, much of its content was nevertheless deemed crucial to halting the contagion of foreign culture and morality. Subsequent chapters describe the state's attempt to fuse the indigenous content with foreign form. Ottoman officials assumed that the secret power of education would work in their favor once a modern educational system had been implemented under the imperial —and Islamic—aegis.

As elsewhere around the world, late Ottoman education was a double-edged sword, possessing both the potential to be a panacea and the danger, vividly illustrated by the advanced position of the competition, to bestow a head start to whoever adopted it first. It is this thinking that explains the urgency of the Ottoman educational mission. The state's response to the challenge represented by its various educational competitors forms the basis of the next chapter.

3

Fighting Back

INTRODUCTION

Faced with the formidable array of competition discussed in the previous chapter, the empire fought back. While the sultans who ruled the Ottoman Empire during its periods of growth had waged their most important battles on the increasingly expanding imperial borders, their late nineteenth-century successors had no such luxury. This was especially apparent to Sultan Abdülhamid II, the longest reigning of the last sultans and the most concerned with stemming the tide of Western influence. He had not only to contend with watching these borders contract, bringing with their shrinkage severe problems such as refugees and lost revenues, but he and his bureaucrats also had to grapple with a more pervasive affliction: the internal meddling of foreign powers and neighboring states. In the educational arena, as we have seen, the Ottoman government was forced to compete on its own territory with foreigners and with minority groups who enjoyed considerable foreign backing. But these competitors from abroad came equipped with a further advantage; they brought with them a cultural and pedagogical model that was increasingly looked upon within the empire itself, by detractors and advocates alike, as containing the secret to success in the modern world. This placed the Ottoman government in the difficult position of emulating the very system with which it was forced to compete.

The Hamidian solution, like the challenge that provoked it, was both pragmatic and ideological. Unwavering in the commitment to imitating the *form* of the Western educational system, the Hamidian state launched a campaign to Ottomanize significant portions of that borrowed system's *content* to render it more suited to the empire's Islamic heritage. We shall return in subsequent chapters to this vetting campaign; here it is important to bear in mind that the formal, systemic aspects of the late Ottoman educational program were indispensable to the delivery of the more ideological aspects that were soon to follow. In other words, the state's educational message depended upon its medium.

But this message was changing. Like its counterparts in Russia and China, the Ottoman government sought to use education to stem the tide of European influence by reasserting consciously *indigenous* material for *indigenous* reasons. In this sense the late Ottoman educational endeavor should be seen as a case study of the *adaptation* of a foreign model to suit reassessed Ottoman requirements. Not an example of inevitable secularism or Westernization, the Hamidian schooling effort should be seen as an example of Ottoman agency, a program with intentions specific to Ottoman objectives. Although the empire's room for maneuver was greatly restricted by an array of competitors, with the foreign missionaries being the most problematic, this only added a sense of urgency to the Ottoman effort.

The example of the Christian missionaries suggests that the combination of religion and science was a formidable one, and it induced a like response. Just as American missionaries rejected as absurd the notion that religious education should be divorced from teaching science,[1] so also was it logical for the missionized to combine their religion with modern methods and concepts. The Ottoman effort bears this out clearly, as we shall soon see.

This chapter explores the specific circumstances, historical and logistic, of the Ottoman state's response to what it perceived to be the increasingly visible and insidious nature of the educational competition. I begin by situating the expansion of the state's school system in the context of the other responses such competition provoked. Although the development of the school system was certainly the chief weapon the state used to fight back, it also had recourse to other, less conventional methods. These included closing foreign schools that were operating in the empire, hiring traveling ulama to inveigh against the dangers of missionary schooling, and deploying a growing number

---

[1] For an intriguing example, see Michael Adas, *Machines as the Measure of Men: Science, Technology, and Ideologies of Western Dominance* (Ithaca, NY: Cornell University Press, 1989), 206–7.

of inspectors to monitor the competition. The main plan of attack, however, was the articulation of a fully integrated and centralized educational system. This chapter revisits the history of the founding and early years of the Galatasaray lycée, also known as the *Mekteb-i Sultanî*, that is, the Imperial School. This institution is important because it became the exemplar for the mainstay of Ottoman secondary education—the idadî (preparatory) school—and because its early history prefigures the changes that the idadîs would undergo when much of their initially French-inspired conception was reworked to accord with the larger Hamidian agenda. As with the lycée in France or the gymnasium in Germany, the Ottoman preparatory school was key to Ottoman educational change.

This chapter demonstrates the crucial role the idadîs played in the overall educational policy of the Hamidian period. Having inherited an inchoate and unevenly advanced educational system from the preceding Tanzimat era, Abdülhamid II's regime identified the preparatory level as that which demanded the most attention. By closing the glaring gap that existed at the idadî level, the state educational bureaucracy took its most pronounced step toward completing the system. The state's overall approach to that system and the place of the idadî within it, therefore, occupies the primary focus of this chapter. Sections exploring the way the state conceived of the idadîs, the fiscal sacrifices it made to ensure their construction, and the ways it recorded and displayed its progress in founding them all underscore the critical importance of the idadîs to the Hamidian educational project.

The entire enterprise of late Ottoman educational change was inherently related to the Ottoman relationship with the West. Whereas once the battle with the West had been largely offensive (and, when defensive, at least at considerable territorial remove from the empire's heartlands), the Ottomans of the late nineteenth and early twentieth centuries were forced to endure the presence throughout their empire of foreign educators-cum-propagandists who, in the perception of many Ottoman officials, were attempting nothing less than the empire's destruction. As we shall see, the Ottoman response increasingly bore the signs of approaching the *ghaza* ethos of the period of Ottoman expansion.[2] The waging of a battle for the hearts and minds

[2] See Cemal Kafadar, *Between Two Worlds: The Construction of the Ottoman State* (Berkeley: University of California Press, 1995), for a recent reappraisal of the notion of *ghaza*

of its subjects in the late nineteenth century had perforce to be pursued both internally and defensively, thereby reducing the state to the status of only one of several combatants. Moreover, due to the empire's fiscal crisis the state's resources were often considerably less than those of its competitors. Nevertheless, the Hamidian state recognized the advantages that flowed from being the state in power. Heir to a long and storied history, Abdülhamid II induced his empire to fight back by mobilizing what resources it had left in order to marshal a response to the challenge posed by the competition.

Education was critical to this response. First, as we have seen in the previous chapter, foreign schools and the missionaries that staffed them provided the most visible form of competition. Yet, as Ottoman bureaucrats were quick to perceive, there was a larger, more sinister agenda behind them. In the eyes of observant Ottoman statesmen, the foreigners were "working behind the curtain of education."[3] Secondly, education was important to Ottoman planners because of its inherently forward-looking agenda. Although late Ottoman functionaries were certainly aware of the empire's declining fortunes, they were rarely pessimistic about its future. If nothing else, the Hamidian educational endeavor reveals a remarkable optimism. Indeed, the pervasive faith in the meliorative, even quasi-magical, power of education is palpable in the entire state school system. Thirdly, state-supplied pedagogy provided the means to reorder patterns of behavior and thought. Education held out the promise of being a social corrective. In the Ottoman Empire, as in so many regions of the contemporary globe, the state's educational initiative should be seen as part of a larger attempt to reform society in order to render it "modern."[4] For Abdülhamid's

---

(i.e. warfare on behalf of Islam) in early Ottoman history. Kafadar argues persuasively for a conception of *ghaza* that was constantly changing and being redefined by social and political forces equally in flux (p. 120). It is important to remember that while much had obviously changed since the fourteenth and fifteenth centuries, this history still formed an important part of Ottoman culture roughly half a millennium later. It is no accident that Abdülhamid II used the term *gazi* as his sobriquet and that his educational campaign should emphasize the heroism of his earliest successors in school textbooks.

[3] ŞD 213/1. 16 Cemaziyelahır 1311 (25 Dec. 1893).

[4] For an account of the role education played in the state's attempt to reorganize Egyptian society, see Timothy Mitchell, *Colonising Egypt*, 63–94. We will return to Mitchell's conception of the physical and metaphysical aspects of the state school in our discussion of late Ottoman school architecture in Ch. 4.

empire, as we will see, such a campaign only began in earnest once the competition had been somewhat checked, the state's own system was in place, and the government was able to refit the content of that largely borrowed education system so as to bring it into accord with overall Ottoman strategy.

THE CENTER'S RESPONSE: FIGHTING FIRE WITH FIRE

The center's response to the alarming level of educational competition was twofold. On the one hand, it remained faithful to the formal aspects of the plan devised with strong French influence in the waning years of the Tanzimat reform era. The state redoubled its efforts to fund and build schools wherever possible in keeping with the vision of the 1869 Education Regulation. Eventually, as the problem worsened, the state overhauled the schools' curriculum that had been spelled out in the Regulation in an effort to ensure the political and religious loyalty of their students. (We return to the question of curriculum reform in Chapter 6.) In continuing to prosecute their plan for establishing an empire-wide school system, the Ottoman statesmen may be seen to have been acting in a positive, pre-emptive way.

On the other hand, the Ottoman response bore mounting signs of reacting to the foreigners' activity. The desiderata of central governmental memoranda increasingly included counter-measures to reduce the number and effectiveness of the foreign schools. The most convenient weapons available to the state were those stipulated in the Regulation of 1869. The part of the Regulation most often cited in the context of educational competition is Article 129.

Article 129

This section of the Regulation defined private, that is, non-government, schools as those institutions founded by societies or individuals, whether Ottoman or foreign subjects, and whose funding and appropriations are administered and supervised either by their founders or by the pious endowments established for their maintenance.[5] For such

---

[5] This copy of the Regulation was found in YEE 37/330. The only date supplied is the Hicrî year 1286, i.e. 1869–70 CE.

schools to be opened, the article stipulated: (1) that their teachers be in possession of certificates either from the Education Ministry or from the local education administration; (2) that the schools attest to the fact that no lessons "contrary to custom and [state] policy and ideology" will be taught in the schools; and (3) that the schools be granted an official permission from both the local education administration and from the governor if the school was in the provinces, and from the Education Ministry if in Istanbul. If these three conditions were not fully met, the article continued, permission would not be granted for private schools.

Although this Regulation had been promulgated during the reign of Sultan Abdülaziz (r. 1861–76), it proved useful in the state's attempt to limit the effects of foreign education during that of his successor, Abdülhamid II. As the inventories described in the preceding chapter demonstrate, Article 129 was honored more in the breach than in the observance. For example, only thirty-seven of the 427 foreign schools recorded in Zühdü Paşa's inventory of 1894 were listed as having official permission.[6] Such flagrant non-compliance with the official regulation afforded Hamidian bureaucrats an opportunity: technically the state had the right to close schools that were operating without permission. There is some evidence to suggest that Ottoman authorities embraced this option, particularly as a means of preventing the missionaries from operating in areas where the population was predominantly Muslim. For example, during the 1884–5 school year Ottoman authorities warned American missionaries in Syria that their schools were operating in contravention of Article 129.[7] When this initial warning went unheeded the authorities closed four schools in the area north-east of Tripoli as a further admonition, prompting a small crisis that included missionary accusations of religious intolerance, a petition signed by a number of Protestant missionaries, and the eventual closing of a total of thirty-three schools.[8] The Ottomans used the weapon of school-closure sparingly and mainly as a means of maintaining the practice,

---

[6] Çetin, "Osmanlı İmparatorluğundaki Yabancı Okullar."

[7] Tibawi, *American Interests*, 259–60. Tibawi's account is largely based on missionary archives. For an interesting account of the schooling rivalry between the Ottoman government, invoking Article 129, and the Orthodox, Latin, and Protestants in Transjordan in this period, see Rogan, *Frontiers*, 140 ff. Rogan shows that the Ottoman measures were not lost on the foreign missionaries.

[8] Tibawi, *American Interests*, 260–1. As Tibawi points out, schools in Christian and mixed areas (e.g. Palestine, Lebanon proper, and in major cities or towns in geographical Syria) were not involved in the closings.

"tacitly recognized by both sides since the inception of Protestant missions in Syria," of restricting missionary activity to the Christian population or to areas where the Muslim population was small.[9]

A telegram sent to all Asian provinces of the empire (except those of the Hijaz and Yemen, where missionary activity was non-existent) in August 1904 reveals both the government's fear of missionary activity and its inclination to take action against it.[10] This bulletin instructed the respective governorates to prevent categorically the continued attendance of Muslim students in American schools. Moreover, the provincial administrators were instructed to ascertain whether or not there were any Muslim schools to be found near the American schools. If not, they were to report confidentially on the feasibility of founding Muslim counterparts. The response from the governorate of Aydın (the area around Izmir), dated five days later, stated that the only American schools in the province were situated in Christian areas where there were no Muslim schools to be found, but assured that, in accordance with the sultan's decree, there were no Muslim students attending American schools. Correspondence between Istanbul and the province of Aydın, an area of considerable foreign presence, shows that the state subsequently continued to tighten the application of Article 129.[11]

A Non-Tanzimat Approach: Traveling Ulama

Some techniques put forward to thwart the competition departed from the official script of the Tanzimat. As we saw in Chapter 2, there were several occasions in which provincial officials argued for permission to send traveling Islamic clerics among the Muslim populace to preach against the evils of non-Muslim education. In all instances where they were known to have been called into service—in Iraq, in Syria, and on the island of Cyprus—the ulama were used in conjunction with the normal antidote, the building of mosques and state schools. The collaborative deployment of Muslim clerics and civil officials to carry out the state's campaign may seem odd, given that the historical literature has tended to brand these schools as "secular."[12] But to ignore the strong religious element in the Hamidian education movement is to overlook

[9] Ibid. 261.
[10] MKP 86/22-2136. 27 Cemaziyelevvel 1322 (9 Aug. 1904).
[11] MKP 86/22-2139. 25 Şaban 1322 (4 Nov. 1904).
[12] On the question of how secular these schools were, see my "Islamic Morality in Late Ottoman 'Secular' Schools," *IJMES* 32/3 (Aug. 2000), 369–93.

a significant component of its *raison d'être* and numerous aspects of its practical application. Hamidian policy-makers, always looking for solutions that would offer prompt results, knew that the time-lag between requesting a school and its actual opening could be substantial. A more expedient solution, traveling ulama, was closer at hand.

Süleyman Paşa's recommendations for establishing a corps of official Sunni proselytizers to combat Shiite influence in the provinces of Iraq, which we encountered in the previous chapter, indicate the plausibility (in his view, the necessity) of harnessing the power of religious propaganda to the state's educational campaign.[13] The paşa's suggestions included both Islamic missionaries *and* ostensibly civil schools. Both were to work for the same end, namely, the creation of a morally guided population capable of "distinguish[ing] good from evil,"[14] and, therefore, of seeing the error of failing to follow the path of Sunni Islam. For Süleyman Paşa in particular and for the state in general there was no inherent dichotomy between the secular and the religious. Even if there were such a dichotomy, the state's strong response to educational competition would have provided more than sufficient grounds to blur the distinction. Hamidian bureaucrats considered themselves engaged in fighting a battle for the very existence of the empire. As such, they were quite willing to adopt any solution that promised to be effective.

Indeed, the proven effectiveness of traveling ulama is what led to their being sanctioned for use in the education battle in Syria. In 1892 the governor in Damascus, Mehmed Rauf Paşa, wrote to the capital on the subject of education. After noting the destructive consequences of missionary schools in his province, Rauf Paşa stressed the necessity of building state alternatives. Since the process of freeing Muslim children from having to attend non-Muslim schools would be gradual, he argued, it would be advisable to continue the policy, begun by his predecessor, of sending members of the ulama throughout the countryside during the holy month of Ramadan to inveigh against the missionary schools.[15] This remedy, he stated, had been successful in

---

[13] On Süleyman Hüsnü Paşa, see also Deringil, *The Well-Protected Domains*, 49.

[14] YEE 14/1188, 4.

[15] His predecessor, Osman Nuri Paşa, had suggested the measure as a remedy for the "intrigues and subversion" of foreign missionaries operating in the province. For the details and a discussion of their broader context, see Selim Deringil, "Invention of Tradition," 16.

causing Muslim children to withdraw from the non-Muslim schools the previous year. The governor's proposal was approved by the palace, showing that the center could respond to provincial initiative.[16] As Rogan has shown, the Ottomans' own "missionaries" were active in the southern districts of the province of Syria in the 1890s, an occurrence which alarmed the Christian proselytizers.[17] This partisan stopgap, a clear departure from the Tanzimat notion of education reform, reflects the urgency of the quest for practical remedies to combat the missionary offensive.

The ulama were also mobilized to combat the ill effects of Christian propaganda, both indigenous and foreign. On the island of Cyprus, for example, local notables holding positions in the civil and religious bureaucratic hierarchy wrote to the şeyhülislam asking for help in preventing further attrition of the Muslim population.[18] They ascribed the growth of apostasy among the island's Muslims to several factors, including: the paucity of Muslim schools in Muslim areas (only sixty-five of 305 villages had schools); the fact that no one had gone to preach to them; the fact that Greek was the mother tongue of many of the Muslims; and, most distressing of all, the fact that the Greek metropolitans had sent priests "to deceive and seduce" the Muslim population. The petitioners singled out three villages and asked for primary schools and teachers, to be drawn from the ranks of the ulama, to teach in them and to preach in the neighboring villages. If such measures were to be taken, "it was not inconceivable that many of the apostates would return to Islam."[19] Furthermore, they requested that the state schools on the island be placed within the purview of the Education Inspectorship and that 300 Qur'ans and an equal number of separately printed verses of the Qur'an and religious treatises be sent to the island.

Whether the threat came from a rival form of Islam, as in the case of Iraq, from foreign missionaries, as in Syria, or from the empire's own minorities, as on Cyprus, the Hamidian response was the same. Traveling clerics were to scour the countryside armed with the Holy Book and rail against the threats posed to the Muslim population. Such activity, moreover, was naturally considered to be complementary to the more long-term solution: school building.

---

[16] İrade Maarif 1310 Ş 5. [17] Rogan, *Frontiers*, 157–8.
[18] Y Mtv. 180/177. 29 Rebiülevvel 1316 (17 Aug. 1898). [19] Ibid.

Inspection

Deploying inspectors was another, more conventional recourse of the late Ottoman response. The Hamidian state charged several independent inspection networks with the surveillance of a wide variety of areas.[20] Ironically, the opposition organization known as the Committee of Union and Progress that would ultimately prevail in its objective of overthrowing the sultan succeeded in large part by spreading its message through the growing inspection and educational networks. As we shall see repeatedly in subsequent chapters, the apparatus of education could frequently produce results that were diametrically opposed to the state's objectives. Just as the Hamidian state had turned the tables on many aspects of the Tanzimat educational agenda, so too could the Hamidian opposition use the Hamidian networks to its own advantage.

In the field of education, the state marshaled two types of inspectors.[21] The first was concerned with the monitoring of the state's own schools. These inspectors were primarily interested in guarding against politically subversive material and what they deemed immoral behavior in the schools. The second set of inspectors was given the task of monitoring the schools run by foreigners and other non-Muslim organizations. In accordance with the general pattern of Hamidian educational expansion, inspection of the non-Muslim schools appeared first in Istanbul and later spread to the provinces. In March of 1886 the education minister Münif Paşa issued a memorandum advocating the need to inspect the non-Muslim schools of the capital.[22] Due to the fact that so far none of the non-Muslim schools had been brought under the inspection of the Education Ministry, he argued, the Ottoman state had no knowledge of what transpired in these institutions. Unlike other states, Münif continued, the Ottoman Empire was completely in the dark about the curricula, textbooks, and moral character and

[20] In the civil bureaucracy alone there were at least three ministries (Interior, Police, and Education) charged with inspection duties. Later, the Justice and Public Health Ministries added their own cadres of inspectors to the mix.

[21] A third and related type consisted of health inspectors (*sıhhiye müfettişi*), instituted in 1899, whose brief included civil educational institutions. Koçer, *Türkiye'*, 127. For an earlier memorandum arguing for such inspections, see Y Mtv. 108/90. 12 Cemaziyelevvel 1312 (11 Nov. 1894).

[22] İrade MM 3580. 28 Receb 1303 (2 May 1886).

behavior of the teachers in its non-Muslim schools. This could be politically dangerous. Münif's answer to the problem was inspection. He proposed that a Greek named Kostantinidi Paşa, formerly a member of the Education Council (*Meclis-i Maarif*) and currently under-secretary (*Müsteşar*) in the province of Salonika, be appointed to the Inspectorship of the non-Muslim schools (*Mekâtib-i Gayrı Müslime ve Ecnebiye Müfettişliği*) in Istanbul, with a monthly salary of 4,000 kuruş to be paid for out of the "new revenues." Münif mentioned that, in addition to Turkish, Kostantinidi had the necessary knowledge of Greek, French, and English. This proposal was reviewed by the *Meclis-i Mahsus*, whose protocol added mention of his "competency, good conduct, and moral qualities," and sent to the palace for final approval.[23]

The state employed non-Muslim inspectors to monitor non-Muslim education in the empire for only another year. Thereafter, these officials were to be Muslims. This decision seems to have been prompted by a petition sent to the palace by one Schneider Efendi.[24] This Schneider was petitioning to be considered for the newly created position of inspector for non-Muslim and foreign schools in Rumelia. His candidacy was supported by the Education Ministry and by the Porte, who also asked that the system of inspectors be expanded to all of the empire's provinces. When the paperwork reached Yıldız Palace, however, a critical objection, presumably the sultan's own, was raised. The memorandum of the chamberlain, Süreyyâ, reads as follows:

The grand vizier's memorandum dated 9 Receb 1304 [3 April 1887] and its attachments concerning Schneider Efendi's petition for appointment to the inspectorship of all non-Muslim and foreign schools in Rumelia have been

---

[23] İrade MM 3580, 1. lef. 27 Receb 1303 (1 May 1886).

[24] İrade Dah. 81089. 10 Receb 1304 (4 Apr. 1887). The correspondence between the Education Ministry and the Porte contained in this file refers to some examples that illustrate the state's reasons for expanding inspection of the non-Muslim and foreign schools. Two such examples are described in the documents as follows: first, an Ottoman subject named R-k-ndes (vocalization unclear) had been sent to Athens to represent the Greeks of Macedonia and had made a speech during festivities celebrating the coming of age of the Greek crown prince that the Ottoman authorities found troubling. Secondly, the actions and circumstances of the teachers in schools run by the Greek millet (*Rum*) and by Greece (*Yunan*) in the province of Salonika were considered to have incited sedition (*fesad*). Inspection was recommended as the means of preventing such dangers in the future.

reviewed by his Excellency. Due to the obvious importance of this work, the Imperial decree requires that inspection be extended to all of the Imperial provinces but that Muslims be selected for appointment as inspectors. Therefore, the above-mentioned memorandum and papers have been returned . . .[25]

While the state had so far been willing to use non-Muslims to carry out inspection duties, presumably because of their linguistic capabilities, the matter was henceforth deemed to be too sensitive to be left to non-Muslims. By the early 1890s the names of the bureaucrats appointed to the major school inspectorships show that they were Muslims.[26] In the following years the network of inspection teams in the Education Ministry expanded to keep pace with the rapidly growing number of schools. A special inspectorship for the idadî schools (*Mekâtib-i İdadiye Dairesi*) was created in 1892.[27] Four years later the Ministry's inspection duties were subsumed under the Inspection and Examination Commission (*Encümen-i Teftiş ve Muayene*), chaired by the education minister himself.[28] Abdülhamid II expanded this Commission's mandate in 1903 when he charged it with reviewing publications in terms of their religious content. Inspection was an increasingly visible and important component of the Hamidian educational program.

Schools

These measures—sending traveling ulama to preach in the provinces, deploying inspectors to monitor the non-Muslim and foreign schools, and, on occasion, actually shutting them down—were all signs that the Hamidian state would not react passively to the threat it perceived from foreign education. The main response, however, came in the form of building the state's own schools. The number of schools built in the

---

[25] İrade Dah. 81089.

[26] In areas where the bona fides of the ostensibly Muslim population were called into question, such as in Shiite Iraq, as we have seen, or in the Alawite areas of Syria, the state also sent inspectors to see that the population practiced Islam in what it deemed to be the proper manner. For example, a memorandum written by Zühdü Paşa in 1896 reveals official concern over Islamic practice in the sancak of Lazkiye (Latakia). Here, traveling inspectors were to be charged with monitoring the imams and teachers in the schools and mosques recently built as part of a campaign "to instruct religious practices and to control Islamic principles," Ibid.

[27] Koçer, *Türkiye*, 126. See also, ŞD 211/17.

[28] Koçer, *Türkiye*, 126. For more on the subject of this commission, see Ch. 6.

empire during Abdülhamid II's reign is estimated to have approached 10,000.[29] The effects of this building campaign were most apparent in the provinces and at the secondary level, the areas most neglected by the previous efforts of the Tanzimat. By creating its own network of institutions, the state hoped to ensure that its own version of education would be implemented. Conceived as it was in response to a political-cultural threat, however, the Ottoman schools were more than mere pedagogical vehicles. A unified curriculum in a centralized, regionally articulated system offered the state the possibility of propagating its own message on its own terms. Once the system was in place, the government could then concentrate on refining its message. As subsequent chapters demonstrate, this message was itself in flux as the Hamidian state refitted the Tanzimat curriculum to accord with its own ideology. Before the late Ottoman schools could perform such service, they had to be built.

But before they could be built they had to be planned. The received wisdom of the secondary literature holds that the Hamidian system was built according to the plan articulated in the Education Regulation of 1869. This is certainly true, but the same literature frequently ignores the circumstances surrounding the adoption of that plan. The role that foreign influence played in the development of the Ottoman state school system compels a closer reading of the way it came into being. It is for this reason that, before we discuss the articulation of the idadî schools, it is necessary to explore the two developments most important to their existence. The first was the 1868 founding and early history of the lycée of Galatasaray, known in Ottoman as the *Mekteb-i Sultanî*, the Imperial School. The second was the promulgation of the Education Regulation of 1869.

GALATASARAY, THE "IMPERIAL SCHOOL"

Much has been written about Galatasaray, the school created through the combined efforts of the French and Ottoman governments.[30] My

---

[29] Corinne Blake, "Training Arab-Ottoman Bureaucrats: Syrian Graduates of the *Mülkiye Mektebi*, 1890–1920," Ph.D. diss., Princeton University (1991), 64.

[30] Works on that institution include: Adnan Şişman, *Galatasaray Mekteb-i Sultânisi'nin Kuruluşu ve İlk Eğitim Yılları, 1868–1871* (Istanbul: Edebiyat Fakültesi Yayınevi, 1989); İhsan Sungu, "Galatasaray Lisenin Kuruluşu," *Belleten*, 7/28 (1943), 315–47; [Louis] de

purpose here is not to duplicate those writings but, rather, to highlight certain aspects of the early history of that institution as a prelude to discussing the founding and spread of the idadî schools intended to replicate the work of the Galatasaray lycée throughout the empire.[31] Because Galatasaray was the model for the idadî schools, the story of its transition from the Tanzimat to the Hamidian period offers a good introduction to the larger history of those provincial institutions that are the subject of this project. As the product of a joint Franco-Ottoman endeavor, Galatasaray represents an intriguing example of Ottoman adoption and subsequent modification of a clearly European institution, a clear harbinger of the refitting that the idadî schools would experience during the reign of Sultan Abdülhamid II. Reaching back in time to the period of its founding allows us, further, to see Galatasaray in its proper context.

That context is one of European Great Power pressure for "reform." It is important to use this term carefully, because it can easily be used to mask the less than salutary results that the powers expected from urging their agenda on the late Ottoman state. Galatasaray did not come about in a vacuum but was part of a larger program being pushed by France in the late 1860s which, in turn, was part of the larger pattern of Great Power rivalry for influence in and over a weakening empire. Impatient over what it considered the slow course of the changes promised more than ten years earlier by the Imperial Rescript (*Hatt-i Hümayun*) of 1856 in the aftermath of the Crimean War, and irritated by the violence that was breaking out in Crete in 1866, the French government sent the Sublime Porte a list of the changes it desired to see enacted in the empire. This correspondence, dated 22 February 1867, reflects the extent to which the French desire for educational change was inextricably linked to a larger campaign to induce the Ottomans to open up their empire to Western interference and financial interests.[32] The French list included such demands as: the inclusion of non-

---

Salve, "L'Enseignement en Turquie: le lycée impérial de Galata-Séraï," *Revue des deux mondes*, 5 (1874), 836–53; and François Georgeon, "La Formation des élites à la fin de l'Empire ottoman: le cas de Galatasaray," *Revue du monde musulman et de la Méditerranée*, 72 (1994), 15–25.

[31] Georgeon, "La Formation des élites," 18.

[32] Le Baron I. de Testa, *Recueil de Traités de la Porte Ottomane avec les puissances étrangères depuis le premier traité conclu, en 1536, entre Suléyman 1er et François 1er jusqu'a nos*

Muslims in state service; the creation of a complete and integrated educational system; the generalization of the new provincial administrative reforms that had been implemented in the Danubian provinces, giving Christians a role in local administration; expansion of the commercial courts; the granting of property rights to foreigners; "reform" of the pious endowments; reorganization of taxation; the lifting of internal customs duties; the establishment of railroads, carriage roads, and harbors, with the proviso that the concessions be given to foreign firms; the rationalization of budget procedures; and guaranteeing the rights of the state's creditors, many of whom were French.[33]

The radical nature of Muslim and non-Muslim children learning, eating, and boarding together should be underscored and considered both as the state's effort to foster Ottomanism and as a part of the French desire to eliminate the barriers between the two groups. While the Russians wanted to support the minorities by advocating their separation from the Empire, the French sought to incorporate them into the mainstream. For their part, the Ottomans saw mixed education as an opportunity to replace multiple religious affiliations with one allegiance to one state. This is clear in the account of the founding of Galatasaray Mektebi written by Safvet Paşa in 1880.[34] Safvet's description clearly demonstrates the extent to which the Galatasaray model, the first experiment in interdenominational education in the Ottoman Empire, was only one part of a larger French plan. In his recounting, the fact that the creation of Galatasaray followed hard upon the heels of Sultan Abdülaziz's 1867 visit to Paris, the first by an Ottoman sultan, was no accident. Nor was it the only effect by any means. Safvet Paşa describes the causal relationship between the Paris tour and the initiative, upon the imperial retinue's return, to expand the Ottoman

---

jours (Paris: Ernest Leroux, 1892), vii. 418 ff. It is important to remember the French plan in the context of Franco-Russian rivalry over the empire. While Russia sought to divide the empire into autonomous areas along religious lines, succinctly described by Sungu in a Franco-Turkish ultimatum as *autonomie veya anatomie* (autonomy or anatomy), the French followed a policy aimed at strengthening the empire through centralization. Georgeon, "La Formation des élites," 17. The price for French support for a strong Istanbul, however, was the opening of the empire to French investors and, as the case of Galatasaray demonstrates, French influence in areas such as education.

[33] Sungu, "Galatasaray Lisenin Kuruluşu," 316–17. The complete text can be found in Testa, *Recueil*, vii. 418 ff.　　　　[34] YEE 31/1140. 22 Safer 1297 (4 Feb. 1880).

railroad network and to reconstitute the Meclis-i Mahsus along the lines of the French Conseil d'État. Infrastructural and bureaucratic influence aside, a more momentous outcome of the French journey was an increased effort by the French to press their advantage into other areas.

The French built upon the favorable impression that Sultan Abdülaziz gained from his visit to France by pressing for the implementation of specific items on their list. For example, the French foreign minister wrote to his ambassador in Istanbul on 23 August 1867, stating that:

> The sultan particularly insisted with his ministers on his resolve to give a vigorous impulse to public education, and to increase the resources of the country by creating numerous railroads as well as a mortgage bank. We can only applaud these intentions. My correspondence with the embassy attests to the lively and constant interest that we hold for the spread of education in Turkey. We are eager to reconcile our active co-operation with the first attempts of the Ottoman ministers to ensure the realization of this idea. We are pleased to see in the sultan's words today the definite sanction of these efforts and the promise of the execution in the near future of the plans elaborated several months ago. In the realm of economic ideas . . .[35]

Without missing a beat, the French minister moves from the subject of education to economic affairs. In this light, the French desire for the expansion of Ottoman education along Western lines must be seen as inextricably linked to its economic and cultural interests, and thus appears more self-serving than it would if considered out of context.

By actively encouraging the Ottomans to reproduce a French-style system, Paris was hoping to extend its political and cultural influence in the Levant.[36] The choice of French as the language of instruction in the school was itself a victory for Paris. Moreover, by exporting teachers, administrators, textbooks, and even bed-frames, the French hoped to cultivate hundreds of potential Francophones and Francophiles.

But the Galatasaray experiment was more than an attempt to expand French influence in the empire. It also marked an effort to restructure the way the Ottoman state treated its various religious groups. By bringing them together in one institution where they would study, exercise, eat, and sleep in common, the school took a radical step

---

[35] Testa, *Recueil*, vii. 495.   [36] Şişman, *Galatasaray Mektebi*, 13.

toward dismantling the formal barriers that separated the empire's subjects according to confessional affiliation.[37] From the perspective of the
Ottoman state, the justification for mixed education centered on the
assumption that communal education would foster a common allegiance to the Ottoman state. The French agenda should not be
ignored, however. For their part, the French hoped that the education
of Muslim and non-Muslim side-by-side would increase the opportunities of the empire's minority groups whose cause they championed.
In fact, most of the items on the French list for Ottoman reforms were
related to improving the situation of the minorities in one way or
another. French support for officially supplied interdenominational
schooling should therefore be seen in the context of the larger French
agenda. I stress this point here because, when the discussion turns to
the subject of the Hamidian effort to reconfigure the educational
arrangements worked out in the Tanzimat period, it will be necessary to remember that there was more at stake than pedagogical
issues. Abdülhamid's changes will be seen as an attempt to reassert
Ottoman interests *at the expense of* their Western, in this case French,
counterparts.

For the time being, however, early results at Galatasaray buoyed
French hopes. The number of students enrolled at Galatasaray
increased markedly during its first few years of operation. It opened in
September of 1868 with 341 pupils.[38] One month later the enrollment

[37] Roderic H. Davison referred to the Mekteb-i Sultanî as "the first breach in millet
barriers to mixed education" (*Reform*, 246). There was, however, an earlier attempt, that
of the Mekteb-i Osmanî in Paris. This earlier Ottoman state experiment with interdenominational education foreshadowed the schools that would later be built within the
empire in several respects. These included both the intention of providing for an official
option to compete with other schools in the French capital being run by Ottoman subjects, and the desire to provide a modern curriculum while ensuring that religious and
Turkish instruction be given. On the particulars, see Richard L. Chambers, "Notes on
the *Mekteb-i Osmanî* in Paris, 1857–1874," in William R. Polk and Richard L. Chambers
(eds.), *Beginnings of Modernization in the Middle East: The Nineteenth Century* (Chicago:
University of Chicago Press, 1968), 313–29.

[38] Salve, "L'Enseignement," 848. According to Salve's figures, 147, or roughly 43%, of
these 341 students were Muslims, the remainder being comprised of Armenian Orthodox (48), Greeks (36), Jews (34), Bulgarians (34), Roman Catholics (23), and Armenian
Catholics (19). Georgeon's numbers, for which he gives no source, are slightly higher for
all categories. His totals are 399 at opening and 620 at the end of 1869: Georgeon, "La
Formation des élites," 19.

had jumped to 430 and reached 530 by year's end. One year later it had reached 640, or almost double the number of students on its rolls when it opened.[39] The early success of the lycée was so great as to encourage the idea of opening other schools in the empire's other cities on its model. An article written by Louis de Salve, the school's first director, shows that curricula were requested from an unspecified party in Beirut and that the Bulgarians solicited a similar institution from the French.[40] The high hopes of Louis de Salve, however, were dashed by the demise of France's prestige in the aftermath of its defeat in the Franco-Prussian War of 1870, and by the deaths of Fuad and Ali Paşas, chief architects of the Tanzimat, in 1869 and 1871 respectively. Thereafter, Salve lamented, French influence was pitifully reduced in the Ottoman capital and the bright promise of French-inspired Ottoman education seemed to fade. The French military mission was being abolished and the French language was falling out of favor in the military medical school, in several other educational institutions, and in the civil tribunals of Istanbul, where, according to Louis de Salve's hyperbole, had been used "from time immemorial." Galatasaray, now coming under attack in the press as an instrument of French interest, saw its enrollment fall and its French director depart, replaced by a series of Ottoman officials.

If Salve was dejected by the diminution of his expansive hopes for Galatasaray and the broader goals it represented, he would surely have been appalled at the changes the institution underwent during the Hamidian period. As we shall see, the Mekteb-i Sultanî underwent several modifications intended to square it with the overall precepts of late Ottoman education policy. These changes prefigure many of the ways in which the idadî schools and, indeed, the entire system laid out in the 1869 education regulation were refitted by the Hamidian state.[41]

---

[39] Salve, "L'Enseignement," 848.

[40] Ibid. 849.

[41] It is necessary to point out that some of the efforts to Ottomanize the Galatasaray lycée occurred in the aftermath of the Franco-Prussian War. The changes that occurred—the French director was replaced with an Ottoman functionary, and the school was physically moved out of the Beyoğlu quarter, with its strong minority tradition, to the grounds of the Gülhane gardens adjacent to the Topkapı Palace complex in old Istanbul, a considerable change of venue—took place before Abdülhamid's accession, but they foreshadowed some of the changes he would bring to that institution.

In February of 1877 Abdülhamid II appointed Ali Suavî Efendi to be director of Galatasaray, a sign of the changes in store for that institution and state-supplied education in the empire in general. Not only the first Muslim to hold the post, Ali Suavî was also a flamboyant and controversial figure.[42] He had risen from humble origins through one of the new avenues of social mobility afforded by the state's expansion in the nineteenth century: the public education system. Although he had received a rüşdiye education, Suavî has generally been considered an odd choice for director of the Franco-Ottoman lycée. A populist member of the ulama and an inflammatory writer and public speaker, Suavî was by 1876 best known for the anti-Western and anti-bureaucratic broadsides he had published in the opposition journal *Muhbir*, published first in Istanbul and then in exile in Paris.[43] His appointment to head the school may, however, be traced to his background in both Western and Islamic sciences,[44] and to the ideas he was propounding in Paris. His championing of the necessity of a strong state led by a strong ruler was an obvious source of endearment to the newly enthroned sultan. His public stance against the Ottoman constitution must likewise have curried favor with Abdülhamid II, who soon suspended it.[45] But it is to his general views on education and the importance of resisting foreign influence in the empire that we should look to understand his appointment as headmaster. One of his articles attacked his fellow ulama for failing to take action when confronted by missionary propaganda, a theme that, as we have seen in Chapter 2, would soon be echoed by Kâmil Paşa.[46] He had also advocated the adoption of Turkish as the language of instruction in Ottoman schools,

[42] On the colorful career of Ali Suavî, see Midhat Cemal Kuntay, *Sarıklı İhtilalci Ali Suavi* (Istanbul: Ahmet Halit Kitabevi, 1946); Bernard Lewis, *The Emergence of Modern Turkey*, 2nd edn. (Oxford: Oxford University Press, 1968); Şerif Mardin, *The Genesis of Young Ottoman Thought: A Study in the Modernization of Turkish Political Ideas* (Princeton: Princeton University Press, 1962); İsmail Doğan, *Tanzimatın İki Ucu: Münif Paşa ve Ali Suavî (Sosyo-pedagojik bir Karşılaştırma)* (Istanbul: İz Yayıncılık, 1991); and, most recently, Hüseyin Çelik, *Ali Suavî ve Dönemi* (Istanbul: İletişim, 1994).

[43] Mardin, *Genesis*, 361.

[44] At the time of his appointment, the newspaper *Sadakât* referred to Suavî as "a highly esteemed individual worthy of being described as a library of the world which contains the learning of the East and the West and the Islamic and philosophical sciences," my translation of the Turkish as given in Çelik, *Ali Suavî*, 311.

[45] For the text of his articles published in *Vakit*, see Kuntay, *Sarıklı İhtilalci*, 90–101.

[46] Mardin, *Genesis*, 370.

a change deemed necessary to further his general goal of increasing popular access to education.[47] His strong stance against the potential divisiveness of the nationalities question in the empire ("Nationality questions would cause our ruin"),[48] as well as his advocacy of Islam as a unifying force around which to rally the empire's core in response to the challenges posed by its adversaries, doubtless found a sympathetic audience in Abdülhamid II. Furthermore, Ali Suavî had raised the subject of the Franco-Ottoman school in the letters he sent to various Ottoman opposition journals published in Europe. In May 1868 in the journal *Muhbir* Suavî expressed his dismay at the exclusive favoring of France, and the French language, that the Galatasaray project represented.[49] Suavî argued that this would only encourage other nations to demand the same treatment. His more general writings on the need to reform Ottoman education likewise contained direct references to Galatasaray. In September 1868 Suavî responded to a discussion in a previous issue of the London-based opposition journal *Hürriyet* concerning the lack of education in the Empire:

In order to acquire the affluence of civilization, neither a large army, nor a huge fleet, nor the assistance of the school in Galatasaray filled with French teachers is necessary. Look to the reordering of your own schools. What is the use of taking a Turkish child out of the hands of the large-turbaned hocas and giving him over to goat-bearded Frenchmen? There is an easier way. First of all, nourish your ulama. For no matter how much outward grandeur the heads of most madrasas acquire due to the thickness of their turbans, it is clear that they are internally just as devoid of it. They should not confine their time only to sciences (*ulûm*) that profit the hereafter; they should also look at useful information (*maarif*) of an earthly necessity such as a little history and geography and the natural sciences. Of course human beings die, but they are created not for death but for life.[50]

Seen in this light, the choice of Ali Suavî as director of Galatasaray seems much more understandable; it jibes with Abdülhamid II's

---

[47] Mardin, *Genesis*, 371–2.   [48] As quoted ibid. 372.

[49] Çelik, *Ali Suavî*, 314.

[50] Turkish given ibid. 315–16, my translation. For the distinction between what is connoted by the terms *maarif* and *ulûm*, see Berkes, *Development of Secularism*, 99. In the passage translated here I have used the term "useful information" as a shorthand for Berkes's "the process of becoming acquainted with things unknown." Elsewhere I have rendered the term as "education" and *ulûm* as "(religious) sciences."

unfolding policy of injecting religious content into the secular system he had inherited from the Tanzimat period.

Whatever the motivation for his appointment, his brief tenure at the Imperial School was one of abrupt change. Ali Suavî wasted little time in setting about to increase Muslim enrollment, to reduce scholarships for minority students in favor of Muslims, and to rid the school of troublesome individuals. Suavî's own memorandum concerning the situation at the school in August 1877 elucidates the specific changes he had effected in his first year there, actions taken without official approval from the Ministry of Education.[51] According to this document, he had increased the number of Muslim students by 37 per cent, from 162 to 220. He also acted to remedy the preponderance of scholarships awarded to non-Muslim students.[52] He ordered the expulsion of all Russian students and those Bulgarian students implicated as the leaders of the disturbances that had taken place in the sancaks of Filibe (Philippopolis/Plovdiv) and İslimye (Sliven) the previous year.[53] (Those from regions free of trouble and those who were deemed "hard-working and well behaved" were not affected.) Suavî also described his expulsion of four of the school's teachers, listing their offenses as ranging from openly lecturing against the state to siding with Russia during the 1877–8 war.[54] Suavî also turned his attention toward the school's

[51] YEE 14/1274. 14 Şaban 1294 (24 Aug. 1877). This document has recently been published in facsimile form in Hüseyin Çelik, Ali Suavî, appendix.

[52] Georgeon, "La Formation des élites," 20.

[53] YEE 14/1274. Suavî identifies some of these students by name: Kaplişku (sp.?) is charged with burning Muslim villages, while Dançof (sp.?) and Siyarof (sp.?), identified as having been captured and condemned for armed brigandage but subsequently admitted gratis to Galatasaray by the Porte, are alleged to have incited Bulgarian students when the Russian army crossed the Danube and to have attached themselves to the Russian army.

[54] Ibid. He states that the teacher named Cakmo (sp.?), whom Suavî describes as having been hired due to the influence of the Russian ambassador Ignatief, whose children he had taught, had his contract annulled and was removed for having openly lectured against the Ottoman state. Zankof, also employed due to the intervention of the Russian embassy, is described as having gone to London during the latest Bulgarian incident and participating in meetings against the Ottoman state. Suavî further charges that he has recently been appointed by the Russians to be a local official in the Danube and therefore was dismissed *in absentia*. A French teacher of geography was dismissed for having become an informant for the Russian embassy during the war. Mihalofski was dismissed along with three Bulgarian monitors (*kalfa*) because the Bulgarian language was no longer to be taught at the school. Mihalofski is described as having been implicated in incitement (*tahrik*).

pedagogical standards. Complaining that there were students who had been enrolled for six years without passing out of the ABC's class, and that although there were students who had worked "day and night like machines" for ten years, the school was still incapable of producing anyone able to write in proper Ottoman or French, Suavî advocated tougher hiring criteria for teachers. "In order to reform teaching, the question of the diploma was taken up and those who were untrained in the practice of instruction were replaced with teachers possessing diplomas and earning lower salaries."[55] Suavî also altered the school's curriculum in a way that foreshadowed the broader changes that the Hamidian era would bring to the entire Ottoman education system. He increased the frequency of courses he deemed useful but that had been previously neglected, such as physical sciences, biology, and statistics. But these European subjects were to be balanced with the study of works in Arabic, Ottoman Turkish, and Persian on such traditional Islamic subjects as *kalam*, *adab*, *insha'*, and *fiqh*.[56] Suavî gave the school's atmosphere a decidedly Islamic character. For example, under Suavî the Muslim students were made to study the fundamental principles (*akaid*) of Islam, a subject absent during his predecessor's tenure.[57] As Chapter 6 will demonstrate, moral education would play a critical role in Hamidian education policy. The cumulative effect of Ali Suavî's changes was to make Galatasaray a more Muslim, a more Ottoman, and a more effective institution.

Ali Suavî was dismissed from the Imperial School in November of 1877 but, as the events of subsequent years bear out, the themes underlying the changes he brought to that institution continued to hold sway.[58] One example of the increasingly Islamized and Ottomanized

[55] YEE 14/1274.

[56] Çelik, *Ali Suavî*, 324–5, citing a letter Suavî wrote to the Istanbul paper *Vakit* while he was director of the school.

[57] Ibid. 327. Çelik suggests that Suavî inserted this course into the Galatasaray curriculum in order to thwart the atheist and missionary influence of several of the teachers who were French.

[58] The reason for his dismissal has never been satisfactorily explained. The issue of incompetence has been raised (Mardin, *Genesis*, 364), as has the question of rumors surrounding the deportment of his British wife (Kuntay, *Sarıklı İhtilalci*, 108), but no hard evidence has been given to justify either charge. Georgeon's ascribing his dismissal to the putatively disorganizing effects of Suavî's changes is no more helpful, given the fact that

official milieu at the Imperial School is the attention paid to the ritual of the Prophet Muhammad's birthday, the *Mevlid-i Şerif*. The first known official observance of this holiday occurred in 1882 when candy was distributed to the school's teachers and students in the name of Sultan Abdülhamid II. The gift seems to have produced its desired effect, for in a note acknowledging the sultan's generosity the school's director stated that:

I had wanted to describe the signs of gratitude, pride, and astonishment that immediately appeared on their faces when we came to distribute the candy to each of the students and teachers, but such things cannot be described or captured on paper; they must be seen with the eye. This much I know, that no one in the school will forget this imperial generosity for as long as he lives and that everyone will remember this fortunate day as long as the school stands.[59]

Even if we discount the fawning normally associated with addressing the sultan, it seems unlikely that the director's distribution of candy would have been met with anything but enthusiasm. In subsequent years the occasion was commemorated with the reading of the *Mevlid* poem. The occasion also included the saying of prayers for the sultan, thereby linking Abdülhamid II with the Prophet Muhammad.[60]

But the changes taking place at Galatasaray during the Hamidian period included some of substance to accompany those of mere symbolism. The state sought to increase its control over what transpired in the school, both inside the classroom and in the extracurricular lives of its students. In 1887 the sultan impaneled the first of several curriculum review commissions which he entrusted to the chairmanship of the highest member of the religious hierarchy, the şeyhülislam, Ahmed Esad Efendi. He was to be assisted in this task by an official from the civil bureaucracy named Mehmed Recai, who was the assistant

---

many of the trends he started continued after his departure (Georgeon, "La Formation des élites," 21). Suavî's own memorandum reveals his frustration with the Ministry of Education over the non-implementation of his plans to reform the school. The friction generated by his persistence and by the radical nature of his ideas may have contributed to his dismissal.

[59] Y Mtv. 8/58, # 2. 13 Rebiülevvel 1299 (2 Feb. 1882).

[60] Y Mtv. 109/17, 22 Cemaziyelevvel 1312 (21 Nov. 1894) and Y Mtv. 109/32, 24 Cemaziyelevvel 1312 (23 Nov. 1894).

director of the *Mekteb-i Mülkiye*.[61] Recai's recommendations for altering the curriculum at Galatasaray give a clear picture of the direction in which the palace wanted the school to move. Recai's memorandum contains the following changes "concerning the Mekteb-i Sultanî:"

1. Abolishing Latin and philosophy courses and allowing nothing to be read of the biographies of European philosophers and writers.
2. The serious instruction twice a week of lessons in Islamic principles (*akaid*), which will be entrusted to qualified ulama.
3. Transferring Arabic, Persian, and Turkish classes, which are called Oriental studies at the Mekteb-i Sultanî, to the supervision of a Muslim official.[62]

By reducing the influence of Western ideas—and Western teachers—and increasing the role of Islamic principles, the commission was consciously attempting to transform the school's mission. In his memorandum, which served as a cover letter to the commission's recommendations, the şeyhülislam mentions the need to prevent Galatasaray students from becoming preoccupied "with Western works and writings that are detrimental to Islamic morals and the exalted Sultanate," to have the students study treatises on belief (*resail-i itikadiye*), and to oversee the performance of their obligatory prayers as a congregation.[63]

While the palace was refitting Galatasaray's curriculum to make it less a French institution and more an Islamic and Ottoman one, there was a simultaneous effort to exert more official control over the behavior of its students. Apart from the rare political incident that naturally

---

[61] On "Haci Recai," and his reputation for being "extremely respectful to authorities," see Blake, "Training," 118. On the role of school vice-principals as enforcers of religio-political propriety, see e.g. *Düstûr*, 1. Tertib, vol. 8 (Ankara: Başvekâlet Devlet Matbaası 1943), 434–5.

[62] Y Mtv. 25/52, # 3, ND, but before 6 Cemaziyelahır 1304 (2 Mar. 1887).

[63] Y Mtv. 25/52, # 2, 6 Cemaziyelahır 1304 (2 Mar. 1887). The issue of school curriculum was one that was hotly contested. An *irade* dated Feb. 1893 decreed that the school raise the salaries of its teachers of religious principles. İrade M 1310 Ş 3. 5 Şaban 1310 (22 Feb. 1893). Documents from the following year show what may have been an attempt to diffuse the increasingly anti-secular direction of the school's curriculum: a proposal, apparently unsuccessful, to increase the number of courses taught in French at Galatasaray and the hiring of more French nationals and French-speaking staff. YA Res. 66/26 and YA Res. 67/5.

attracted prompt official intervention,[64] school and other government officials demonstrated an increasing vigilance against what they perceived to be immoral and, in some cases, criminal behavior. An incident in which shots were fired by a Galatasaray student occasioned a top-level discussion of recent student activity at the school.[65] I return to the particulars of this unusual case in discussing school discipline in the next chapter. Suffice it here to note that school officials were on guard against any untoward, especially immoral, student behavior, particularly given the school's location in a section of Istanbul known for its raucous night-life.

Just as the Hamidian government responded to the expansion of foreign missionary educational activity by increasing the inspection of non-Muslim schools, so also did it respond to the perception of rising immoral activity on the part of students in its own system with a pattern of increased surveillance. In December 1893 the education minister Zühdü Paşa wrote a memorandum requesting the hiring of inspectors to monitor the movements of students in the idadîs, the higher schools, and Galatasaray.[66] Zühdü Paşa complained that students from these institutions had been frequenting "beerhouses, *cafés chantants*, and similarly inappropriate places." In order to prevent this sort of licentious behavior, the education minister proposed that ten inspectors be hired and charged with "patrolling the suspicious places day and night." In the event that any students were seen in these inappropriate places, he continued, the inspectors were to remove them and to make a report to the school in question.[67] Zühdü's memorandum was forwarded to the Council of State, where it was read, approved, and then forwarded to the palace where it became an imperial decree.[68]

The early history of Galatasaray displays many of the themes that run through the history of the idadî schools. Founded as part of a plan recommended by the Education Ministry of one of the Great Powers

---

[64] See e.g. MKP 86/6-551, for a reference to a Galatasaray student from Filibe who objected so vigorously to the 1886 Bulgarian annexation of Eastern Rumelia, his own province, that he threatened to assassinate the sultan with a revolver.

[65] İrade MM 4628, 9 Rebiülahir 1307 (1 Dec. 1889).

[66] ŞD 212/61, 17 Cemaziyelahır 1311 (26 Dec. 1893).

[67] Ibid.

[68] İrade Maarif 1311 B 5, 25 Receb 1311 (1 Feb. 1894).

whose encroachments the late Ottoman state was increasingly preoccupied with repulsing, the institution underwent a series of alterations
that brought it into line with the main tenets of Hamidian policy.
Through changes in staff, curriculum, and the rules governing the
extracurricular activity of its students, the Mekteb-i Sultanî evolved
into an institution that was both more Ottoman and Islamic. Increasingly concerned with the pernicious effects of Western European
influence and with the concomitant moral dissipation of its subjects,
the Hamidian state worked to overhaul the curriculum of its schools
and to assert itself as the moral guardian of its children. The seriousness with which the state approached this mission ensured that such
moves were not confined to one institution in the capital, but rather
were extended to the provinces so as to affect as many of its subjects
as it possibly could. Although its financial resources were severely
limited, the Hamidian state acted to extend the fledgling school system
it inherited from the Tanzimat to the far corners of the empire. As it
built these schools, it worked simultaneously to refit their curriculum
and the rules that governed them in order to align them with its
increasingly visible program of religious anti-imperialism. In doing so
the state took advantage of the centralized, systemic nature of the education plan it was following.

The story of Galatasaray illustrates that the late Ottoman education effort was both helped and hindered by the extent to which it
borrowed from the West. On the one hand, the importation of the
French-style system afforded a ready-made plan. This plan offered
a number of attractions to a state determined to increase the control
of the central bureaucracy over diverse territories and to play a
much stronger role in the daily lives of the subjects who lived there.
On the other hand, the imported system came with many attendant problems. The greatest of these was the unspoken assumption
that the answers to the Empire's problems could be found in the
West. On a more practical level, many of the notions imbedded in
the curriculum of the new system were diametrically opposed to the
Hamidian worldview. The state opted to reorient the curriculum
toward what it felt to be the proper direction. Presented with such an
inherited system, the Hamidian state set about adapting it to its own
needs.

THE SYSTEM

The plan the Hamidian regime inherited was that articulated in the Education Regulation (*Maarif Nizamnamesi*) of 1869. We have already encountered this document, in its promulgation as a result of French interference during the Abdülaziz era, its subsequent role as educational touchstone, and its provisions for licensing and inspecting competing forms of education. The chief importance of the 1869 Regulation is that it served as the blueprint for the network of schools that was largely implemented during the reign of Abdülhamid II. Since the document has been summarized elsewhere,[69] it suffices here to mention only its most salient features. The Regulation called for a highly rationalized and centralized state school system. Schools were to be built according to the size of the local population and, for schools like the idadî, according to the status of the city or town involved. For example, each town consisting of more than 1,000 houses was to have an idadî school. The system that the Regulation described was little different than most centrally planned education systems built in most places around the globe in the last century. In the context of the Ottoman Empire, where education had traditionally been provided by the various religious hierarchies, what was unprecedented was the fact that the central government was now assuming the responsibility, at least theoretically, for educating the entire population of the empire. The other major thrust of the Regulation was its insistence on providing the provinces with the same array of educational institutions as was available in the capital, with the obvious exception of higher, specialized academies. The Regulation envisioned a complete, integrated network of schools that would stretch across the length and breadth of the empire and would work as a pyramid to funnel the top students to the capital for specialized training at the advanced level or directly into the scribal service of the central government.

Throughout the Hamidian period the 1869 Regulation provided the guidelines for the state's massive educational initiative. Officials charged with implementing its details made constant reference to the Regulation. As we have seen in Chapter 2, Ottoman officials serving in

[69] Koçer, *Türkiye'*, 82 ff.; Kodaman, *Abdülhamid*, 22–7, 114–17.

the provinces frequently invoked the Nizamname to justify requests for permission and funding for schools to be built in their administrative districts. In most cases, given the ambitious scope of the plan and the straitened condition of the treasury, these officials had frequent opportunity to point out that the provisions of the Regulation had yet to be carried out in their provinces and to urge the central government to produce the funds needed to meet its targets. Bureaucrats in Istanbul likewise paid lip-service to the Regulation in recommending that these requests be approved and funded by the Porte and, ultimately, the palace.

The aspect of the 1869 Regulation that most recommended it to the government of Abdülhamid II was its systemic and centralized nature. The regularity of the proposed school system appealed to a government bent on creating an expansive and highly rationalized network of government institutions throughout the empire. The educational edifices erected in the Hamidian period represent only one facet of this expanding governmental apparatus. Alongside the growing school system appeared parallel networks of government bureaus, each charged with extending Istanbul's influence and reach into the provinces. Thus, parallel to the schools appeared telegraph and railroad lines, commerce offices, mapping crews, health inspectorships, Interior Ministry inspectorships, Justice Ministry inspectorships, census teams, tribal reform teams, and untold networks of political informants, to mention only a number of the civil bureaucratic networks that the Hamidian government created outright or greatly enhanced. The expansion of the state school system was thus only one of many examples of the arrogation of authority by the central government over areas that had previously lain outside its jurisdiction.

Given the nature of education, however, the school system was unique in that it was precisely that government branch that had the potential, indeed the intention, of affecting the lives of the vast majority of the empire's subjects. While the railroad lines might transport a growing share of the empire's subjects and reshape local economies, and census bureaus might record their physical presence, education was the only state apparatus that had as its mission the task of affecting the way the young population thought. In an increasingly literate age, education was in many ways the best investment the government could make in its future. As we shall see in discussing the economic context of the Hamidian educational endeavor, the Ottoman state realized the potential that education offered, and thus made the difficult financial sacrifices necessary to effect educational expansion on a broad scale.

Thus, while qualitatively different from the parallel networks of the central government's expansion, the state educational apparatus conformed to the formal, systemic attributes of those networks. Indeed, important late Ottoman functionaries recognized the form of the school network—the fact that it was an integrated system—as being critical to its success. Many archival documents testify to the government's preoccupation with its systemic quality. Bureaucrats frequently criticized the early incarnation of the state's educational apparatus as failing to be sufficiently systematic. What was needed, these memoranda urged, was a mechanism that would produce a steady supply of talented school graduates who would enter into government employ. The common metaphor these officials used was that of a chain, the links of which would represent the interlocking levels of educational training.[70] A few officials, aware of educational trends in Europe, referred to the German tracking system as an object of emulation. But it was the highly centralized French model, already internalized in the 1869 Education Regulation, that provided the main source of imitation.

In concrete terms this "system" appeared, naturally enough, in the form of individual schools. The spate of school building from 1884 onward resulted in the appearance of newly opened Ottoman schools in every province of the empire. Our analysis of the architectural form these schools took and their symbolic import must wait until the next chapter. It suffices here to say that their effect upon the local population must have been dramatic, given both the distinctively modern style of the new buildings and the fact that their impact was multiplied by a supporting cast of similarly constructed government buildings. These new buildings provided the most visible impression of the changes the state was effecting in the empire.

The Gap

The importance that the Hamidian state attached to the systemic nature of its school network explains the state's emphasis on building schools at the idadî level. Educational expansion in the Tanzimat period

[70] See e.g. Y Mtv. 25/52, Y Mtv. 37/56, İrade Maarif 1310 M 7, among others.

had the effect of building schools from the bottom of the system up and from the top down, leaving a large gap in the middle.[71] Such a gap had not emerged by design. The original plan for the state school system contained three levels: sıbyanî (elementary); rüşdiye (middle); and the *Darülfünun* (the University).[72] However, due to a number of problems, including a funding shortage and the delays inherent in training teachers in accordance with the new system, the lower two levels of the system were unable to produce students sufficiently qualified for the higher levels. Therefore, the rüşdiye-class schools were essentially demoted to the status of advanced primary schools intended to remedy the deficiencies below. This demotion, a tacit admission of partial failure of the initial effort, created the need for a new level of schooling to fill the gap between the rüşdiye and the sultanî schools. (The sultanî level was abolished during the Hamidian period but reappeared during the Young Turk era.)

Awareness of such a gap pre-dated the accession of Sultan Abdülhamid II in 1876. In 1873 the influential Ottoman cleric, reformer, and scholar Ahmed Cevdet Paşa had drafted a memorandum in which he urged construction of the idadî level schools.[73] He worried that the failure to do so would endanger the empire's progress. Referring to the terms of the 1869 Education Regulation, Cevdet Paşa pointed to

[71] In a recent article François Georgeon describes Ottoman education in the mid-1860s as "fragmented and compartmentalized. Fragmented, because of the lacunae, notably a 'gap' between the preparatory schools and the higher schools; one could not therefore speak of an education system, nor truly of a public education policy. Compartmentalized, because there were neither links, organization, nor 'formation' among the various types of schools . . ." (Georgeon, "La Formation des élites," 16). While his negation of the existence of an Ottoman education policy is debatable, his assessment of the presence of a gap in the proto-system accords with what the archival evidence presented here makes plain, namely, official Ottoman awareness of that gap and the resulting push for idadî school construction. This gap has also been noted by Şişman, *Galatasaray,* 11 and Salve, "L'Enseignement," 844.

[72] YEE 18/1860. 24 Şaban 1309 (24 Mar. 1892). Ahmed Cevdet Paşa gives a full account of the early history of educational reform. The changes that occurred in the levels of schooling (see below) explain some of the confusion over school nomenclature and type. For example, even though the rüşdiye school was essentially demoted from a preparatory function to that of an advanced primary institution, it has continued to be referred to as an intermediary institution, probably due to the derivation of the name rüşdiye, which comes from the Arabic term for adolescence (*rushd*).

[73] YEE 18/553-419. 6 Kanun-ı evvel 1289 (18 Dec. 1873).

the lack of idadî schools, particularly in the provinces, and urged that steps be taken to reverse this deplorable situation. Always practical, Cevdet suggested the creation of an idadî in Istanbul that would serve as the model to be emulated throughout the provinces, where the civil idadîs were to appear alongside their military equivalents.

Calls for the implementation of the idadî level of education continued to appear in the early years of the Hamidian period, and the consequences ascribed to the state's failure to act were increasingly presented as dire. Kâmil Paşa's memorandum of 1881, discussed in Chapter 2, placed the necessity of completing the preparatory level of schooling in the context of the empire's struggle with the West, thereby raising the ante for the state.[74] His recommendations, which included the founding of an idadî in every major city of the empire, marked a subtle but important change from Cevdet Paşa's approach. Whereas Cevdet had considered the failure to complete the proposed school network a potential deviation from the empire's path to progress, in Kâmil Paşa's view the situation was more menacing. For him, the failure to complete the school system did not merely represent a missed opportunity but was tantamount to allowing the foreigners to succeed in their persistently sinister attempts to seduce Ottoman youth away from the empire in accordance with their own national aims. With the passage of time and the accompanying increase in missionary activity, the reaction of Ottoman officials assumed an increasingly alarmist tone concerning the need to complete the empire's education system.

As Chapters 5 and 6 will demonstrate, the ultimate objective of creating such a fully articulated system was the Hamidian state's ability to alter the schools' content to conform to the state's overall agenda. Before such content could be manipulated, however, the form of the school system had to be completed. Recognizing that the lack of schooling at the preparatory level constituted the single most important flaw in the imperial education project, Abdülhamid's bureaucrats set out to correct the situation. Their actions may be grouped into two categories: (1) the procuring of the funds for school construction and administration, and (2) the reorganization of the bureaucratic apparatus necessary to accommodate the new schools.

---

[74] MKP 86/1-55.

Funding

The most important sign of the Hamidian state's campaign to build the idadîs was the creation of the financial mechanism to make possible the bulk of school construction. The creation of the Education Fund in 1884 was the breakthrough that would allow the state to overcome the chief barrier to the realization of its integrated system, the chronic lack of funds.[75] The Education Fund was created by increasing the amount of the tithe (*öşr*) levied on agricultural production. Previously one-tenth of the tithe, or 1 per cent of the total harvest, had gone to the Public Works Fund (*Menafi sandıkları*), which included some monies for education; now 1.8 per cent of the tithe would be taken. This would henceforth be divided into thirds, with 1.2 per cent continuing to cover Public Works and the other 0.6 per cent forming the Education Fund.[76] The specific mechanics of the Fund are important,[77] but two of its broader ramifications need first to be underscored. First, by creating a permanent income stream for schooling, the Hamidian state was making a major commitment to education. This was, after all, a time of acute financial crisis. Since the time of the Crimean War

[75] Shaw and Shaw, *History of the Ottoman Empire*, ii. 249; Kodaman, *Abdülhamid*, 158; Akşin Somel, "Das Grundschulwesen in den Provinzen des Osmanischen Reiches während der Herrschaftsperiode Abdülhamid II (1876–1909)," Ph.D. diss., Universität Bamberg (1993), 96–7. Also translated as the Education Benefits Share, the Ottoman term is *Maarif Hisse-i İanesi*, meaning the share of the [popular financial] assistance for education. It was also referred to in less official parlance as the Education Tax (*Maarif Vergisi*). The first date associated with the measure is 26 Cemaziyülevvel 1301/12 Mart 1300 (24 Mar. 1884), the date given for the grand vizier Said Paşa's memorandum, Mahmud Cevad, *Maarif-i*, 236–8.

[76] AYN 1243, 286. 13 Şaban 1301 (8 June 1884). So that the fund would not single out the agricultural sector, a corresponding percentage of the tax on fixed property (*müsakkafat vergisi*) was also to be taken for the fund. This source is also referred to by Kodaman, *Abdülhamid*, 158, and Somel, "Das Grundschulwesen," 96–7.

[77] The formula for calculating the *hisse* was initially expressed in a somewhat convoluted manner. It called for taking the sum of one-seventh of the tithe and one-quarter of that seventh, i.e. roughly 1.8% of the tithe. This formula can be found in a variety of official documents. Perhaps the most informative is İrade MM 3400, # 3, which offers both an example of calculating the tax on a hypothetical farmer's crop on a step-by-step basis and a table to aid in the collection of virtually any amount necessary. Details concerning the mechanics of collection of the *hisse*, including the role played by the *Ziraat Bankası* in transferring the moneys, can be found in the special Regulation (*Nizamname*) compiled for this purpose. One copy can be found, in both draft and printed forms, in İrade MM 4462.

the Ottoman state had been incurring massive foreign debt. High rates of interest, combined with the seemingly insatiable demands of a rapidly growing government apparatus and such short-term shocks such as poor harvests, wars, and war reparations, created a precarious situation for the Treasury. Moreover, the creation in 1881 of the Public Debt Administration turned over various state revenues into the hands of mostly foreign overseers charged with servicing the now consolidated Imperial debt. With its revenues thus in short supply, the allocation of even 0.6 per cent of the tithe revenues amounted to significant support for public education.

Secondly, from its creation, the Fund was specifically linked to the campaign for idadî school construction. It was envisioned as the way to finance the large number of idadîs projected.[78] Precisely whose idea this linking was is unclear. Most accounts credit Mehmed (Küçük) Said Paşa, grand vizier at the time, with arriving at the formula.[79] Said Paşa, a close and trusted adviser to Abdülhamid II, had long been advocating the implementation of the school system called for in the 1869 Regulation. As minister of justice in 1878 he had recommended, *inter alia*, the establishment of lycée-level (sultanî) schools in the provinces.[80] But while he took full credit for founding numerous idadî and other schools during his various tenures as grand vizier, he did not claim authorship of the Education Fund. Said Paşa's rival, Mehmed Kâmil Paşa, on the other hand, seems to have been at least partially responsible. In his memorandum advocating educational change, referred to in Chapter 2, he mentioned the need to establish idadî schools in the major cities of the Empire.[81] In order to fund these and other institutions, he recommended a temporary solution until such time as the state could undertake a more concerted effort: "It is without a doubt that if a very small amount such as 1 per cent. be taken from the general harvest in every province, then the people will not feel [the loss of] this amount at the time of tithing and, moreover, when they understand the wisdom behind spending it for future public works,

---

[78] Somel, "Das Grundschulwesen," 96.

[79] Kodaman, *Abdülhamid*, 158; Somel, "Das Grundschulwesen," 96.

[80] Mehmed Said, *Said Paşa'nın Hatıratı* (Istanbul: Sabah Matbaası, 1910), 393. A memorandum of Said Paşa's that he included in his memoirs also recommends transferring the expenses for ibtidaî and rüşdiye schools to the public and creating a university with the money saved by such a restructuring.   [81] MKP 86/I-55.

they will be pleased."[82] Kâmil Paşa's idea would seem to be the source of the Education Fund. Furthermore, his related suggestion that revenues from abandoned pious endowments (*vakıf*) be diverted to help defray the costs of local schools seems also to have later been adopted as official policy. Whatever the origin of the Education Fund, its creation in 1884 paved the way for the tremendous growth in the number of the idadî institutions with which it was so closely associated.

Only two years after the Fund's inception officials at the highest level were able to set high targets for idadî construction. Correspondence in August 1887 between Münif Paşa, serving as education minister, and the grand vizier, Kâmil Paşa, concerning disbursing funds for student incentive prizes (*mükâfât*) to be awarded to hard-working students in the idadî schools reveals the escalation in the numbers involved.[83] Whereas the number of idadîs projected for the empire in 1884 had been "up to ninety,"[84] Münif Paşa now described a total of 104 schools, a clear sign of the expansion.[85]

The Education Fund was the major structural innovation of the Hamidian period in the field of education. It made possible the expansion of schooling on the preparatory level intended to close the most glaring gap in the embryonic Ottoman system. As the perception of foreign educational encroachment gathered strength during the latter half of the nineteenth century, the official impetus to turn the state's educational plan into reality increased dramatically. The state's recognition that educational expansion at the idadî level was critical to the realization of this plan explains the commitment so tangibly represented in the creation of the Education Fund.

Reorganization

While the Education Fund marked the first and most tangible evidence of the state's strong commitment to the school building campaign at

---

[82] MKP 86/1–55.

[83] İrade MM 3912. 23 Zilhicce 1304 (12 Sept. 1887).

[84] İrade Dah. 73753. 27 Muharrem 1302 (16 Nov. 1884).

[85] İrade MM 3912, 1. lef. İdadîs in the provincial centers would receive 1,000 kuruş per year for these awards, while those in the liva centers would receive 750 kuruş, funds which would come from the newly created Fund. The grand vizier wrote back, asking how many such schools were intended. Münif answered that, according to sultanic decree, there were to be 28 idadîs in provincial centers and 76 in the liva centers, making a total of 104 schools throughout the provinces.

the idadî level, there was also considerable administrative reorganization as part of the effort to realize the state's project. There were three
stages in this restructuring. First, the Education Ministry acted to
ensure that a number of "rogue" institutions at the preparatory level
were brought into line with the idadîs proper. This explains the closing
of the school in Beirut, originally called the Mekteb-i Sultanî, and the
incorporation of the roughly analogous institution in Crete into the
broader system.[86] In both locations idadîs were reopened in confor-
mity with the overall plan.

The second administrative adjustment made to accommodate the
idadî building campaign was the restructuring of the Education
Council (Meclis-i Maarif).[87] In 1884 the Council was reconstituted so
as to be able to handle the work associated with the founding of all of
the idadî schools made possible by the newly available education
funds.[88] The Council had been composed of members of the Education Ministry staff and had met only twice each week. The Imperial
Decree of 16 November 1884 reorganized the body with the intention
of making it more productive. It was thereafter composed of well-
respected officials from outside the Ministry, thereby freeing the Ministry's bureaucrats to devote their attention to their specified tasks, and
it was convened on a daily basis. The formidable religious scholar
and poet Ali Haydar Efendi, described in the decree as "a member of
the Council of State well versed in the virtues of the religious sciences
and Islamic sagacity," was chosen to be its head.[89] He was to be assisted
by four others, including the multi-talented Selim Sabit Efendi.[90]
The reorganization of the Education Council to accommodate the
additional work associated with the preparatory level further illustrates

---

[86] On the closing of the Beirut school and its reopening as an official Ottoman institution, see Martin Strohmeier, "Muslim Education," 215–17.

[87] For the various permutations of the Meclis-i Maarif between its founding as the
sixteen-member body called the Meclis-i Maarif-i Umumiye in 1846 and its first reorganization in the period of Abdülhamid II, see Kodaman, *Abdülhamid*, 11–29.

[88] İrade Dah. 73753. Text also provided in Mahmud Cevad, *Maarif-i*, 242–4 and
Düstûr, 1. tertib, v. 5 (Ankara: Başvekâlet Devlet Matbaası, 1937), 604.

[89] On Ali Haydar Efendi, see Gövsa, *Türk Meşhurları Ansiklopedisi*, 35–6.

[90] On Selim Sabit Efendi, see ibid. 350. A good example of the transitional late
Ottoman bureaucrat, Selim Sabit received both a madrasa and a Western-style education.
His name reappears in several important Hamidian educational positions, including that
of director of the empire's rüşdiye schools and the chair of the important *Encümen-i Teftiş
ve Muayene*. He was also the author of a large number of school textbooks.

the central role of the idadî schools in the Hamidian educational campaign.

Five years later the state's drive to build idadîs produced a third administrative restructuring: the closing of a number of rüşdiye schools and the creation of idadîs in their stead. On 8 January 1890 Münif Paşa blamed "the present condition of the Treasury" for the capital's appropriation of an additional one-quarter of the hisse funds. This diversion of funding resulted in the failure to build the anticipated number of idadî schools.[91] Münif proposed a compromise: the closing of the rüşdiyes in towns where no idadîs had yet been built and the transfer of these rüşdiyes' financial appropriations to the idadîs. Teachers from the rüşdiyes would be used in the idadîs and the buildings assigned to serve as "well-ordered ibtidaî schools."[92] In other words, the idadîs would assume the task of the rüşdiyes, a tacit admission of both the weakness of the rüşdiyes and the scaled-back aspirations for the idadîs. In essence, the acceptance of this proposal marked the continuation of the demotion of the state school levels that necessitated the adoption of the idadîs in the first place. As in the plan of 1869, the contrast between the high aspirations for and the disappointing results from the lower rungs of the state's educational hierarchy resulted in a scaling back of the system. As the apparent lack of concern for the integrity of the individual levels demonstrates, what mattered most to the senior bureaucracy was to ensure the articulation of the system. If that entailed an effective demotion of two important levels of schooling, so be it. Given the importance that Ottoman planners attached to producing a system able to match up with the competition, as demonstrated in the previous chapter, the specifics of that system seem to have been less important than its completion.

Numbers

Ottoman officialdom was frequently just as concerned with producing quantitative as qualitative results. In this they were remarkably successful. However, providing accurate statistical information about the number, size, cost, and founding date of the idadî schools built during this period is not a strong point of the secondary literature, for all of its interest in descriptive and numerical evidence. Discrepancies con-

---

[91] İrade MM 4704. 11 Cemaziyelahır 1307 (2 Feb. 1890).   [92] Ibid.

cerning a variety of details, ranging from the time elapsed between the first proposal to open a school in a specific location and its first day of operation, to varying figures concerning the costs involved, and, as we have just seen, the changes in the level of some schools, have hindered attempts to provide an accurate statistical picture of the schools present in the empire at any given time.[93] For our purposes, the exact numbers involved matter less than their relative and contextual significance. Whether the Hamidian state produced sixty-eight or seventy institutions at the idadî level is ultimately less significant than an appreciation of either of these figures in comparison to figures generated by previous and subsequent administrations. Furthermore, it is far less significant than understanding the context, both local and imperial, in which these schools were produced. That being said, it is nevertheless important to have some idea of the magnitude and chronology of the undertaking we are discussing. The following represents such an attempt.

Tabulating the dates when the provincial idadî schools were founded between 1882 and 1894 illustrates their chronological development (see Table 3.1).[94] These numbers show that the creation of the Education Fund in 1884 was critical to establishing the idadîs in the provinces on a uniform basis. Thereafter, priority seems to have been given to establishing boarding schools first. The reclassifying of a number of rüşdiyes as idadîs in 1890 explains the late acceleration in openings of day idadîs.

The inventories of foreign and minority schools cited in Chapter 2 illustrate the Hamidian bureaucracy's concern with monitoring the competition. The state was no less interested in keeping track of the progress of its own school building effort. Such an interest manifested itself in internal record-keeping, in the presence of school statistics in official government yearbooks that had a broad dissemination, and in

[93] Cf. the statistics of earlier historians, such as Koçer and Unat, *Türkiye Eğitim*, and with the official Ottoman statistics provided in the various yearbooks (*Salname*).

[94] Source: Kodaman, *Abdülhamid*, 125–6. There are several cases where Kodaman's statistics conflict with those presented in the official yearbooks. For example, Kodaman lists the date of the Edirne idadî as 1890 while the yearbook gives 1884. He also gives no mention of the idadîs in the province of Yemen where schools were opened in San'a and in Ta'iz. *Salname-i Nezaret-i Maarif-i Umumiye* (Istanbul: Asır Matbaası, 1321 [1903]). Kodaman's figures are presented here unchanged on the assumption that they are internally consistent.

TABLE 3.1. *The expansion of Ottoman secondary schooling, 1882–1894*

Year	Number	Running total	Location
1882	0	0	—
1883	1	1	Rhodes
1884	5	6	*Bursa, Adana, Manastır,* Balıkesir, İzmit
1885	4	10	*İzmir, Kastamonu, Erzurum,* Manisa
1886	5	15	*Salonika, Trabzon,* Drama, Siroz, Mamuratülaziz
1887	5	20	*Damascus, Beirut,* Gümülcine, Gelibolu, Bolu
1888	1	21	*Konya*
1889	10	31	*Yanya, Ankara, Diyarbekir, Midilli, Üsküp, Biga,* Dedeağac, Kütahya, Aydın, Jerusalem, Baghdad
1890	11	42	*Edirne, Sivas, Aleppo,* Kırklareli, Tekirdağ, Muğla, Çankırı, Sinop, Samsun, Tripoli, Latakia, Hama
1891	2	44	Denizli, Görice
1892	2	46	Kırşehir, Amasya
1893	4	50	Kayseri, Yozgat, Nablus, Mosul
1894	1	51	Acre
TOTAL	51	51	

Note: boarding schools are listed in italic and day schools in plain type.

Source: Bayram Kodaman, *Abdülhamid Devri Eğitim Sistemi* (Ankara: Türk Tarih Kurumu, 1988), 125–6.

the schools' being heavily featured in photographic form in albums sent overseas. Internal government correspondence tabulated the progress and expenses to date of the schooling campaign, both as a matter of bookkeeping and as a way of justifying the mission and the efforts of those who worked on its behalf. For example, a document dating from 1892 records the amounts of money spent on various levels of education in the empire.[95] It shows that within a decade of the creation of

---

[95] İrade Maarif 1310 M 7. 25 Muharrem 1310 (19 Aug. 1892).

the Education Fund, the Ministry of Education had opened a boarding idadî school in fifteen of the empire's provinces. By 1892 several provinces could boast day idadîs in cities or towns other than the provincial seat. Edirne province is listed as having the most, with one boarding and six day idadîs.

DISPLAYING PROGRESS

While the Hamidian bureaucracy was busy tabulating the achievements in education for its own internal purposes, it was also clearly interested in a more public display of such progress. The first instance of such official demonstration of educational success can be seen in the official Ottoman yearbooks (*Devlet Salnamesi*). These volumes were compiled by the central government and included a variety of facts about the state apparatus, ranging from general information, such as lists of the Ottoman sultans and the achievements of their reigns and guides to calculating the date and the hour for prayer, to more specific information such as the many government positions and who held them in a given year. Anyone wishing to ascertain the identity of a given official could find that information in these annuals. As the state bureaucracy grew, the state yearbooks increased in detail and in heft. Another symptom of this expansion was the appearance of yearbooks that concentrated on individual provinces (*Vilayet Salnamesi*). The expansion of state education during the Hamidian period produced such a wealth of statistical information that the section of the state yearbooks soon became too large to be contained therein. As of 1898 the Ministry of Education began producing its own yearbooks (*Salname-i Nezaret-i Maarif-i Umumiye*). These appeared consecutively thereafter until 1903 when, for reasons unspecified, they ceased.[96] The sheer existence and size of the education yearbooks, which could run to as many as 1,600

---

[96] Although the yearbooks were produced over a span of six years, only five seem to have been published. The fifth of what might have been a six-part series seems not to exist. Organization of Islamic Conference, *Ottoman Year-Books (Salname and Nevsal)* (Istanbul: Research Centre for Islamic History, Art and Culture (IRCICA), 1982), 98. See also, Mehmet Ö. Alkan, "Osmanlı İmparatorluğu'nda Eğitim ve Eğitim İstatistikleri, 1839–1924," in Halil İnalcık and Şevket Pamuk (eds.), *Osmanlı Devleti'nde Bilgi ve İstatistik/Data and Statistics in the Ottoman Empire* (Ankara: T. C. Başbakanlık İstatistik Enstitüsü, 2000), 136–7. I thank Jun Akiba for this reference.

pages in length, attest to the physical growth of the state's pedagogical apparatus in the period of Sultan Abdülhamid II. They are also
important in revealing the state's desire to display—and claim—the
progress it was making. Not only did these yearbooks list the various
schools in each province, the number of students they were educating,
and other information about curriculum and staffing, but they also
began to present visual evidence of the schools in question. Starting
in 1901, the education yearbooks began to include photographs and
occasionally architectural plans of the schools being created in the
Hamidian educational expansion.[97] By including these photographs
and plans in the yearbooks, the state presented evidence of educational
advances to the empire's domestic audience.

While propaganda was probably not the chief motivation for the
education yearbooks, the photographic collections Abdülhamid II sent
abroad as gifts to foreign powers reveal a concerted attempt to show
the empire in a favorable light. Apart from catering to Abdülhamid's
personal interest in photography, the sultan's extensive photograph collection served two main purposes. First, it was a means by which the
notoriously reclusive Abdülhamid II could have the empire brought to
him.[98] This also suited Abdülhamid's penchant for organizing and creating inventories of the contents of his empire, apparent in his affinity
for census-taking and list-making. Secondly, the collection provided
him the opportunity to display his accomplishments to others. As
Selim Deringil's recent study makes clear, the sultan was particularly
interested in countering the negative attitudes concerning the empire
prevalent in the West.[99] His presentation of photographic albums and
other works to the American and British public should be seen as an
attempt to improve popular opinion of the Ottoman Empire in those
countries. It is no accident that educational institutions figure prominently in these collections.[100] The albums sent to Washington and

---

[97] *Salname-i Nezaret-i Maarif-i Umumiye* (Istanbul: Matbaa-i Amire, 1319 [1901]).

[98] Carney Gavin, "Historical Introduction: Abdul-Hamid's Gift-Albums as an
Imperial Self-Portrait," *Journal of Turkish Studies*, 12 (1988), 7.

[99] Ibid. 7. Deringil, *Well-Protected Domains*, 151–2.

[100] Abdülhamid II presented the US government with a set of albums containing over
1,800 photographs selected from among his much larger Yıldız Palace collection in 1893.
A virtually identical set of 51 albums was sent to London the following year. Gavin, "Historical Introduction," 3.

London contain a high percentage of material displaying the empire as modern. The new schools are depicted as highly organized and up-to-date. Students are aligned in meticulous rows in front of the buildings' façades, or grouped so as to display such signs of progress as scientific instruments and globes. They therefore complement such scenes as a mechanized fire brigade, the Imperial yacht, schools for the deaf, and lifeboat crews. Abdülhamid II sent these images to the West in an attempt to demonstrate just how modern his empire had become by the early 1890s.

CONCLUSION

Like other non- or partially Western empires in the late nineteenth and early twentieth centuries, the late Ottoman Empire was reassessing its relationship with the West, and taking action to ensure that indigenous concerns were at the top of the agenda. Parallels with the nationalist re-evaluation of educational policy in Tsarist Russia and the self-strengthening movement in China have been addressed in previous chapters. The Ottomans likewise saw it necessary to reformulate key elements of its policy, both internal and external. This did not mean that Western models and ideas were eliminated. The pursuit of "progress" via emulation continued to operate in full force; if anything formal emulation increased rapidly as the school system expanded to reach more of the empire's population. It was rather that the new schools should be freed from what Ottoman bureaucrats now saw as an undue reliance on Western influence. Just as in Russia Ushinsky objected to the 1869 schools program as excessively indebted to importation from Western Europe, the Hamidian government was acting to ensure that Ottoman schools be informed by domestic requirements, rather than a passive aping of Westernization for the sake of Westernization.

The Hamidian education project must thus be seen in the overall context of the Ottoman dynamic with the West. While the state's campaign was carried out first and foremost by and for Ottomans, it was nevertheless shaped by the geopolitical and cultural relationship with the West. Chapter 2 illustrated the extent to which Ottoman bureaucrats involved in the Hamidian educational endeavor viewed the empire's educational agenda in conscious distinction to that of the foreigners operating in their midst. This chapter has demonstrated the importance Abdülhamid II's state attached to completing the formal aspects of the Western-style school system outlined during the Tanzimat period. The Hamidian state quickly realized that the educational plan adopted under Western pressure during the Tanzimat period actually offered opportunities for the empire to fight back against Western influence. The Hamidian state could take advantage of Article 129 of the Education Regulation of 1869 to close almost any private school. While the state was loath to invoke this article frequently, it appears that its occasional invocation served to maintain the tacit understanding that the missionaries should keep away from predominantly Muslim areas of the population. Furthermore, by deploying teams of traveling ulama to preach against the dangers of missionary education and cadres of inspectors to monitor the foreign and minority schools, Abdülhamid's state combined *ad hoc* methods with formally sanctioned regulations to monitor the competition.

Meanwhile, the Hamidian state was giving unprecedented attention to completing the state school system envisioned since the early years of the Tanzimat period. By finding a solution to the fiscal obstacles thwarting earlier implementation of the planned educational network, and by making the necessary administrative changes to accommodate the large number of schools it contained, the Hamidian state demonstrated a remarkable dedication to education. Yet, even as it set about to fulfill the formal aspects of the Tanzimat-era plan, Abdülhamid's bureaucrats were beginning to revamp the ways in which these schools would operate. The history of the idadîs' model institution, the lycée of Galatasaray, reveals the way in which Hamidian policy altered the heavily Western orientation of the earlier Ottoman educational agenda. The appointment of the activist Ali Suavî Efendi to head the school was only the most visible and symbolic of the changes the Hamidian era had in store for Galatasaray and for the many provincial idadî schools for which it served as an exemplar. By increasing the Muslim share of the enrollment and scholarship money, by expelling students implicated in actions taken against the empire, and by reorganizing instruction at Galatasaray, Ali Suavî effected changes that prefigured the systemic alterations yet to come during the course of Abdülhamid's reign.

As soon as the funding and reorganization of the new schools were secured, Abdülhamid II convened the first of several commissions he would charge with vetting the curriculum of the entire school system. These commissions, composed of both civil and religious officials, were chaired by the empire's highest religious dignitary, the şeyhülislam. As we will see, the main thrust of the changes his commissions effected was to replace clearly European and secular material with what conformed to Ottoman and Islamic tradition. Far from providing the "secular education" of most historical accounts, the educational program that emerged was thus a complicated hybrid of West and East. Chapters 5 and 6 will demonstrate that the instruction that took place in these schools underwent a major transformation as the Tanzimat agenda was adapted by the Hamidian agenda. Before analyzing two critical elements of this transformation, however, it will be useful to set the stage by examining the architectural milieu in which Hamidian instruction transpired.

4

Buildings and Discipline

INTRODUCTION

The architectural and disciplinary record of the late Ottoman schools reveals the state's program to distinguish its educational offerings from the competition by adopting a conspicuously Ottoman and Islamic stance. The use of symbolically powerful architectural motifs matched the politico-moral policies of the Hamidian regime. Complementing the schools' external forms and lesson content was a state agenda that sought to instill a suitably Islamic mode outside the classroom. As both the buildings and the disciplinary agenda of the Hamidian schools are subjects that must be situated in the context of relations between the Ottoman Empire and the West, this chapter begins with a poignant scene taken from one of the most important contemporary literary attempts to address the issue of education against the backdrop of the East–West dynamic.

In the opening pages of the late Ottoman novel *Turfanda mı Yoksa Turfa mı*, the protagonist approaches Istanbul via steamship in a scene fraught with implications for the Ottoman educational predicament.[1] As the ship makes its way down the Bosphorus from the Black Sea, Mansur Bey, the zealously patriotic and earnestly energetic young medical doctor and educator, and the other passengers on deck begin to discern the landmarks on both the European and Asian sides of the Straits. The early morning light allows them to distinguish first Rumeli Feneri and Rumeli Kavağı, and eventually places such as Sarıyer and

---

[1] Mehmed Murad, *Turfanda mı Yoksa Turfa mı* (Millî Roman) (Istanbul: Mahmud Bey Matbaası, 1308 [1890–1]). The title has been translated as "First Fruits or Forbidden Fruits?" and as "The Early or the Spoiled Seed?" Its subtitle announces that it is a "national" or perhaps "patriotic" novel.

Büyükdere. Characteristically absorbed in deep thought, Mansur Bey is described as oblivious to the passengers' voices as they identify the sites along the shore. Only the mention of the summer residences of the embassies alters Mansur's trance-like state. The mention of Hünkâr İskelesi and Balta Limanı, sites of infamous treaties with the Russians (1833) and the British (1838) respectively, provokes a similarly visceral stirring in the protagonist. Then, after a long passage describing the tremendous religio-patriotic importance that Istanbul holds for Mansur Bey, one of the passengers calls out that they have reached Rumeli Hisarı, the fortress built by Mehmed II in preparation for his conquest of Istanbul in 1453. This lifts the hero's spirits and adds to the rising expectations as the boat moves closer to the Ottoman capital. Looking at the impressive new building on the hill above the fortress, Mansur Bey imagines that patriotic Ottomans must have constructed this building to allow their fellow subjects to pay homage to Mehmed the Conqueror. Here Mansur Bey receives a shock:

It was at exactly this moment that a man wearing a fez who was explaining the points of interest and an English tourist who was listening to him came close to Mansur Bey.

The one wearing the fez said: "This tall building that may be seen above that tower is Robert College, established and administered by American missionaries."

The Englishman said: "Did you say missionary school?"

The Englishman was not able to conceal his surprise.

At first, Mansur Bey was unable to believe his ears. Later, when he realized that the fingers of the English [sic] had extended to the building that he had deemed to have been built by patriotic charity and appreciation, his eyes gleamed strangely and his color changed.[2]

Mansur Bey's visceral reaction to the existence of a missionary school building on soil that for him carried extraordinary historical and patriotic resonance is a fictional response to the late Ottoman predicament in general and the Western educational presence specifically.

This passage provides a fitting introduction to the current chapter, which focuses on the architecture of the new schools and on the schools as arenas of disciplinary activity. It resonates with the main theme of the preceding analysis, namely, the importance of competition in

[2] Mehmed Murad, *Turfanda mı Yoksa Turfa mı*, 13.

driving late Ottoman educational policy. It also allows us to move from a discussion of the context surrounding the late Ottoman state's creation of a school system to one which focuses on what took place inside these structures. Mehmed "Mizancı" Murad's introductory scene is helpful to our discussion for two reasons.[3] First, like the world of late Ottoman education, the novel's opening scene is replete with contrasts between East and West. Murad's heavy-handed didacticism employs dichotomous pairings to get his point across. For example, the passengers on the steamship are marked as either Eastern or Western by their headgear; those in the former category are described as *fesli*, that is, wearing the fez. The steamship, a vessel of the Lloyd line, is described as being "crowded with European tourists" eager to experience and enjoy the splendid views of Istanbul and the Bosphorus, which "the literati and poets of East and West have failed to find the appropriate words to describe."[4] Contemporary Ottoman readers would likewise have been struck by the Francophone references to the geography of the Istanbul region. The tourists cry out "Bosfor, Bosfor!", referring to the straits by the French term (*Bosphore*) in place of their Turkish analog (*Boğaz*).

So far this passage seems to substantiate the notion so prevalent in the scholarly literature of a culturally distinct and mutually exclusive "East" and "West." The novel's description of Mansur Bey's first interaction with the surrounding characters and with the geographical setting, however, suggests that a more nuanced reading is possible. Our first clues that the tidy boundaries separating discrete cultural worlds are inadequate appear in several forms. While the boat contains many

---

[3] Mehmed Murad (1854–1917) was born in the Caucasus and received a traditional Islamic education before attending Russian schools in the Crimea. He moved to Istanbul in 1872 and subsequently was employed in various branches of the Ottoman bureaucracy, including the Ministry of Education, in which he served as history teacher, member of the Inspection Committee, and director of the Darülmuallimin (the teacher-training college). When he ran afoul of Abdülhamid II in 1895 he left the empire, first returning to the Crimea before continuing to Europe and Cairo. He published the influential *Mizan* (Balance) which, for a time, was recognized as the official journal of the opposition Committee of Union and Progress. His return to Istanbul in 1897 was deflating for the exiled opponents of the regime. Ahmet Evin, *Origins and Development of the Turkish Novel* (Minneapolis: Bibliotheca Islamica), 117; EI2, s.v. "Mīzandjı Meḥmed Murād," by M. O. H. Ursinus. For a further treatment, see Birol Emil, *Mizancı Murad Bey: Hayatı ve Eserleri* (Istanbul: Edebiyat Fakültesi Basımevi, 1979).

[4] Mehmed Murad, *Turfanda mı Yoksa Turfa mı*, 5.

European passengers, it is actually sailing a southerly route, from Varna on the Black Sea to Istanbul. Russia, straddling two continents, is perhaps the perfect point of departure for the protagonist, who works throughout the novel to effect Western-inspired change within the equally multi-continental Ottoman realms. While pursuing a Western agenda in his medical, educational, and agricultural labors, he does so for unquestionably patriotic purposes. Secondly, Mansur Bey's curriculum vitae itself suggests a synthesis of influences, both Eastern and Western.[5] Having grown up in an Ottoman Turkish family in Algeria and been educated in Paris, Mansur speaks Arabic, Turkish, and French. In fact, at one point in the introductory passage the hero is addressed in a manner that combines the French "Monsieur" with its Ottoman analog, as "Mösyö Mansur Bey." The mixture of linguistic and cultural references in this appellation underscores Mansur Bey's role as a man of synthesis.

But the clearest example of the inadequacy of the East–West dichotomy appears when Mansur inverts the process which deems that schools patterned after Western models are therefore automatically to be labelled "Western." As we have seen, the protagonist mistakes the imposing edifice of the American missionary school, Robert College, for an Ottoman structure. Unlike later historians, for whom the buildings' exterior was only further inducement to declare that the schools were Western, Mansur Bey naively assumes that a major edifice commanding such a historic piece of Ottoman territory would have to be an Ottoman one.

Mansur Bey's assumption raises the complicated issues of appearance and origins in the context of late Ottoman education. This chapter addresses the physical appearance and disciplinary environment of the idadî schools as points of departure for discussing what actually transpired within their walls. As we will see, appearances frequently *are* deceiving. Given the fact that the idadî schools were perceived by the

---

[5] Mansur Bey's strong integrative aspect recalls another multi-talented Franco-Ottoman character, the non-fictional Said Bey. As Paul Dumont has demonstrated, the late Ottoman official cum educator need not resemble the caricatures standard in much contemporary fiction. See Paul Dumont, "Said Bey—The Everyday Life of an Istanbul Townsman at the Beginning of the Twentieth Century," in Albert Hourani, Philip S. Khoury, and Mary Wilson (eds.), *The Modern Middle East: A Reader* (Berkeley: University of California Press, 1993), 278.

Hamidian state that built them as an indigenous response to Western encroachment, it is instructive to consider their outward appearance and architectural form as a function of the presumed dichotomy between East and West. I say "presumed" dichotomy because Abdül-hamid II's policy, in which many attributes of the Western systems of education were incorporated into a system that was increasingly emphasizing its Ottoman and Islamic heritage, defies classification into one or the other category. This idea of an either/or dichotomy has doubtless been buttressed by the prevailing but problematic notion that late Ottoman society must be seen as "schizoid" or as exhibiting "cultural bifurcation" or "cultural dualism," as discussed in the first chapter. In what follows I examine the evidence provided by the late Ottoman schools, institutions that assimilated key elements from both traditions and therefore call into question the utility of insisting upon a divide between East and West.

Late Ottoman state schools have been described as "new," as "secular," and as "European." In many respects these institutions do in fact represent a radical break with learning as traditionally understood in the Islamic world, and the Ottoman Empire in particular. They removed pedagogy from the traditional locus of religion, separating it physically from the precinct of the mosque, church, and synagogue. This new dispensation of education might have effected a more nearly ecumenical basis of identification, but for the aggressive presence of religiously—and nationally—motivated educational competition. As we have seen, the Ottoman state's response amounted to an attempt to compete with the West by using the West's own educational apparatus. While this might seem paradoxical to those who persist in perpetuating the "East is East and West is West" dichotomy, taken from the perspective of the Yıldız Palace this *modus operandi* had all the hallmarks of the pragmatism for which the Ottoman state was renowned.

State education policy in the reign of Abdülhamid II eagerly embraced what Ottoman officials considered to be the positive, successful aspects of Western-style schooling. From its organizational structure to the façades of its buildings, the Ottoman educational institutions built in this period clearly reflect the influence of Europe. At the same time, beyond the obvious systemic and architectural similarities with their European analogs, the Ottoman state schools exhibit a syncretism of influences that defy easy categorization. Such a

1. The idadî school of Trabzon. Note the classical style of the building, and the Black Sea in the background. (Source: Istanbul University Rare Book Library)

synthesis is a theme that recurs continuously in the architecture and daily life of the Ottoman schools.

These schools have tended to produce results akin to those of a Rorschach test among observers. Depending on their time and bent, historians have chosen to emphasize certain of the schools' constitutive elements to buttress their arguments. Taking, for example, the schools' physical setting as our point of reference, it is easy to see how some would choose to characterize the new schools as embodying a critical step along the path toward the cherished and apparently triumphal notion of state secularism. Those influenced by such a worldview could point to the physical distance of the schools from the traditional milieu of religion and to the fact that many of the schools were built away from the urban core as evidence of a major shift taking place due to the active stewardship of the state. With respect to the idadî schools, such an argument might refer to the schools built in Ankara, Aleppo, or Trabzon (Fig. 1). Photographs taken of the idadî buildings in these cities at the time of their construction or shortly thereafter reveal imposing structures that stood alone on the edge of town.[6] Their bright

---

[6] Istanbul University Rare Book Library, Photograph Collection of Abdülhamid II, Album nos. 90431, 90454, and 90441, respectively.

2. The idadî school of Jerusalem. In the background stands the Dome of the
Rock. (Source: Istanbul University Rare Book Library)

stone façades would thus seem to herald a fresh start for the empire's
future.

On the other hand, the schools built in Edirne and Jerusalem suggest
a much closer alignment with the Ottoman and Islamic past. In the
former Ottoman capital of Edirne, the Education Ministry opened its
new idadî building in the center of the city, only a few blocks from
the famous sixteenth-century Selimiye mosque complex. In Jerusalem
the idadî was erected inside the walls of the Old City not far from the
Ḥaram al-Sharīf, site of the Dome of the Rock and the Al-Aqṣā mosque
(Fig. 2). Its location in the holy city's Muslim Quarter is particularly
significant, given the fact that much contemporary building was taking
place outside the walls of the Old City.[7] One can only speculate about
the greater significance of these schools' location vis-à-vis the religio-
political center of the towns in which they were built. The location
of the schools may well have been determined by the availability and
ownership of land, but it does seem intriguing that cities more laden

[7] Ruth Kark and Shimon Landman, "The Establishment of Muslim Neighbourhoods
in Jerusalem, Outside the Old City, during the Late Ottoman Period," *Palestine Exploration Quarterly*, 112 (1980), 113–35.

with Ottoman and Islamic significance found room for the schools near the center of town.

Concentrating on the schools' physical remove from the center of their towns' religious life, however, creates a false impression of their divorce from the practice of the Islamic cult: the schools had their own mosques and *imams*.[8] While we have little evidence that sheds light on the way communal prayer affected school life, it is clear that these features were not merely included as some sort of vestigial remain of the Ottoman past. Attendance at communal prayers was noted by the school authorities and affected the student's cumulative standing, as reflected in his "moral report card," a feature of school life to which I return in Chapter 6.

Religion played an important role in student life. Moral education, with an overtly Islamic flavor, occupied a prominent place in the new schools' curriculum.[9] As often as not, courses in Islamic morals were taught by ulama who filled a variety of faculty and administrative positions in the schools and in the provincial educational bureaucracy.[10] Because of the state's rush to create the new schools, ulama were hired to serve as interim instructors while the appropriate personnel could be trained (Fig. 3). While little is known about the critical area of training and staffing policy, anecdotal evidence suggests that the presence of the ulama in the schools was not merely a temporary phenomenon. The schools commonly employed ulama, particularly for the purpose of teaching Islamic subjects. To cite only two examples, the staff of the idadî in Diyarbekir included a certain Mahmud Efendi who was identified in one document as the teacher of religious sciences (*Ulûm-u diniye muallimi*).[11] In Mamuretülaziz men of religion constituted the entire staff of the idadî school.[12] In any event, the institutionalized presence of so many *hoca*s (members of the ulama) alone blurs the distinction generally drawn between the old- and new-style schools.

---

[8] This can be seen in a number of places, e.g. the schools' architectural plans, the lists of school personnel provided in the state yearbooks, the rare interior photograph, and in anecdotal reports preserved in the Ottoman archives.

[9] Ch. 6 discusses the emphasis placed on moral education.

[10] For a description of the crossover between civil and religious officials in the province of Damascus, see Deguilhem, "State Civil Education," 240–1.

[11] Y Mtv. 114/140. 11 Şaban 1312 (7 Feb. 1895).

[12] *Salname-i Nezaret-i Maarif-i Umumiye* 1319 [1901].

3. Students with their teacher, a member of the ulama, in Konya. Ulama played a much larger role in state education than is usually recognized. (Source: Istanbul University Rare Book Library)

Likewise, the primacy given to observing the Muslim holy days throughout the year necessarily reinforced the religious aspect of school life. The birthday of the Prophet Muhammad (*mevlid*) was an occasion for special celebration. To mark the occasion, students received candy. Education Ministry personnel were favored with a less toothsome but clearly no less desirable form of sultanic appreciation: cash.[13] As we have already seen, students at the Imperial School of Galatasaray demonstrated their appreciation for the mevlid candy that they received by writing a letter of thanks to the sultan. As the disciplinary case to be discussed later in this chapter reveals, the question of Islamic legitimacy was a paramount feature of life in the schools. The state attempted to adopt the posture of a benevolent protector, keeping its charges' activity within the bounds of morally upright behavior. Its agents worked to assure that the students avoided such places as beer-halls and night-clubs. Daily prayer and the fasting and

[13] Y Mtv. 164/261. 15 Rebiülevvel 1315 (14 Aug. 1897).

the pre-dawn meal associated with the holy month of Ramadan likewise were prominent features of the school calendar.

ARCHITECTURE

At first glance, the physical appearance of the new schools would seem to provide further evidence of their constituting a radical break with the past. One could point to the architectural evidence to support the assertion that the new-style schools were a conscious importation from Western Europe.[14] The former grand vizier Mehmed "Küçük" Said Paşa states in his memoirs that he ordered architectural plans for the idadî schools to be gathered by the Ottoman Embassy in Paris and sent to Istanbul for distribution to the provinces.[15] This presumably is the process to which Mahmud Cevad refers in his account of the *hicrî* year 1302 (i.e. 1885–6): "Eighty sets of plans, placed in protective cases, for the first- and second-class idadî schools to accommodate 300 and 200 students [respectively] that were to be newly established in the provincial and sub-provincial centers were sent to the districts."[16] The architectural evidence seems to corroborate the notion that the idadîs were modeled on French counterparts. Most of the Ottoman structures are, like their contemporary buildings in France, highly symmetrical, both in plan and elevation, and neo-classical in design.[17] In general, the idadî buildings were undertaken on a grand scale. Almost all were constructed of dressed stone masonry and featured such elaborate details as arched or pedimental windows, ornamental staircases and entrances, and articulated cornices.

The new Ottoman schools marked themselves as being distinct from the established tradition of education in the empire. The combination

---

[14] For an overview of the architecture of the idadî schools, see Burcu Özgüven, "İdadî binaları," *Tarih ve Toplum*, 14/82 (1990), 44–7.

[15] Mehmed Said, *Said Paşa'nın Hatıratı* (Istanbul: Sabah, 1328 [1910]), 157.

[16] Mahmud Cevad, *Maarif-i*, 246.

[17] For examples of contemporary French schools, see Anne-Marie Châtelet, *Paris à l'école: "qui a eu cette idée folle . . ."* (Paris: Picard, 1993). Photographs of the Ottoman buildings may be seen in Kodaman, *Abdülhamid*, unnumbered plates following p. 181; in Carney E. S. Gavin (ed.), *Imperial Self-Portrait: The Sultan Abdul-Hamid II's Photographic Albums* (Cambridge: The Harvard Semitic Museum, 1989); and in the Istanbul University, Library of Congress, and British Library collections.

of their highly ordered and classicizing (in the Western sense) external appearance, their physical detachment from the context of religion and, in many cases, their considerable distance from the center of town— all this marked the new schools as novel. It is easy to see how this physical distinctiveness combined with other aspects of the state schooling endeavor, ranging from the frankly Western influence associated with its inception to the more mundane, but perhaps no less distinctive, appearance of the uniforms worn by the students,[18] to create the impression that the new schools represented a fundamental break with the past.

But while it would be foolish to deny the novel aspects of the Hamidian educational project, it is equally unsound to overlook those aspects which aligned it with its Ottoman and Islamic roots. As with the curriculum, the architecture of these structures reveals significant Ottoman modification of an originally European inspiration. Through the mediation of ornament and the creation of areas for prayer and ceremony, the Ottoman school buildings incorporated central elements of Ottoman and Islamic tradition. For example, it was a common feature of the idadî buildings to include such symbolic elements as the sultanic monogram (*tuğra*), a panel of text concerning the dedication of the school and the role of the sultan in its founding, or the crescent moon in an otherwise classical façade. Clear examples of this can be seen in a number of schools, for example, Trabzon, Salonika, and Yanya. The seeming omnipresence of framed calligraphic phrasings of the widely used slogan "padishahım çok yaşa" (Long live the sultan!) on the walls of the schools' interior reinforced the exterior use of such elements as the monogram and crescent to connect the buildings with the central government and its ultimate authority, the sultan.

Late Ottoman school buildings reveal other affinities with an indigenous architectural tradition. Strong parallels in style existed between the schools and other contemporary structures, not only other government edifices, as previously mentioned, but also the much more clearly symbolic structures built during the Hamidian period. These included fountains, libraries, monuments, and, most conspicuously, the Hamidiye mosque built near Abdülhamid II's Yıldız Palace and the

---

[18] Whereas the madrasa students wore robes and turbans, the state school students donned tightly fitting frock-coats, trousers, and the fez.

buildings associated with the Hijaz Railway, such as the station in Damascus.[19] It is clear from the strong architectural parallels between these types of structures that the late Ottoman style was not merely confined to educational institutions. In her work on late Ottoman architecture in Bursa, Beatrice St Laurent has referred to this common style as "Ottomanization."[20]

Another important but less obvious connection to be drawn between the architecture of the late Ottoman schools and indigenous patterns is suggested by Henry Glassie. In his richly researched and elegantly composed volume entitled *Turkish Traditional Art Today*, Glassie explores the relationships between various contemporary artists and craftsmen and the traditions within which they work.[21] Glassie's reading of the work of a particular present-day carpenter reveals connections with esthetic sensibilities of long standing. In the three-paneled yet symmetrical façade of Mustafa Sargın's dowry chests, Glassie finds affinities with central elements involved in the construction of traditional Turkish houses and in the design of Turkish carpets.[22] All three media create a central unity by working with a tripartite design that produces both a complete whole and two symmetrical halves. The façades of the great majority of late Ottoman schools, with their tripartite division, visible both in elevation and in plan, fit this schema. Glassie's work opens the possibility, at least, that idadî school architecture may have had more in common with an ambient and therefore more receptive indigenous esthetic than the Western-looking literature on the subject of modernization in the late Ottoman Empire would lead us to expect.

For all of their common elements, the state schools were far from

[19] For an account of such monuments, see Klaus Kreiser, "Public Monuments in Turkey and Egypt, 1840–1916," *Muqarnas*, 14 (1997), 103–17. For a more general account of architectural change in the Ottoman capital, see Zeynep Çelik, *The Remaking of Istanbul: Portrait of an Ottoman City in the Nineteenth Century* (Seattle: University of Washington Press, 1986; repr., Berkeley: University of California Press, 1993).

[20] Beatrice St Laurent, "Ottomanization and Modernization: The Architectural and Urban Development of Bursa and the Genesis of Tradition, 1839–1914," Ph.D. diss. Harvard University (1989); "Ottoman Power and Westernization: The Architecture and Urban Development of Nineteenth and Early Twentieth Century Bursa", *Anatolia Moderna/Yeni Anadolu*, 5 (1994), 199–232.

[21] Henry Glassie, *Turkish Traditional Art Today* (Bloomington: Indiana University Press, 1993).   [22] Ibid. 165 ff.

uniform. Given the centralized planning inherent in the articulation of the Ottoman school system, it would have been easy for the state to build identical schools throughout the provinces. As we have seen, the Ottoman bureaucracy procured architectural plans for the idadî schools from France and distributed them throughout the Ottoman domains.[23] Similarly, Mahmud Cevad notes that eighty such plans, each in a protective case, were dispatched to the provinces at this time.[24] This distribution arrangement certainly implies a centrality of planning. The architecture of these schools, however, exhibits considerable diversity. First, not all of the schools were housed in new buildings. In several instances previously existing structures were converted into schools, perhaps for reasons of economy. The most notable examples of such reuse of buildings were in Damascus,[25] where the building originally constructed as a residence of a wealthy merchant and subsequently used as a private school was converted into an idadî—the famous Maktab 'Anbar—and in Baghdad, where the idadî set up operations in the hospital for the poor.[26]

When new buildings were built, in the vast majority of cases, they differentiated themselves in a number of ways. First, their relative location varied from city to city. Quite frequently, as we have already seen, the new buildings were placed on the outskirts of town, away from the traditional center. Clear examples of this can be found in Mağnisa,[27] Trabzon,[28] and Aleppo.[29] In other cases, however, being near the city center seems to have been an important criterion in the choice of a site. As we have seen, this was the case in Edirne, where the new educational structures were grouped together in a location that was not far from the Selimiye mosque complex.[30] Similarly, in Jerusalem the idadî school was situated on the grounds of the ruined al-Ma'mūniyya madrasa.[31] As noted, this placed it within the Muslim Quarter of the Old City, in close proximity to the Dome of the Rock and Al-Aqsā mosque, the holiest Muslim sites in the city. The school was therefore not part of the new building taking place outside the walls to the north of the city that was led by the leading notable families, representatives

[23] Mehmed Said, *Said Paşa*, 157.   [24] Mahmud Cevad, *Maarif-i*, 245–6.
[25] Istanbul University Rare Book Library (IU), Photograph Collection, 90876.
[26] Library of Congress (LC) USZ62-81297.   [27] IU 90561.
[28] IU 90441.   [29] IU 90454.   [30] IU 90425 (includes a city map).
[31] İrade MM 4280. 16 Safer 1306 (22 Oct. 1888). IU 90504.

4. The idadî school of Gelibolu. This was one of the smaller idadî schools.
(Source: Istanbul University Rare Book Library)

of which were involved in planning the new schools.[32] Instead, the
school remained inside the walls, closer to the majority of the city's
Muslim population and to the Ḥaram al-Sharīf.

The buildings also varied according to size, degree of formality and
finish, whether they were free-standing structures (as in most cases) or
integrated into the fabric of the city block (for example, Manastır), and
other factors, such as the degree of ornamentation of their façades. The
idadî at Gelibolu (Fig. 4) would have been dwarfed in comparison to
one of the larger schools, such as the building at Aleppo. A photograph
taken of the former building shows a two-storey edifice with eight
windows across the front of each floor and four along the side.[33] In
Aleppo, by contrast, there were twenty-eight windows, some of which
were double windows, across each storey of the building's massive
façade.[34] A similar contrast in appearance occurs between the highly

[32] Kark and Landman, "The Establishment of Muslim Neighborhoods," 113–35.
[33] IU 90455.   [34] IU 90454.

5. The idadî school of Erzurum. The dark, undressed stonework contrasts with the more usual finished appearance of the schools. (Source: Istanbul University Rare Book Library)

dressed stonework of the school at, say, Sivas[35] and the rough appearance of its counterpart in Erzurum (Fig. 5).[36]

Such variation was due to a combination of factors, including the use of numerous architects, the wide range of building materials involved, and, perhaps most important, the delegation of considerable decision-making authority to local administrative bodies, such as the provincial Administrative and Education Councils. Since the officials who composed these bodies were long-time residents of the cities or towns in question (and not part of the ruling circles of the capital), there was obviously a strong degree of local input. A photograph taken on the steps of the idadî in Mağnisa is one of several showing the members of the local Education Council standing proudly before the institutions they helped to establish.[37] Such decentralization in educational administration explains the considerable variation apparent in the school buildings themselves.

In spite of all of this variation, however, the schools are nevertheless recognizable as like institutions, both similar to one another and to

[35] LC, USZ62-81124.   [36] IU 90504.   [37] IU 90561.

other architectural expressions of centralized Ottoman authority. In Edirne, for example, photographs taken of the main government building (*hükümet*) suggest that it could have been taken for any state school.[38] They are buildings that accommodated regional differences and practical concerns while still maintaining a unity of purpose and imperial identification. The architecture of these school buildings thus demonstrates the combination of idealistic and pragmatic tendencies that are the hallmarks of the late Ottoman educational endeavor.

The question of the schools' uniformity cannot be answered without equivocation. On the one hand, the system exhibited aspects of centrally mandated uniformity that were without precedent in the educational history of the empire. In what looked like an administrator's dream, students all across the empire followed the same curriculum, read from the same textbooks, observed the same daily schedule, wore similar uniforms, and attended schools that shared common architectural features. On the other hand, as we have seen, there were important differences that distinguished these schools one from another. Important regional distinctions in financing (as in the case of Damascus), in the instruction of regional languages, and in the relative physical location and ornamentation of their buildings suggest that the Hamidian state's approach to provincial education was considerably less uniform and more pragmatic than might have been anticipated. Now, the issue of whether or not the state intended such exceptions could be disputed. But either way (whether it planned for such exceptions or whether they occurred in spite of the state's best efforts), they force us to recognize the limits of the power and reach of the central government in this period—and, therefore, the shortcomings of the monolithic, mechanistic view of the Hamidian state.

LIVING AND LEARNING

Late Ottoman state schools introduced new ways of living to thousands of the empire's young. The novel regimen involved a variety of features, ranging from the mundane to the, at least potentially, profound. If the new-method schools did not initiate their young students into the world of the knife and fork, the raised desk and bed, the single

[38] IU 90455.

blackboard, the wall map, and the study of geometry, then they certainly inured them to the daily use of these items that traditionally had formed no part of the daily routine of education in the Ottoman Empire. For all of these features had a novelty that mirrored the unusual spatial organization of the new buildings in which they were to be employed.

As with the exterior architecture of the school buildings, much in the interior environment of the new schools suggests a Western derivation. The fact that students at these schools slept on raised beds and ate with cutlery off separate plates, it has been implied, meant that they were perforce absorbing the discipline of the West.[39] The very orderliness of students lined up for a school portrait, or of their beds positioned in two long, straight lines in the dormitory, to cite only two examples, has been taken as evidence of the pervasiveness of Western influence in the schools. As was the case with the buildings' façades, it is unwise to ignore the clearly Western provenance of such items as the bedstead, whose very name in Turkish, *karyola*, reveals its European—in this case, Italian—origin. It is equally imprudent, however, to assume that the existence of these objects in the school regimen necessarily implied an acceptance of the broader methods and ideology of the social milieu from which they derived.

In discussing cultural borrowing, we need to distinguish between two related but distinct phenomena. The first is the importation of certain physical devices and techniques, such as the bedstead, either directly or via locally produced imitations. Now, the existence of raised bed-frames in Ottoman secondary schools suggests only that the state planners responsible for provisioning the buildings believed them desirable. Perhaps these officials were acting on specific instructions from their superiors. On the other hand, perhaps they were merely attempting to satisfy the *perceived* desiderata of the officials higher up on the organizational ladder. All we know is that the beds were procured; we can see them in photographs taken during the Hamidian period and read their description in contemporary accounts.[40] That the

---

[39] Blake, "Training Arab-Ottoman Bureaucrats," 92–3. Blake mentions Timothy Mitchell's work on discipline in connection with schooling in Egypt.

[40] Photographs can be found in the Istanbul University Rare Book Library, the Library of Congress, and the British Library. A plate taken of a dormitory of Maktab 'Anbar is reproduced in Blake, ibid., facing p. 93.

Ottoman state supplied its idadî schools with bedsteads does not necessarily imply a more insidious invasion of Western discipline. Bedding on the floor could just as easily have allowed school officials to observe their charges as raised beds did. It is interesting to note that at least one Ottoman official objected to their use.[41] The use of knife and fork likewise appears to have been an innovation associated with the new-style schools. Introduced to the Ottoman palace only after 1860, the knife and fork and the use of separate plates were, according to one contemporary observer,

generalized among middle-class families by the public schools, boarding schools in particular . . . The young people who spent many years in these boarding schools forcibly assumed there new habits imposed by the organization and discipline of the school; they then took them to their families. It is in this way that the boarding schools powerfully contributed to the modification of traditional Turkish practices, inasmuch as they could be modified; it was the young people who had attended the boarding schools who little by little generalized European-style dress, beds raised off the floor, chairs, benches, desks.[42]

But what does this tell us about student lives? Just as the external appearance of the late Ottoman schools can be deceiving, so also can the focus on the supposed intent of the schools cloud our view of the way they may have operated in practice. Recent scholarship on education in the late nineteenth-century Middle East has emphasized the extent to which the new schools were instruments of order and discipline.[43] Indeed, there did seem to be a strong interest in creating an orderly, centralized system. But that does not necessarily mean that the schools functioned like Napoleon's dream of mechanical precision and certainly not like Jeremy Bentham's celebrated Panopticon. The same recent literature has focused largely on regulations and plans. Little

[41] On the questionable grounds that they were part of a larger impetus drawing Muslim students away from trade and industry and into government service. ŞD 213/50. 5 Şaban 1312 (1 Feb. 1895).

[42] Leïla Hanoum, *Le Harem imperial au XIXe siècle* (Paris: Éditions Complexe, 1991), 139, n. 1.

[43] Mitchell, *Colonizing Egypt*. Brinkley Messick, *The Calligraphic State: Textual Domination and History in a Muslim Society* (Berkeley: University of California Press, 1993). While neither work is devoted exclusively to education, both dwell at length on the subject.

evidence is taken from actual cases. The following pages represent an attempt to move beyond both the cataloguing and inventorying that characterizes much of the earlier literature on education in the late Ottoman Empire and the view that the "new-method" schools mainly functioned as instruments of state control. By addressing the cases of individual students, I approach the schools as arenas of human activity and interaction, not merely as mechanistic vehicles of state-imposed hegemony.

Consider the following attributes which define a particular group of students in a province of the late Ottoman Empire: they wear a specific type of clothing that marks them as distinct from the rest of the population; they follow a fixed daily schedule; they ascribe to clearly defined rules of conduct; they live communally, isolated, for the most part, from the rest of the community in which they live (some of the students board at the school); they approach their studies both by memorizing their lessons and by working in pairs or groups; and they receive special food on religious holidays. Some readers will have surmised that the students described are those of the new-style idadî schools, or at least those that had been converted to boarding institutions. But this description is, in fact, based on Messick's depiction of madrasa students in Yemen.[44] The parallels between the two groups are so many and so striking that the description can apply to either group, further evidence arguing for a more nuanced approach to the "new-style" schools. While there was much that was new, if not radical, in the state schools, there was also much continuity with the Ottoman madrasa tradition.[45] Like their madrasa counterparts, many of the students who attended the late Ottoman preparatory schools seem to have developed a common identity that set them off from their peers. Just as the schools' architecture and approach to learning marked them as up-to-date, so also were the students of the new institutions identified as belonging to a world apart from the daily life of their towns where their schools were located.

This separateness naturally imbued a stronger sense of communal identity among the students attending the rapidly growing number of

[44] Messick, *The Caligraphic State*, 82–4, 95.

[45] For a discussion of the continuities and breaks with traditional schooling as seen through the eyes of its students, see my "Education and Autobiography at the End of the Ottoman Empire," *Die Welt des Islams*, 41/1 (2001), 1–31.

boarding institutions. Even in an environment like that of Damascus, known for the emergence of anti-Ottoman feeling in the early decades of the twentieth century, it was nevertheless Ottomanism that was taking root among the students of the state preparatory school there during the Hamidian period.[46] During this era the Arabists were in the clear minority; most students at a school like Maktab 'Anbar were taking on the dress, language, manners, and, generally speaking, the prestige of an institution associated with the Ottoman elite. As Rogan has argued, the idadî in Damascus played an important role in

shaping an elite bound by a common school experience, rather than any particular ideology. From the frock-coat trousers and fez of their uniforms to the new habits of eating and sleeping communally, the 'Anbar school imparted a distinct socialisation to its students of diverse backgrounds. The subjects which students were taught and the new languages they learned gave 'Anbar graduates a culture and patois all their own, in which Arabic was mixed with Turkish, Persian and French—a cosmopolitanism which would have made them incomprehensible to all but others educated in the Ottoman system.[47]

The schools were vehicles for social mobility and for the fusing of a common Ottoman identity.[48] As we shall see, the identification with the sultan and with correct moral behavior figured strongly in the students' educational formation.

A word of caution is needed here. However much these schools may have encouraged a common identity, we nevertheless need to remember that individual experiences must have varied considerably. Following a lead proposed by Şerif Mardin,[49] I found the work of Mikhail Bakhtin to be helpful here. Bakhtin's interest in the natural environment led him to appreciate the different ways that organisms responded to stimuli. In human beings the complexity of the body's composition makes for a greater level of unpredictability. In fact, individual unpredictability lies at the core of Bakhtin's theory of answerability. Although seemingly simultaneously present in time and place, humans have different reactions to the "same" event because of

---

[46] Deguilhem, "State Civil Education," 246.
[47] Rogan, "The Political Significance of an Ottoman Education," 5.
[48] Deguilhem, "State Civil Education".
[49] Mardin, "Projects as Methodology," 77.

differences in "placement." No two people can hold the same place, and thus cannot observe an event or experience in the same way. For Bakhtin, answerability is directly related to the question of authorship, which is for him the chief difference separating humans from other species.[50] At the very least, Bakhtin's unbounded assumptions provide an interesting counterpoint to the much more restricted, deterministic approach of, say, Pierre Bourdieu's more recent work on education.[51] Ideally, perhaps, studies on educational effects would benefit from a productive tension between these two views, but my reading of what has been written about late Ottoman schools generally suggests that the less bounded approach needs a broader airing. For unless we wish to ascribe a subhuman status to students in late Ottoman schools (or in any other, for that matter) we must hold out the possibility, at the very least, that they just might have reacted in very different ways to the stimuli of state education. With this caveat in mind, we can move on to the subject of discipline.

DISCIPLINE

Our account of school life would be incomplete without considering the subject of discipline, a concept critical to the highly centralized and ordered realm of the state school system. Given the geographically far-flung dispensation and inherently hierarchical nature of the late Ottoman school system, some degree of order was clearly required. Precisely what type of ordering was desired and the steps taken to implement that ordering tell us a good deal about the ways in which the Hamidian state viewed its educational endeavor. We have already discussed such aspects of the state's schools as their systemic and integrated qualities. There is, in the almost obsessive nature of school administration, ample evidence of the state's intent, at least, to create a highly structured and centralized organization, an ordering principle that is impossible to ignore.

On the other hand, as we have seen, recent literature on discipline

---

[50] Katerina Clark and Michael Holquist, *Mikhail Bakhtin* (Cambridge, Mass.: Belknap, 1984), 65 ff.

[51] Pierre Bourdieu, *The State Nobility: Elite Schools in the Field of Power*, trans. Lauretta C. Clough (Cambridge: Polity Press, 1996).

in the modern Middle East has called attention to the coercive power of the state to such an extent that readers are forced to remind themselves that these were in fact human and not mechanical institutions. Timothy Mitchell has led us to appreciate the importance of both the liberal and the colonial impact on forms of education in Egypt, but his reliance on the little-practiced Lancaster method and the disciplinary element in general overemphasizes the prison-like quality of schooling. A thorough critique of Mitchell's approach and, as a result, a considerably more nuanced reading of the Egyptian case have recently appeared in Gregory Starrett's eloquent volume.[52]

These studies reveal the danger in relying heavily on the regulations produced by the state to govern the schooling process. Not surprisingly, these regulations create the distinct impression that school life was a highly mechanistic enterprise. Strict schedules are listed for any number of human activities, ranging from the daily schedule of waking, bathing, praying, eating, and so on, to the precise number of school personnel required to be present at various functions of the weekly schedule. While such rules are clearly critical to our understanding of the way the state *wanted* the schools to function, relying on them excessively would be akin to assuming that, for example, everyone possessing a driver's license in our own day followed the rules of the road contained in the state-supplied regulations. The pedestrian knows all too well that such is not the case. In what follows, although we refer to the regulations governing school behavior, we shall weigh them against the events that transpired in two specific disciplinary cases.

The state's attempt to control student life may be divided into two rough categories. The first includes state supervision of the written word. We have seen how the state expended considerable attention on monitoring the curriculum and textbooks used both in its own and in the competing school systems. Anecdotal evidence pertaining to disciplinary cases surrounding the presence of banned material in the schools adds credence to the notion of an abiding Hamidian concern with the spread of politically sensitive ideas. In one case, idadî students were caught with copies of *Osmanlı*, the main organ of the opposition organization Committee of Union and Progress.[53] But this does not

---

[52] Starrett, *Putting Islam to Work*, 30 ff.

[53] MKP 86/15-1443. 2 Nisan 1318 (27 Apr. 1902).

add to what we already know about Hamidian preoccupation with interdicting banned material and staunching anti-regime activity. State schools, particularly the higher schools of the capital, are known to have been areas of opposition to Abdülhamid II, although activity occurring at this level of schooling and in the provinces has not been adequately documented.

The second category of discipline cases involves student activity not specifically associated with banned texts, namely, behavioral issues and the question of punishment, corporal and otherwise. Some of these cases could work to the students' benefit, for example, in a case that arose when a teacher allegedly wounded one of his pupils.[54] Other cases, such as those centering around an official's venality, did not directly affect the state's relationship with the students.

Disciplinary cases document what is perhaps the only type of truly contemporary source that presents school life as something other than abstract and routinized. (Autobiographies are, of course, composed much later and thus require separate treatment.[55]) In the disciplinary cases students appear both as individuals and as members of a group. While the state may be seen as trying to recruit the young students to its "side" or "team" through the moral component of the schools,[56] it was frequently unsuccessful.[57] Whether alone or as part of a collective, these young men frequently acted on their own volition, despite the education system's obsession with order and regulations. As these cases demonstrate, such action could be in flagrant disregard for authority. The existence of such evidence should sound a cautionary note for the historical writing on late Ottoman education that relies solely on idealized regulations and anonymous statistical information. What follows is an attempt to provide some anecdotal detail to a subject that has been conspicuously lacking in the human element.

[54] ŞD 217/33. 22 Ramazan 1319 (2 Jan. 1902).
[55] On the subject of autobiography, see my "Education and Autobiography."
[56] On the notion of the "team" recruitment in connection with the Sufi brotherhoods in Ottoman history, see Şerif Mardin, "The Nakşibendi Order in Turkish History," in Richard Tapper (ed.), *Islam in Modern Turkey: Religion, Politics and Literature in a Secular State* (London: I. B. Tauris, 1991), 137.
[57] For a fictionalized but highly realistic account highlighting the absurdity of the Iranian state's attempt to induce nation-building through sartorial uniformity in a later period, see the appendix to Houchang E. Chehabi, "Staging the Emperor's New Clothes: Dress Codes of Nation-Building under Reza Shah," *Iranian Studies*, 26/3–4 (1993), 230–3.

Istanbul, 1889

The first of the two cases to be discussed here took place in the capital in the autumn of 1889. At this point in its history Istanbul was, in the words of one historian, in "the throes of westernization," a phrase that is particularly appropriate for discussing the quarter of Galata in which the case unfolds.[58] The facts of the case, as recorded in the official correspondence concerning the event, are as follows. On the evening of Monday, 28 October, an external watchman on the staff of the Galatasaray lycée saw a student named Feyzî together with his companions in a drinking establishment, a clear violation of the expected norms of student behavior.[59] The watchman consequently apprehended the student and turned him over to the local gendarmerie station, whereupon Feyzî was reported to have threatened to kill the school employee. This threat resulted in Feyzî's dismissal from the school. Later, when the same unnamed watchman was leading a group of students to the bathhouse, as was customary, Feyzî ambushed him at the bathhouse door. Suddenly entering the bathhouse, Feyzî drew a revolver and fired at the watchman, but missed his target. At this point the description of the events of the case ends and discussion turns to such subjects as the necessity of taking measures to prevent similar crimes and immorality, and the appropriate punishment to be meted out to Feyzî.

Although the documentation available provides only skeletal information about the events, and the principal figures involved remain obscure, several points are clear. First is the gravity of Feyzî's original infraction, frequenting a place known to serve alcohol. The seriousness of Feyzî's action is underscored both by the watchman's behavior and, perhaps, by that of Feyzî himself. Whereas the watchman might have chosen to settle the matter within the confines of the school's

---

[58] For a highly original account of Ottoman Istanbul, see Edhem Eldem, "Istanbul: From Imperial to Peripheralized Capital," in Edhem Eldem, Daniel Goffman, and Bruce Masters (eds.), *The Ottoman City between East and West* (Cambridge: Cambridge University Press, 1999), 135–206.

[59] İrade MM 4628. 9 Rebiülahir 1307 (3 Dec. 1889). The functionary's title was that of *harici mubassır*, which might be translated as external watchman or overseer. The place is described in the supporting document as "a tavern-like place" (*meyhane gibi bir yer*). I have referred to this case in Ch. 3 in the context of that institution's transition from the Tanzimat to the Hamidian eras.

disciplinary procedure, he nevertheless turned the student over to the authorities. Feyzî's dramatic response, both the verbal threat and the attempted murder of the guard, likewise seems either to indicate his awareness of the seriousness of his offense, or, perhaps, his having been blinded by rage. It is possible that he was distraught at having brought shame on his family; it would have been considered a source of pride to have a son at this school. Whatever the underlying reasons, it is clear that the incident produced an extraordinary response in this student.

Second, the office of external watchman suggests a comprehension on the part of the authorities that student behavior outside of school grounds warranted close scrutiny. The existence of local bars and the presence of several of Feyzî's companions at the one in question seems to bear out the administration's fears. Given the school's location in the heart of Beyoğlu, a district of Istanbul known for its large Christian population and, then as today, for its night-life, it is not surprising that, as the authorities must have viewed the matter, one of their charges had fallen in with a bad crowd. As we have already noted, just this sort of behavior, apparently magnified by similar cases in the year 1894, provoked the education minister to request approval for the hiring of ten additional inspectors to be charged with "patrolling the suspicious places day and night."[60]

The third and more general observation we may draw from the case of Feyzî is that the state was attempting to act as moral arbiter of the lives of its students. The education bureaucracy felt itself obliged not only to carry out the letter of the regulations regarding student activity but also to undertake the policing of an unspecified normative moral code. Given what we know about the role that Islam played in determining the spirit of this morality in the Hamidian educational context, it is not surprising that a strictly Islamic notion of behavior obtained, even in a school such as Galatasaray which had the highest non-Muslim enrollment of any Ottoman state secondary school. The particulars of the case unfolded in an environment in which the state was on guard against what it deemed to be threats to moral rectitude, acting *in loco parentis* with respect to these boarding students who, in a radical experiment, had been entrusted to the state for education and upbringing.

---

[60] ŞD 212/61. 18 Cemaziyelahır 1311 (27 Dec. 1893). Approved as İrade M 1311 B 5. 25 Receb 1311 (1 Feb. 1894).

Therefore, the case turns not only on the proximal event, that is, Feyzî's presence in an establishment where the primary activity was presumably the consumption of alcohol, the Qur'anic injunction against which is famous. It must also be seen in the context of the state's attempt to supervise student life. It is the link between such a drinking establishment and the moral laxity of the venues which the education minister would later describe as "beer-houses, *cafés chantants*, and similarly inappropriate places" that infuses the situation with its tension, a tension which, in fact, may explain Feyzî's violent reaction to his having been caught in an act known to be both against the rules and at variance with the religio-moral dictates of Hamidian education policy.

Although Feyzî had taken direct action, it was nevertheless the state that took charge of the situation, first expelling him and then sentencing him to prison. It was able to interdict activity that flagrantly affronted Islam and thereby to act as the arbiter of morality, a role with considerable advantages for a state that was attempting to resurrect a proud heritage by championing the Muslim faith.

Manastır, 1903

The second case unfolds in a different time and place. The date is late November 1903, and the setting is the provincial capital of Manastır, present-day Bitola in Macedonia and then the second city, after Salonika, of the Ottoman Balkans.[61] The chronological and physical remove from the events that occurred in Istanbul invites comparison with the situation that obtained at the time of the case of Feyzî, some fourteen years earlier. In those intervening years much had changed in the world of Ottoman secondary education. By 1903 almost all of the idadî construction in the provincial capitals had been completed. Many of the schools that were still being planned or were in the initial stages of construction in 1889 had now been expanded into boarding institutions that, like the school in Manastır, could now boast of eight grade levels. The details of the Manastır case reflect the fact that the aims for the expansion of secondary education that Ottoman statesmen had made a priority in the 1880s had by the 1900s become a reality.

The same period in which the state was expanding its school system

---

[61] For an excellent overview of Manastır in this period, see Lorry and Popovic, "Au carrefour des Balkans, Bitola 1816–1918."

also saw an increase in Great Power pressure on the empire. As the case in Manastır highlights, this pressure was most acutely felt in the Ottoman Balkans. The repository for the documents that enable us to know about the Manastır case at all, the institution of the inspector-general for Rumelia, was created due to pressure that the powers brought to bear over the question of Macedonia. Manastır province in the first years of the twentieth century was particularly bloody, the result of a violent cycle featuring massacres by armed gangs and the inevitable reprisals of the Ottoman army. The Mürzteg agreement between the Russian tsar and the Austro-Hungarian emperor (9 November 1903) included provisions by which the local Christian population could seek redress for the instances of abuse or misrule that acted as a lightening-rod for public outcry in the West. The creation of the Inspectorship was one of these "reforms." It is against such a stormy background that the case of students at the Manastır idadî school unfolds. Yet the violence in Manastır province rarely affected the town of Manastır itself, which enjoyed a period of prosperity and dynamism. In this period the city boasted large, glass-fronted shops, a municipal theater, and a railway connection—"a European city ready to compete with Salonika."[62]

Before turning to the details of the case, it is necessary to make clear that the wealth of detail and the quality of the source material in the 1903 Manastır case makes for a lopsided comparison with the scant evidence available in the case of Feyzî. Whereas the sum total of information concerning the Istanbul events was limited to several lines of second-hand observations by the grand vizier, the Manastır case presents a relative treasure trove of evidence. The documentation consists of a petition signed by twenty-five students at the Manastır idadî that they submitted to the offices of the Ottoman inspector-general of Rumelia,[63] in which they voice complaints both general and specific concerning the school authorities, as well as the texts of five individual

---

[62] Lorry and Popovic (ibid.) describe this period as a "belle époque" for Manastır.

[63] Located in Manastır, the office of the *Rumeli Müfettiş-i Umumiliği* was created by Abdülhamid II in November of 1902 in response to pressure from the signatories of the Treaty of Berlin, Russia and Austria-Hungary in particular, for "reform" in Macedonia. İsmet Binark *et al.*, *Başbakanlık Osmanlı Arşivi Rehberi* (Ankara: T. C. Başbakanlık Devlet Arşivleri Genel Müdürlüğü, 1992), 379–80. See also, Shaw and Shaw, *History of the Ottoman Empire*, ii. 207 ff.

depositions taken from students involved in the case.[64] This case thus represents the only available example (at least of which I am aware) of a source in which Ottoman state idadî students speak in their own words. It therefore offers a clear contrast to the textbook we shall encounter in Chapter 6 that places words in the mouth of a hypothetical student.

Unlike the case of Feyzî in Istanbul, the documentation of the Manastır case contains no third-person account of what transpired. Rather, the file contains only the students' extremely critical petition (*arzuhal*) and the five depositions (*ifade*). Determining the events of the evening of 21 November 1903, therefore, requires interpretation. According to the students' petition, the problem began on the first night of the holy month of Ramadan, when the school's director summoned the students for a roll-call at approximately 10:30 in the evening.[65] He then ordered the students to go to sleep, an order they resisted, claiming that in past years the students had been able to stay awake until two or three o'clock in the morning, at which time they had eaten the pre-dawn Ramadan meal (*sahur*). This request apparently had the effect of infuriating the director, who expelled approximately ten of the students. These students, not properly dressed for the street, were left to wander in the rain and mud for an hour and a half before finding a petition-drafter (*arzuhalci*) and having him draft a petition which they presented to the inspector-general.

By the students' own account, the inspector-general advised them to return to the school, an action which precipitated further threats against them. Of what happened next, the only verifiable event seems to be the fact that the authorities took five of the students aside and recorded their answers to a set of similar, but not identical, questions. It is these five depositions which, along with the original petition, constitute the documents in the available file. Apart from the standard office marking, "After taking the necessary action, save," that appears on the petition, there is no information that would explain what steps, if any, were eventually taken to resolve the matter.

---

[64] TFR.1.ŞKT 2327. 8 Teşrin-i sani 1319 (21 Nov. 1903).

[65] Times in these documents are given in old-style reckoning which counted hours after sunrise and sunset. The student petition places the time of their being summoned as "four thirty" in the evening, which corresponds roughly to 10:30 in the evening by today's clock, if we assume sunset to have been at 6:00. *İslâm Ansiklopedisi*, s.v. "Sâat."

Further information supplied in the petition and in the depositions offers perspective and nuance to the skeletal form of the case presented thus far. Several interesting details about the school come to light in these documents. Most of the students involved were in the seventh or eighth grade of the Manastır idadî, testimony to the fact that the school system had expanded vertically (in terms of the age-group enrolled) as well as horizontally (in geographical terms). The school's students are identified in these documents both by student-identification number and by place of origin. We know from photographic and archival evidence that student-identification numbers were a prevalent feature of the late Ottoman school system. Photographs of students from several, but not all, idadî and other state schools reveal that their school numbers were sometimes sewn into the collar of their uniforms.[66] While it is to be expected that the authorities would refer to the students by their numbers, the documents from the Manastır case reveal that, at least in an official context, the students also occasionally adopted that mode of identification. Thus, in his testimony Kâzım Efendi, a student from the seventh grade, refers to his fellow students as "number two Şevki Efendi, a student of the eighth grade," and as "2 Şevki, Ali Rıza Efendi, 47 Sadık Efendi, Lazaraki Efendi, 3 Hâlid Efendi . . ."[67] At least to a certain extent, the students had internalized the rationalized organization of the school.

Of relevance to the ongoing official attempt to regulate student activity outside the school is the fact that school officials had apparently established a particular coffeehouse for student use, described by one of the students most involved in the grievance procedure as "the coffeehouse near to and designated by the school."[68] Another describes the establishment in similar terms as "the coffeehouse designated for the school and frequented by the school's students."[69] The same coffeehouse is also referred to in another student's deposition as being

---

[66] See e.g. the photographs from the Library of Congress collection showing students in uniform at the following idadî schools: Üsküdar, LC# USZ62-81104; Sivas, USZ-62-81125; Kastamonu, USZ62-81129; Salonika (Selânik), USZ62-81131; and Damascus, USZ62-81270. These photographs were taken before the collection was bequeathed to the US government by Abdülhamid II in 1893. For evidence of the students at the Aşiret Mektebi being referred to by school number, see the tables in Eugene L. Rogan, "Aşiret Mektebi: Abdülhamid II's School for Tribes (1892–1907)," *IJMES* 28/1 (1996), 83–107.

[67] TFR.I.ŞKT 2327. 6. lef.

[68] Ibid. 1. lef. The text reads: *mektebe yakın ve mektebin tahsis eylediği kahve.*

[69] Ibid. 5. lef. In the original: *mektebe tayin ve mekteb talebelerinin gittiği kahve.*

"Ali Ağa's coffeehouse," possibly a reference to its proprietor or manager. However described, it was in this coffeehouse that the students gathered to sign the petition after it had been drafted by the *arzuhalci*. The students' choice of such a semi-official venue for attaching their signatures to the petition that severely criticized their superiors is, as we will see below, perhaps just one sign of their boldness.

Although these documents offer information about other miscellaneous aspects of school life, for example, that timeless student complaint, the poor quality of the food provided, the most important lesson to be drawn from this case is the extent to which the students involved had developed a sense of group identity, even solidarity. This mutual affinity is defined both by their common circumstances and in distinction to the school authorities. The features these students had in common fall into two categories: those associated with what we can surmise about their identity prior to arriving at the idadî school in Manastır, and those associated with their school-derived identity. In the absence of such potentially helpful information as, say, the socio-economic background of the students or their fathers' occupations, information concerning the students' pre-school origins can nevertheless be deduced from the ways in which the students are referred to and from their descriptions of themselves. All of the students involved in this case appear to have come to Manastır from other parts of the Ottoman Empire. Four of the five students deposed are associated with another place: Hanyalı Ali Rıza (that is, Ali Rıza from Hanya, on the island of Crete), Gramos Kazalı Kâzım bin Mehmed (Kâzım, son of Mehmed from the subprovince of Gramos), Pirlepeli Hâlid (from Pirlepe, a town north of Manastır), and Dibreli Eftim (from Dibre, in present-day Albania). Only Şevki is identified as being from Manastır. But even this assignation is ambiguous; it may refer to his origins in the province of Manastır and not to the city of the same name. In their petition the students clearly state that, since they were all from the countryside, they had no place in which to seek refuge when they were thrown out onto the street.[70] One of the students even went so far as to state that he was a stranger and that he did not know Manastır at all.[71] As this case demonstrates, the late Hamidian boarding schools

[70] Ibid.
[71] Ibid. 6. lef. Cf. Rogan, "Political Significance," who describes the experience of one student arriving as a rank outsider to the Damascus idadî school, so much so that the other students laughed at his unsophisticated ways.

were bringing together students from different parts of the empire to live and learn together. Their common bond as strangers in a strange city no doubt contributed to their common identification.

The students' shared religious background must also have added to this sense of shared identity. Judging from the names of the students involved in this case, almost all of them were Muslims. Of the more than twenty student names discernible from their signatures on the petition and their being named in the documents, only two are clearly non-Muslim. The rest are almost certainly Muslim, including such names as Ali Rıza, Hâlid, Sadık, Mahmud, Muammer, Fuad, Abdurrahman, Receb, Selim, and so on. The fact that the event that triggered the students' protest involved an important event in the Islamic calendar, namely, the first day of the holy month of Ramadan, lends credence to the impression that the students' religious affiliation was an important factor shaping their group identity. Although perhaps coincidental, it may be significant that of the five students deposed the one who attempted to distance himself the most from the rest of the group was Greek. He stated that he signed the petition without reading it because everyone else was doing so, and only became apprised of the contents after the fact. Although agreeing that the students had discussed the poor quality and undercooked nature of the food served at the school, he further disavowed the more serious of the students' complaints by stating flatly that, "There is nothing to complain about at the school." Given the background of interdenominational violence in Macedonia in the period just prior to events of this case, it would not be surprising to find that the students at the Manastır idadî were increasingly drawn together—and apart—by their religion. Yet, as was the case in Damascus, the events portrayed are not charged with political significance. Attempts to read such motives into cases like these run the risk of injecting a dimension which may not have been present at the time.

The students' complaints further suggest that their common experience in the school amplified their pre-existing mutual affinities. Their school-derived identity was based on common experience. The documents available from this case indicate that their mutual bond was forged by a number of common grievances. Apart from the complaints about food and the more specific charge of being denied their customary Ramadan fast observance, the Manastır idadî students' petition exudes a deep sense of resentment toward the school's authorities. The students single out one staff member in particular in their complaint. They charge Şevki Efendi, whom they identify as one of their assistant principals and teachers (and therefore not to be confused with the student of the same name), with "inefficacy and, what's more, indifference."[72] Even worse than his "sinister practice," in the students' eyes, is the charge that other school officials have colluded to conceal this official's behavior in order to keep him out of trouble.

The perception of official collusion reinforces the dominant theme that pervades the students' complaint and testimony, namely, the existence of a wide gulf separating the students from the administration. The students refer to the officials who supported Şevki Efendi as the "director and teachers who are his companions." There is a clear sense that the students perceive the authorities to be acting in collusion against them.[73] The testimony of Hâlid Efendi includes the charge that, while the students were given little at mealtimes and had to buy food from the greengrocer, the school's director and local education director were joined at table by the storekeeper, who was not registered to receive meals at the school. The presence of this interloper was, moreover, particularly common on holidays.[74] This must have been especially galling to the students, who were clearly upset at not being allowed to celebrate Ramadan as they had in the past. Their petition ascribes this deprivation to less-than-flattering motives on the part of the school officials. In the students' view, the officials heaped abuse on the students when they returned from the inspector-general both in order to exact revenge from them for their actions and because they wanted to be able to frequent the theater and coffeehouses themselves

---

[72] The Education Yearbook for 1903–4 lists Şevki Efendi as the school's Second Assistant Principal (Muavin-i Sani) and also as a teacher of such subjects as cosmography, arithmetic, and geometry. *Salname-i Nezaret-i Maarif-i Umumiye* (Istanbul: Matbaa-yı Amire, 1321), 661.

[73] For an autobiographical account of several incidents in the idadî in Damascus that share much with the cases presented here, see Rogan, "Political Significance." In one such incident the principal sided with the students against a school official seen drinking alcohol and kissing a student. This case, which attracted the attention of Istanbul, also featured depositions taken from students. But it differed from the Manastır case in that it created rifts between the students and between the staff, further evidence of the unpredictable quality of school life.

[74] TFR.1.ŞKT 2327. 7. lef.

in complete freedom and to assure their personal comfort and repose.[75] The lines were clearly drawn between students, who were neglected and undernourished, and their superiors, who made the students go to bed early so that they could enjoy the cosmopolitan entertainments of the town with their cronies.

The gulf in privilege and behavior that existed between the students and the authorities seemed to empower the students to act with unexpected boldness. The students actively involved in this case exhibited a remarkable confidence and defiance toward their superiors. This attitude is clear both from their initial refusal to go to bed when ordered to and from their subsequent petitioning of the inspector-general. Hâlid Efendi's deposition contains the following statement: "Even though the school director ordered me to go to bed, I did not. I said, 'If my friends go to bed, then I will also.'"[76] Both in its original context and as recounted in the form of a deposition, this is a bold assertion. Its defiance is in marked contrast to the respectful language of the official petition. In that formal document the students' refusal to retire for the evening is referred to as a request (*istirham*), and the extent of their disobedience toward the school officials is not revealed.

In an attempt to place their predicament in a context larger than one of petty complaints and vendettas, the students framed their appeal to the inspector-general in the context of their concern for the welfare of the Ottoman Empire. The petition states that,

As a result of his inefficacy and, what's more, his indifference, Şevki Efendi, one of our assistant directors and teachers, far from effecting progress (*terakki*) among the children of the fatherland (*evlad-ı vatan*), has rather engendered incidents and so forth that make one recall the education (*terbiye*) of the era of the Janissaries with affection.[77]

In a stunning inversion of the relationship between students and state that obtained in the case of Feyzî, the Manastır idadî students seized the moral high ground. Perhaps emboldened by the establishment of the office of the inspector-general for Rumelia, they turned the tables

---

[75] TFR.1.ŞKT 2327. A municipal theater had been founded in 1897. Lorry and Popovic, "Au carrefour," 86.

[76] TFR.1.ŞKT 2327. 7. lef. The original reads: *Bana Mekteb Müdiri yat diye emir verdiği halde yatmadım[.] Arkadaşlarım yatarsa ben de yatarım dedim.*

[77] Ibid.

on their superiors by identifying the shortcomings of the school's officials whom they associate with the Janissaries (who appear here as emblematic for all that was backward in Ottoman history), recounting their resulting deprivations, and associating themselves with a religiously correct and patriotic agenda.

These two cases occurred in institutions of a different time and place, but they underscore the degree to which combining Western disciplinary techniques with Islamic notions of morality afforded the Hamidian state a potentially effective means of projecting its Islamic stance. But they also reveal how much depended upon the individuals, both officials and students. These cases remind us that the historical record has overlooked certain important aspects of late Ottoman education. Far from being statistical entities that functioned according to their prescribed regulations, these schools were, as these cases remind us, first and foremost human institutions. The individuals who administered them and the students who attended them were alike subject to the vices and virtues of humanity.

CONCLUSION

Here we come up against the crux of state education, namely, the attempt to bridge the gap between great intentions and practical abilities, between broad inspiration and local possibilities, and between sweeping societal concerns and individual lives. In the late Ottoman case, a complicating and seemingly omnipresent factor was the East–West dynamic. The Ottoman educational endeavor was inextricably bound up with the relationship between the empire and the West. In its very *raison d'être*, its organizational model, and various features of its architectural form and lesson content, the idadî revealed considerable Western influence. In this chapter we have seen echoes of the Western presence in the form of French architectural detail, in the background presence of such places as nightclubs and *cafés chantants* that are clearly associated with the West, and, more instrumentally, in the office of the inspector-general of Rumelia, a post created at the insistence of the Western powers.

In direct response to what Hamidian officials perceived to be the dangerous effects of Western encroachment, the Ottoman state built schools that were to act as alternatives to the Western educational offerings. The buildings, although based on French architectural plans, sought to mitigate their Western derivation by accenting specifically Ottoman and Islamic elements. In parallel fashion, the content of the new schools was designed to instill Ottoman notions of loyalty and an Islamic sense of propriety in daily behavior.

Like the buildings which represent an effort to mediate the opposing tendencies of East and West, daily life in the Ottoman state schools was a matter of negotiation and accommodation. There were no regulations covering the subtler aspects of school life, and no ground-rules to help students and staff cope with the inevitably individual ways in which the new schools affected them. The students and officials alike were left to their own devices in navigating their own course through a number of competing influences. The state presented clear markers in the form of buildings, regulations, teachers, administrators, ulama, mosques, and textbooks. While this array of state-supplied references undoubtedly prescribed much in the daily life of the Ottoman school, the disciplinary cases show us that there was clearly much room for maneuver.

5

Maps

INTRODUCTION

We have seen how the aggressive presence of Western educational competition spurred Ottoman officialdom to create its own educational system. The increasingly adversarial Ottoman approach to education manifested itself very clearly in the way the system envisioned during the preceding period of the Tanzimat reforms was refitted or "Ottomanized" in the Hamidian period (1876–1909). Some measures, such as the restructuring of curriculum to include more patently religious material for instruction while eliminating subjects like Western philosophy, were relatively overt. Others were more subtle. Geography is one area where it is possible to discern a significant movement away from the construct of the Tanzimat—and one with far-reaching consequences.

In his incomparable study of Ottoman and Turkish Republican education, *Türkiye Maarif Tarihi*, Osman Nuri Ergin recounts that when the rüşdiye schools were introduced in 1862, their maps provoked a violent reaction. Irate that images were being presented as part of the schools' curriculum, gangs of reactionaries rushed into the schools, seized the offending maps, and, declaring them to be "drawing" and therefore blasphemous (*resimdir, küfriyattır diye*), threw them down the toilet.[1] This incident illustrates both the power associated with the cartographic image and its novelty as a pedagogical tool in the late Ottoman Empire.

This chapter is concerned with the role maps played in the rapidly

---

[1] Osman Nuri Ergin, *İstanbul Mektepleri ve İlim, Terbiye ve San'at Müesseseleri Dolayısıyla Türkiye Maarif Tarihi*, 5 vols. (Istanbul: Osmanbey Matbaası, 1939–43), ii. 460.

expanding Ottoman state educational system. It begins with a description of an outdoor map created by the Ministry of Education to inform the public of Istanbul about the 1877–8 war with Russia. In its didactic intent and attention to detail, this three-dimensional map prefigures important aspects of the two-dimensional cartographic images that hung from the classroom walls of the "new-style" schools. After placing late Ottoman school maps in the context of both the Ottoman cartographic tradition and late Ottoman educational policy, this chapter goes on to analyze the generally suspicious but increasingly curious official attitude toward maps during the Hamidian period. A close examination of the maps used in the state schools reveals an abrupt shift in official cartographic production. In the mid-1890s the state bureaucracy directed its sole supplier, the military, to begin producing maps that displayed all Ottoman territory within one frame, thus ending the near monopoly of continent-oriented school maps that effectively truncated the Ottoman domains. The Hamidian state was refitting the education plan it had inherited from the preceding Tanzimat period so as to make it conform to its overall agenda. It is no accident that the state emphasized the cartographic unity of its territory as it sought to promote a renewed sense of loyalty to the empire and its ruler. The maps created for this endeavor undoubtedly altered student perceptions about the empire. As one important memoir reveals, the results may not always have been those the state intended. Such were the risks that came with using a new pedagogical device that was as powerful as it was unproven.

A WARTIME MAP

On 13 October 1877 Münif Paşa, the Ottoman minister of education, informed the palace about an unprecedented project to create a large-scale, three-dimensional map in Istanbul. The outdoor map was to represent the western front in the war with Russia that had begun the preceding April and would end the following January with disastrous results for the Ottomans. The 1877–8 war was undoubtedly the most important event in the early years of the reign of Abdülhamid II and a chief reason why his state was unable to direct much initial attention to education. Indirectly, however, the war produced a map that prefigured many of the important features of the Hamidian educational effort. Münif Paşa's map project demonstrates the state's interest in the educational potential of maps, a potential that the state would actively utilize when it could devote more attention to expanding its school system in the ensuing decades.

The use of maps in the service of education was, as we will see, unprecedented in the history of the Ottoman Empire. Yet the educational objective behind Münif Paşa's wartime map is clear. The map's intended audience were the people of Istanbul, and it aimed both "to demonstrate the military terrain to them in a clear way" and "to facilitate the progress of those engaged in the science of geography."[2] In other words, it was designed both to educate the inhabitants of the capital about the strategic situation of the war and to encourage the hands-on learning of geography in the process.

Münif Paşa reported that the map had recently been completed and that he was now writing to obtain permission for it to be opened to the public. His description of the map is quite detailed and allows us to glimpse its underlying agenda. Located in the courtyard of the idadî school in the vicinity of the mausoleum of Sultan Mahmud II (that is, just off the central Divan Yolu in the heart of old Istanbul), the map covered an area of 400 square meters and conformed to a scale of 36 : 1,000. It included the provinces of the Danube (*Tuna*) and Edirne, portions of the provinces of Salonika and Bursa, the proximal areas of the Mediterranean and Black Seas, the Golden Horn (*Haliç*), Istanbul, and the Sea of Marmara.[3] It thus was designed to instruct its viewers in the strategic aspects of a war whose front was coming dangerously close to the imperial capital. Presumably, this approach was intended to rally popular support for the war effort.

The map's didactic intentions are palpable from several of its features. First, the map was intended from the start to be open to the public, as we will see below. Second, it was designed to be easily interpreted by those with little or no cartographic experience. Seas, lakes, and rivers were represented by actual pools and flows of water, mountains and hills were shown in bas relief, and forests were depicted with actual greenery (*sebze*). Furthermore, models of cannon, lighthouses, railroads, bridges, and military headquarters provided more

---

[2] İrade Dah. 61754. 12 Şevval 1294 (20 Oct. 1877).   [3] Ibid.

pedagogical detail than most standard maps of the period could provide. Third, all of the places had their names written on the map. Fourth, "several talented officials were to be trained to present the necessary explanations of the most important places, encampments, and battle sites." Lastly, Münif Paşa continues, "it is hoped that the inhabitants of Istanbul, particularly those who are incapable of perusing normal maps, will benefit from this spectacle."[4] The intention behind this display was to reach out and educate the public. Like the maps used in Ottoman schools, this project marks an attempt by the state to expand cartographic literacy among its subjects.

Even the financial arrangements concerning admission to the map conformed to the state's didactic mission and wartime footing. A nominal entrance fee was to be taken from visitors, with the exception of soldiers and students of state schools, who were to be admitted gratis. Once enough money had been collected to recoup the costs of construction, all proceeds were to be handed over to the War Assistance Fund (*İane-i Harbiye Sandığı*). If the map proved successful, the project was to be expanded to include another map depicting the eastern front and, eventually, should it meet with the approval of the sultan, a map depicting the empire in its entirety.

While the ultimate fate of Münif's plan to reproduce this public cartography elsewhere remains unclear, the existence of this wartime map and the agenda behind it indicate state recognition of the important role maps could play in reaching the public. Ultimately, the thinking that lay behind Münif's large-scale map resurfaced in the Ottoman school system. Just as Münif Paşa's public map was intended to teach the inhabitants of Istanbul about a war that had a direct bearing on their lives, so too did Ottoman state schools in the Hamidian period attempt to effect a more direct identification between students and the empire to which they belonged.

The late Ottoman state saw public education as a means to construct a new basis of loyalty to the empire. The old arrangement by which individuals found themselves connected to the empire was the *millet* system. Although the reform decrees of the Tanzimat period insisted on the equality of all subjects, the state's attempts to reorganize the millets actually served to undermine the unifying intent of the reform

---

[4] İrade Dah. 61754. 12 Şevval 1294 (20 Oct. 1877).

edicts.[5] To replace confessionalism—and to forestall the divisive effect of increasingly separatist nationalisms—the Hamidian state sought to re-emphasize "Ottomanism," a construct intended to garner allegiance to the state and, by extension, to its ruler, the sultan.

In his ground-breaking article on late Ottoman attempts at image building, Selim Deringil discusses the importance of such symbols as the musical anthem, the coat of arms, the pilgrimage, and education in the empire's "mobilization" and "inclusion" effort (to use, as Deringil does, Anthony Smith's terms).[6] Deringil states that the resultant "public image of the state" formed the basis for its legitimization and its attempt to rally the loyalty of its subjects as potential citizens.

As Münif Paşa's project suggests, one additional area with important implications for the Ottoman attempt to effect identification with the state among its subjects is found in its use of maps. While music and heraldic imagery were marshaled to represent and to identify the empire, the rendering of the empire in map form provided an even more graphic form of representation. Of all the potential icons that can represent a state—flag, ruler, coat of arms, animal, and so on—the map offers perhaps the most direct impression. The personality cults that attempted to equate the state with the person of its ruler, for example, in the case of Mustafa Kemal Atatürk and Gamal 'Abd al-Nāṣir, developed later with the use of two- and three-dimensional imagery; the iconic value of the ruler became dominant only in the twentieth century. In the late Ottoman Empire the ruler was only indirectly present; only a relative few would see him on his way to Friday prayers in the vicinity of Yıldız Palace. But even if he was physically withdrawn, his symbolic presence was ubiquitous in the form of his monogram, chanted and calligraphic slogans proclaiming his long life, and the various fountains, schools, and libraries that he had bestowed upon the public. In retrospect, as will become apparent in the course of the present discussion, the late Ottoman state was beginning the process of attempting to effect a pattern of identification that would link its subjects to the geographical entity of the empire, with the state acting as the necessary intermediary. This process was inherently difficult,

---

[5] On the Tanzimat attempts to reorganize the millets, see Davison, *Reform*, 114–35.

[6] Selim Deringil, "Invention of Tradition," 329. See also Anthony D. Smith, *The Ethnic Origins of Nations* (Oxford: Blackwell, 1987).

given the almost complete absence of cartographic imagery available to Ottoman subjects prior to the elaboration of the state school system. Maps offered their inherent iconic and didactic capabilities in the service of the state's program.

In what follows I explore the ways the state used the science of geography to further that program. My focus is the map, the prime instrument of the technology of geography, because of the critical role that it plays in constructing identification between individuals and their territory.[7] On the face of it, representing a particular territory in the form of a map seems straightforward enough. Yet, choosing what is to be included (and what excluded), how territory should be represented, and what text, if any, should accompany the print—all require a bewildering array of decisions. The way these and other choices are made reflects both the way their maker sees the world and the way he wants it to be seen by others.[8] More scientifically stated, "the meaning and use of maps is, like all human actions, set in a cultural context of values and beliefs that reinforce, and are reinforced by, the act of mapping itself, *and* the people behind the scenes."[9] Understanding the Hamidian state's use of geography is critical to our comprehension of the overall effort to inculcate a new form of loyalty to the empire. Maps formed a critical part of that attempt, both because of their power to effect political identification and because, like the overall public education effort, they reveal the attractions and the risks of the state's initiative.

As we have seen, the Ottoman state was forward-looking in its educational policy. It saw the young generation as the natural place to begin inculcating the various aspects of its agenda—political, social, and moral. Schools were the obvious place to introduce and strengthen the ideals and concepts it sought to impart in order to establish long-term allegiance to the empire. Before turning to an analysis of the

[7] This chapter follows the notions of cartography employed by Thongchai Winichakul, *Siam Mapped: A History of the Geo-Body of a Nation* (Honolulu: University of Hawaii Press, 1994). Much of the theoretical understanding of his work relies on Robert David Sack, *Human Territoriality: Its Theory and History* (Cambridge: Cambridge University Press, 1986).

[8] Mark Monmonier, *How To Lie With Maps* (Chicago: The University of Chicago Press, 1991).

[9] Robert A. Rundstrom, "Mapping, Postmodernism, Indigenous People and the Changing Direction of North American Cartography," *Cartographica*, 28/2 (1991), 1.

school maps themselves, it is important to locate them in historical perspective, both in the broad scope of Ottoman cartography and in the more restricted context of Hamidian educational policy. Establishing this background will then allow us to distinguish those attributes of Hamidian state school maps that further past Ottoman practice from those that depart from it.

SCHOOL MAPS IN THE CONTEXT OF OTTOMAN CARTOGRAPHY

By the time of Abdülhamid II's accession in 1876, Ottoman cartography was nearly five centuries old.[10] In the long and varied tradition of Ottoman map-making, several features stand out. First, there was a strong tradition of state patronage. Ottoman map-making can be divided into two categories—that sponsored by the state and that sponsored or undertaken privately—but it is the former tradition that is obviously more germane to our discussion of maps in late Ottoman state schools. There is no known record of the Ottoman state's having used maps in its traditionally limited involvement in pedagogy. The state created maps for military, nautical, administrative, public works, and architectural purposes only. The second feature of the Ottoman cartographic tradition is that, as in the Islamic world generally, maps were usually not produced on their own but were adjunct to a larger text or manuscript. While a full spectrum in the relation of map to text did exist, spanning a range from complete subordination to a text at one extreme to independence of any text at the other, most could be described as falling on the side of subservience.[11] Ottoman high culture was largely textual.

Thirdly, the audience for which the maps were produced was generally very small and select, consisting of those individuals specifically involved in the issue at hand, such as navigating a sea passage,

---

[10] The following discussion of Ottoman cartography relies heavily on the articles by Ahmet T. Karamustafa in J. B. Harley and David Woodward (eds.), *The History of Cartography, Vol. 2, Book 1, Cartography in the Traditional Islamic and South Asian Societies* (Chicago: The University of Chicago Press, 1992).

[11] Karamustafa, "Introduction to Islamic Maps," in Harley and Woodward (eds.), *History of Cartography*, 5.

building a bridge, or administering a province. Even those produced for a more general purpose were restricted to the thin stratum of the urban cosmopolitan elite. Fourthly, Ottoman cartographers showed a sustained openness to adopting the techniques of foreign map-makers, most notably those of Western Europe but also occasionally of China. This tendency to borrow was particularly apparent in the early years of the empire as the Ottomans consolidated the formerly Byzantine lands. It was natural for them to adopt the techniques used by their neighboring and predecessor states. The trend toward adoption gathered momentum again toward the end of the eighteenth century for a quite different reason: "increasingly rapid assimilation of contemporary Western European cartographic practices into Ottoman culture almost completely squeezed out older 'traditional' patterns of map making."[12]

The late Ottoman use of maps for pedagogical purposes was novel, but not because of a lack of collective Ottoman experience with maps and map-making. Cartography was a science in which no small number of Ottoman subjects had excelled. Some, like Pirî Reis (d. 1554) and Kâtib Çelebi (d. 1657), incorporated the latest in European navigational findings and gained reputations that extended beyond the borders of the empire.[13] Indeed, one wonders whether it was precisely their having adopted the European standard of their day that has won them immortality in both European and modern Turkish historiography. The history of Ottoman cartography as currently written stops somewhere in the eighteenth century. Thereafter, European map-making takes over.[14]

Where do the maps that appeared in the new Ottoman state schools of the late nineteenth century stand within the empire's cartographic tradition? As products of an increasingly centralized government appa-

[12] Karamustafa, "Introduction to Ottoman Cartography," ibid. 206.

[13] On Pirî Reis and Kâtib Çelebi, see e.g. Halil İnalcık, *The Ottoman Empire: The Classical Age 1300–1600* (New Rochelle, NY: Caratzas, 1989), 180.

[14] It is practically impossible to find any specific information about late Ottoman cartography in the secondary literature. The one authority on Ottoman map-making dates the time of greatest Ottoman absorption of European cartographic influence to the eighteenth century, and places "the demise of traditional Ottoman military cartography about two centuries later, at the end of the nineteenth century." Ahmet T. Karamustafa, "Military, Administrative, and Scholarly Maps," in Harley and Woodward (eds.), *History of Cartography*, 213. His two other articles in the same volume provide a general introduction to Ottoman cartography.

ratus, they are consistent with the tradition of Ottoman state patronage. These maps were produced by military officials at the behest of
the central bureaucracy expressly for use in the state's schools. Furthermore, that many school maps were clearly versions adapted from
Western European models indicates that they represent a continuation
of the Ottoman tradition of incorporating the cartographic developments of other lands. Thus, in terms of state sponsorship and foreign
influence, the maps used in Ottoman state schools stood solidly within
Ottoman cartographic tradition.

In other respects, however, school maps of the Hamidian period represent a break with that tradition. Their lack of textual apparatus marks
their formal deviation from most of their cartographic precursors.
What little text they display in the way of title or legend is clearly sub-
ordinate to the map as visual image. Furthermore, the agenda behind
this project included the goal of expanding the number of Ottoman
subjects familiar with maps and able to read them. Students in the state-
run rüşdiye and idadî schools spent two hours per week in geography
class, the same amount of time their schedules devoted to such standard courses as Arabic, arithmetic, or history.[15] Cartographic literacy
was clearly an important objective of the Hamidian school system.

Ottoman school maps seem at first glance to confirm the ascendancy
of Western cartography; they share the major features of the typical
map produced during the nineteenth century in Western Europe. They
divide territory by continent, use lettering and colored shading to
demarcate political features, and include legends and scales—all easily
recognizable attributes of Western European cartography. In fact,
many maps and atlases produced in the Ottoman Empire during the
Hamidian period were "translations" into Ottoman Turkish of maps
originally produced in Western Europe. Of the many maps and atlases
available in the archives of Istanbul, many refer to their Western origin.
For example, a map of Europe dated 1308 AH (1890–1 CE) states in
its upper left-hand corner that, although it was produced with the
Ministry of Education's permission by two employees of the General

---

[15] *Salname-i Nezaret-i Maarif-i Umumiye* 2. defa. (Istanbul, 1317 [1899–1900]), 230.
Anecdotal evidence suggests that students in a number of higher schools in Istanbul were
engaged in map-making projects. See e.g. the student-drawn map of the Mekteb-i
Mülkiye on deposit in the Istanbul University Rare Book Library, 93583.

Staff in Istanbul, it was "a rendition of the latest map of the famous Kiepert."[16] Similarly, a world atlas produced in Istanbul in 1311 AH (1893–4 CE) by the same two General Staff cartographers acknowledges that it was a translation of the atlas organized by a commission of members of the French Geographical Society and produced by "the famous Hachette."[17] Such borrowings even extended to representations of Ottoman territory. A large cloth map of the empire produced by the General Staff in 1317 AH (1899–1900 CE) announces that it was patterned after "Kiepert's famous atlas."[18] (Fig. 9). Numerous other quite similar maps share these borrowed origins whether or not they acknowledge them in their legends.

Yet these maps and many others like them were produced by Ottoman cartographers working for the Ottoman government and were specifically intended for use in Ottoman state schools. In terms of their technique and modeling, they obviously bear a strong Western influence. Yet their source and function are clearly Ottoman. Yet whether they are "Ottoman" or "European" is largely immaterial. What is important is that by combining features associated with both traditions they represent the long-standing cartographic tradition of the Muslim world, a tradition which, as Karamustafa has shown, is one of synthesis. Once they are incorporated into the context of their new surroundings, the Ottoman state school classroom, their provenance is less relevant than the use to which they are put. The same is true of the various textbooks that we will discuss in the following chapter and, broadly speaking, of the entire notion of Ottoman importation of Western education.

[16] BOA, Harita, $13\frac{C_1}{3}$. These two cartographers, Ali Şeref Paşa and Mühiddin Bey, reappear frequently in connection with Hamidian map-making. "The famous Kiepert" is Heinrich Kiepert (1818–99), a geographer and cartographer of the classical world. He was particularly interested in Anatolia, traveling there four times between 1841 and 1888. His *Atlas von Hellas und den hellenischen Kolonien* (1846) and his *Karte des osmanischen Reiches in Asien* (1844 and 1869) established him as the foremost European authority on the area. *Encyclopædia Britannica*, 11th edn., s.v. "Kiepert, Heinrich."

[17] BOA, Harita, $3\frac{A}{1}$.

[18] My thanks are due to Mr Mühittin Eren for allowing me to examine this map in his gallery, *Ottomania*, in Tünel, Istanbul, in April 1995. A similar map, also dated 1317 AH and acknowledging its debt to Kiepert, can be found in the British Library map collection, 43305.(59.). See Fig. 9.

GEOGRAPHY IN LATE OTTOMAN EDUCATION

It is necessary, first of all, to place the subject of geographical instruction within the context of the history of late Ottoman education generally. Maps played an important role in articulating the late Ottoman worldview. This worldview was not static but, rather, one that changed considerably in the course of the transition from the Tanzimat to the Hamidian eras. Abdülhamid II inherited a fledgling school system that had been initiated during the Tanzimat. The earlier nineteenth-century Ottoman approach to education had largely been informed by the desire, so prevalent in that period, to emulate Western Europe. The 1869 Education Plan, the blueprint for the construction of an imperial public education system based largely on a report submitted by the French Education Ministry, epitomizes the European influence on Ottoman educational "reform."

While Abdülhamid II went to great lengths to implement the quantitative goals of the 1869 plan, his school system was qualitatively different in many respects. It was symptomatic of a larger process of rethinking the relationship between the empire and the West. In general, Abdülhamid II's policies reflect a distancing from the closer relations between the Porte and the European powers that obtained in the Tanzimat era. Engin Akarlı's work on Hamidian statecraft has shown how the Hamidian state used the European diplomatic process as a means to reduce European control over Ottoman affairs.[19] In some areas, as, for example, in the case of the Public Debt Administration or administrative reform in Macedonia, there was not much that the empire could do to diminish the control being exerted by the Great Powers.

Education, however, was one field where Hamidian policy could show a more independent bent. This independence increased over the course of Abdülhamid II's reign. As we have seen with curriculum reform, Hamidian educational policy represented significant movement away from the secular lesson plans inherited from the Tanzimat. While this policy continued to uphold the universalistic appeal of an educational system open to all Ottomans, several factors militated against the secular approach. First, the loss of the bulk of Ottoman

---

[19] Engin Deniz Akarlı, "Friction and Discord."

territory in Europe increased the Muslim percentage of the population in the remaining Ottoman lands.[20] Secondly, the increasing stridency of nationalist or proto-nationalist activity among the empire's minorities forced the state to adopt a less sanguine approach toward inter-communal education. Thirdly, the fact that missionary and millet educational offerings provided for almost all of the educational demand for the Christian and Jewish subjects of the empire meant that the state school system was increasingly seen as *de facto* Muslim. By this I mean both that the students enrolled in Ottoman state schools were overwhelmingly Muslim and that the culture that obtained in these institutions was increasingly Muslim as well. Fourthly, the preponderance of missionary and millet schools, combined with Ottoman suspicions of their underlying intentions, placed the Ottoman bureaucracy on the defensive. The resulting adversarial approach ensured that, as we have seen, Ottoman bureaucrats perceived the state schools as a means of defending its Muslim population—increasingly the bulwark of the state's loyalty base—against European and minority influence. Thus, the state attempted to foster allegiance to Ottomanism while increasingly emphasizing the pre-eminence of the Muslim component of such loyalty.

Abdülhamid II's policy in education, as in so many other areas, was to retain important elements of the European-inspired Tanzimat agenda, but to integrate these elements with those derived from the state's Islamic and Ottoman traditions. While it might be tempting to view such distinct influences as indicative of the dichotomous or even schizophrenic nature of the late Ottoman state,[21] a pragmatic explanation is more plausible. The Hamidian regime saw no reason to scrap

---

[20] The percentage of Muslims in the empire increased for two reasons: (1) the fact that the lands remaining in the empire's possession had larger Muslim populations than those lost in battle, and (2) the influx of Muslim refugees from the lands lost to Christian armies.

[21] As we have seen, the notion of cultural dualism in late Ottoman society has been addressed by some of the most prominent scholars in the field, including Niyazi Berkes, Carter V. Findley, and Şerif Mardin. What they mean generally is the split effected between those exposed to Western-style education and thought against those who received an Islamic education. In this context, the state schools are generally conceived of as contributing to this dichotomous situation. However, as our analysis of the state's conception of its schools and of the way in which it restructured their curriculum makes clear, Hamidian policy went to great lengths to synthesize the competing worldviews.

the fledgling school system it inherited from the Tanzimat. The success of the European states argued for emulating them, even if, or perhaps particularly because, the system that was copied in this case was of relatively recent date. All that was needed, Hamidian bureaucrats seem to have thought, was to make some adjustments of pedagogical content to ensure that what was imported accorded with the overall Ottoman agenda. A prime example of Hamidian curricular adjustment is the strong emphasis given to moral education, the subject of the next chapter. Properly refitted to coincide with the state's program, the school system was intended to combine the organization of the Western model with an Ottoman content designed among other things to foster loyalty to the state.

THE HAMIDIAN ATTITUDE TOWARD MAPS

In order to assess Ottoman school maps in this light, it is first necessary to describe the Hamidian approach to maps in general. Before we turn to some positive examples of how cartography was used in state schools, a few negative examples indicate Ottoman preoccupation with the adverse effects that could arise from maps produced outside of the control of the Ottoman state. Normally suspicious of uncensored texts, the Hamidian state was particularly alert to the dangers presented by those pertaining to geography.

The state's cartographic vigilance was particularly acute concerning maps and geographical texts produced in the West. One book concerning the geography of the Hijaz published in Istanbul in 1888–9 went so far as to alert its readers to the perfidy of foreign maps.[22] In a brief appendix following the text, the historian and major general Eyyub Sabrî included the following: "Warning—When some European maps are studied, many errors and flagrant mistakes are visible in the colors and markings that indicate the sovereignty of the places named in the explanatory text."[23] For example, it was pointed out in 1891 that a geography textbook widely in use in the Ottoman

---

[22] Eyyub Sabrî, *Mir'at ül-Haremeyn* (Kostantiniye [Istanbul]: Bahriye Matbaası, 1306 [1888–9]). On Eyyub Sabrî, see *Türk Dili ve Edebiyatı Ansiklopedisi*, iii. 133–4 (art. Eyyub Sabrî Paşa). I thank Şükrü Hanioğlu for bringing this item to my attention.

[23] Eyyub Sabrî, *Mir'at ül-Haremeyn*, 329.

school system contained false and corrupting information.[24] This was the book entitled *Mufassal Coğrafya* (Comprehensive Geography) written by the Frenchman Cortambert.[25] The offending issue was the way Ottoman Asia was divided in the text, although the memorandum provides no specific information as to what was objectionable. A geography teacher from a rüşdiye school in Istanbul had petitioned to request that the textbook be removed from circulation, lest it deceive any naive students and, further, because it was being used by students in most of the empire's higher-level and idadî schools. Another case from the same period shows that geography texts and atlases imported from France for use in an Armenian Catholic school in Erzurum had been seized by customs officials.[26] These works were impounded because they contained "harmful ideas" and were "in contravention of the order given by the Education Ministry." Other examples abound which reveal the state's interest in cartographic accuracy, particularly where the borders of the empire are concerned. Whether acting to ensure the accuracy of a newly printed set of maps showing the border with Greece,[27] demonstrating concern over a Russian map of a section of Ottoman Europe and its border with Serbia,[28] or acting to ban a Bulgarian geography textbook that contained geographical divisions deemed to be contrary to the Ottoman state,[29] the central government was both alert to and wary of maps produced outside of its control.

The Ottoman state's own efforts at representing the world reveal a similar attention to detail. Consider a seemingly simple development: the introduction of wall maps in school classrooms. This fact, innocu-

---

[24] AYN 1428, 390. 20 Cemaziyelevvel 1309 (22 Dec. 1891).

[25] Presumably a translation into Ottoman Turkish of Pierre-François-Eugène Cortambert, *Cours de géographie, comprenant la description physique et politique et la géographie historique des diverses contrées du globe* (Paris: Hachette, various edns. 1846–93). This information is taken from *Catalogue général des livres imprimés de la Bibliothèque nationale—Auteurs, Ministère de l'instruction publique et des Beaux-Arts, tome XXXII* (Paris: Imprimerie nationale, 1907), 738 ff. Cortambert (1805–81) authored and edited a large number of works on geography. My thanks are due to Charif Kiwan for making this information available to me.

[26] AYN 1428, 326, 4 Cemaziyelevvel 1309 (6 Dec. 1891).

[27] Y Mtv. 185/8. 3 Şaban 1316 (17 Dec. 1898).

[28] Y Mtv. 189/108. 15 Zilhicce 1316 (26 Apr. 1899).

[29] Mahir Aydın, *Şarkî Rumeli Vilâyeti*, Türk Tarih Kurumu Yayınları 14/12 (Ankara: Türk Tarih Kurumu, 1992), 218. For yet another example, see Deringil, *Well-Protected Domains*, 95.

ous though it may seem on the face of it, is of central importance to
our discussion for two reasons. First, the very presence of any sort of
illustration in the classroom was both historically unprecedented and,
as we have seen with the anecdote about the violent reaction produced
by the introduction of maps in the rüşdiye schools mentioned earlier
in this chapter, potentially incendiary.

The second reason the schools' wall maps were important derives
from the way they were constructed. Photographic and archival evidence shows that, for the most part, the first Ottoman pedagogical
maps depicted the territory of the earth by dividing it into continents
and representing each continent on a separate map.[30] While there was
a strong Ottoman tradition of classifying territory by continent for
administrative purposes,[31] isolating the world in visual fashion into
separate continents made little sense for an empire whose dominion
extended over land on three continents. Division by continent effectively truncated the lands of the empire. Moreover, as all Ottoman
territory lay on the edges of three continents, focusing on them
individually ensured that Ottoman territory be relegated to the maps'
margins. Although the way the maps were bordered often permitted
Ottoman possessions on a contiguous continent to fit into the frame,
the colored shading of the continent chosen for attention renders it
virtually impossible for the viewer to gain any sense of the integrity of
Ottoman territory. For example, a school map of Asia produced for
the empire's rüşdiye and idadî schools in 1897–8 includes most of the
European portion of the empire as well, in its upper left-hand corner.[32]
But because the map emphasizes only the Asian portion of the
empire—by coloring it pink, marking its distinguishing features with
topographic shading, identifying its bodies of water, cities, and so on—

---

[30] For one of the many instances of archival evidence of continent maps, see e.g. BEO
83073 and İrade Dah. 60285. Numerous requests for new maps to replace supplies that
have run out refer specifically to maps which are to represent one of the "five continents."
Before the mid-1890s school maps depicting the Ottoman Empire *per se* were generally
limited to atlases and therefore did not appear on classroom walls.

[31] The chief distinction made was that separating the European provinces (*Rumeli
vilayetleri*) from those in Asia (*Anadolu vilayetleri*).

[32] Istanbul University Rare Book Library (IU), Map Collection, 92456. This map states
that it was produced by Ali Şeref Paşa who, along with his assistant, produced the 1890–1
map of Europe based on Kiepert. It is therefore possible that these later maps were also
based on the work of that German geographer.

6. School map of Asia. Until the 1890s, continentally divided maps were the
norm in Ottoman schools. (Source: Istanbul University Rare Book Library)

and leaves the African and European lands unshaded and devoid of
political and geographic detail, all sense of sovereign continuity is
lost (Figs. 6 and 7). A companion map of Europe produced the previous year treats territory in much the same way.[33] Such maps offer no
indication that Ottoman rule held sway over land on three continents.

Why were these maps drawn in this way? While there is a general
dearth of scholarship concerning late Ottoman cartography, it can
safely be assumed that Ottoman map-makers were following European
practice. To begin with, the military was the sole source for maps used
in the empire's schools. The Ottoman military was, after all, precisely
that institution which had a tradition of borrowing heavily from the

[33] IU 92455. This map offers more detail concerning marginal territory than the
example mentioned above. For example, it does show the topography of North Africa
and Anatolia. However, the only areas that receive full shading are those that fall within
the limits of Europe. Ottoman territories outside Europe are, to the extent that they fit
inside the map's borders, delineated by a thin pink outline.

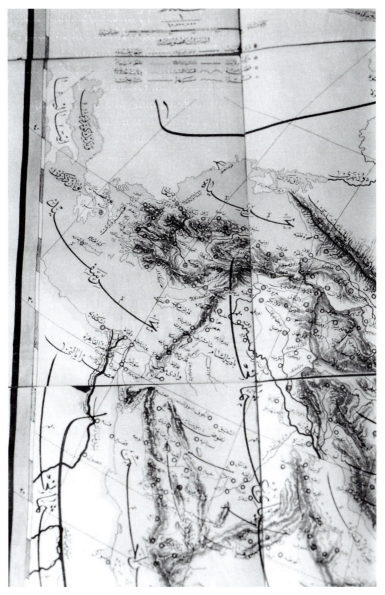

7. School map of Asia, detail. Note the lack of detail accorded the European portions of the empire, which are left virtually blank. (Source: Istanbul University Rare Book Library)

West, particularly in the area of technology, and had been doing so the longest. In the case of cartography, the military had been training cartographers domestically and sending them to England, France, and Prussia since the establishment of the War College (Harb Okulu) in 1834. In 1880 the Fifth Department of the General Staff was established in order to produce maps for the empire.[34] In 1895 archival evidence shows the Ottoman military importing experts and map-making equipment from Europe and convening a Map Commission.[35] In the late nineteenth century the influence of Western European cartography was paramount in the Ottoman military, the official source of the empire's maps.

In fact, as we have already noted, the tradition of importing Western techniques went back many centuries. Some of the most celebrated Ottoman cartographers were those, like Pirî Reis and Kâtib Çelebi, who adapted Western advances to meet the needs of the Ottoman state. Their maps and those of others generally owed their existence to such practical applications as navigation or military preparedness. The maps produced for the late Ottoman schools did have a utilitarian function, that is, pedagogy, but the way they were drawn contradicted the state's attempt to fashion a single imperial affiliation. In the Ottoman context the artificiality of dividing land by continents is clear: it necessitates the fracturing of the very political entity toward which the young subjects and proto-citizens were being asked to turn their loyalty.

In the European context, the continental approach makes more sense. This is so for geographical, political, and philosophical reasons. Geographically, it was (and remains) in the interest of Europeans to promote the notion of division by continents precisely because of the artificiality of Europe's own claim to be a continent. Politically, the magnitude of the colonial experience in the collective history of modern Europe demands that attention be paid to overseas (that is, non-European) possessions. This is just as true in the cartographic sense as it is in any other, and probably more so. British fondness for that part of the world colored pink on their nineteenth-century maps is well known. Maps and atlases in schools and through the popular

---

[34] Binark et al., Başbakanlık, 443.
[35] e.g. Y Mtv. 125/60. 7 Safer 1313 (30 July 1895); and Y Mtv. 132/211. 28 Cemaziyelevvel 1313 (16 Dec. 1895); Binark et al., Başbakanlık, 443.

press imparted knowledge of and pride in overseas domains over which "the sun never set." It is interesting to note in this context that Ottoman state cartographers also used the color pink to denote "the protected possessions."

But while the imperial agenda demanded maps that would display the entire globe, there was a simultaneous move in the other direction, namely, toward a taxonomic approach to territory. For related to this inculcated sense of politico-geographic mastery is a philosophical construct. The rational, positivist mode of thinking so prominent in Western Europe in the nineteenth century—and so attractive to many an Ottoman thinker as well—was bent on dividing up the things of the world, the better to analyze them. Ernest Gellner has described this tendency to separate as the "unitary conceptual currency" of the modern world. In the West, he argues, we refer to "one coherent world" in which it is legitimate to relate one thing to another and to separate things for analysis.[36] "Equalization and homogenization of facts is incomplete unless accompanied by what may be called the separation of all separables, the esprit d'analyse, the breaking up of all complexes into their constituent parts . . ."[37] While in the European geographical context it might make sense philosophically to divide the globe into continents, in the Ottoman Empire this approach produced tension between the unifying attempt of official rhetoric and the splintered representation of Ottoman territory displayed on the walls of the state's schools. The way its territory was framed was out of step with the empire's efforts to unify its far-flung lands.

The paradox represented by the presence of the continental maps illustrates the dislocations associated with establishing a system that had the blessing, or curse, of being simultaneously foreign and new. In hindsight such an inconsistency seems peculiar, yet it is easy to see how the Western mode was adapted—and how such a tension could come about. The curriculum of the new schools, at least initially borrowing heavily from Europe, emphasized geographical pedagogy and enlisted maps and textbooks to this end. This curriculum naturally approached geography on the basis of the Western analytical approach; even the lessons on Ottoman territory were organized continent by continent—

---

[36] Ernest Gellner, *Nations and Nationalism* (Ithaca, NY: Cornell University Press, 1983), 21–2.   [37] Ibid. 22.

first Europe, and then Asia and Africa.[38] As we have seen, the maps used in this endeavor owed much to European cartography. Their inclusion in the late Ottoman school project reflects pragmatism and inertia more than it does the official ideology of the Hamidian state. Due to the more pressing fiscal and financial concerns of the early years of his rule, Abdülhamid II was unable to devote much attention to the question of education until after the initial crises of his reign—war with Russia, fiscal insolvency, and so on—had subsided. In the meantime, the Tanzimat approach continued to hold sway by default. With respect to geographical pedagogy, the persistence of the Western ways of perceiving and presenting the world typical of the Tanzimat can be seen in a number of instances. We have referred above to the incorporation of maps and atlases of Western European provenance into the Ottoman educational endeavor. In this context, the epitome of this sort of borrowing must be the use of maps arranged according to the continents. Indeed, this borrowing made good practical sense.

   With the coming of the Hamidian period, however, the state demonstrated a new awareness of the power that maps could bring to furthering its agenda. There is a sense that, more than being a device made indispensable by the perceived necessity of imitating the sources of Western "progress," maps were a tool that could aid the state's effort to educate its subjects. The Hamidian period introduced a way of presenting territory—particularly Ottoman territory—that was more consonant with its overarching imperial agenda.

IMPERIAL SCHOOL MAPS

The maps designed to be hung in the classrooms of the state schools provide the most important set of cartographic images produced for the schools. There were, of course, maps to be found in atlases and geography textbooks as well.[39] Many of these were inspired by

---

[38] *Salname-i Nezaret-i Maarif-i Umumiye* 2. defa. (Istanbul, 1317 [1899–1900]), 288 ff.

[39] An early example of a document that refers to such a text is İrade Dah. 60285 which dates from Nov. 1876. This decree grants the education minister permission to replenish the stocks of a text entitled *Coğrafya-yı sagir*, intended for the lower primary (*sıbyanî*) schools, which contains maps of the five continents as well as a map of the Ottoman Empire in its entirety.

European works, and sometimes were actual translations. Here we are concerned specifically with wall maps, clearly the most public form of cartography possible after the three-dimensional offering of Münif Paşa's project discussed above. Because they were mostly non-retractable, these permanently visible wall maps played a critical role in shaping the students' geographical imagination, as we shall see shortly.

Unlike school textbooks, which frequently announce on their title-pages that they were published for use in a certain school or even a certain grade level, state-produced maps provide far less detail about their *raison d'être*. However, several circumstances make it possible to identify specific maps as having been used in the Ottoman school system. First of all, there exists a series of photographs which show maps in use in a school built during the reign of Abdülhamid II.[40] This is, as far as I am aware, the only instance of school maps photographed *in situ* during this period. These are photographs taken of a girls' rüşdiye in Yanya (Janina), which shows interior photographs of the school's various classrooms. Each photograph reveals a classroom with chairs and desks arranged in rows facing the raised teacher's desk. Behind the teacher's desk and to the side hangs a map depicting a particular continent (Fig. 8). (Occasionally, a blackboard or a second continental map is also present.) Each room shows a different map. The continental maps pictured in these photographs appear to be the same type as those extant in the map collection of Istanbul University. Secondly, the sheer size of the orders that the Education Ministry was placing for school maps makes it clear that they were being purchased for the entire school system. Orders were typically approved for the purchase of 5,000 units of each map in the set of continents, a number that would easily include all the state's rüşdiye and idadî schools.[41] Orders made to replace depleted Education Ministry stocks were generally made in lots of 500 and frequently reached the size of 3,000 units.[42] Thirdly, using descriptions in documents and literature (see below), it is possible to link the school maps we have identified with their descriptions.

[40] The photographs can be found in BOA, YEE 12/151 and IU 90496.

[41] e.g. İrade Dah. 60285, an order for 5,000 sets of maps of Europe, Asia, Africa, America, and Australia. 12 Zilkade 1293 (29 Nov. 1876).

[42] İrade Dah. 97584, 24 Safer 1309 (29 Sept. 1891).

8. Continental school map *in situ*. A rare photograph of a school interior, showing the maps in use in a primary school in the Balkans. (Source: Istanbul University Rare Book Library)

The most striking cartographic change to be observed in Hamidian cartography is the wide-scale introduction of maps depicting the Ottoman Empire in its entirety. While this might not sound like a momentous break with tradition, it nevertheless marked a decisive change from the practice of the Tanzimat period. Prior to the middle of the last decade of the nineteenth century, Ottoman state school maps were, as we have seen, overwhelmingly organized by continent. Despite the extreme unsuitability of such territorial division for an empire encompassing land on three continents, the maps that the Education Ministry sent out to its schools throughout the provinces followed the European custom of continental demarcation. Thus, the maps drawn to incorporate all Ottoman land inside a single border on three continents that were assigned to the schools in the 1900s marked an important cartographic milestone. Benedict Anderson has described such maps by the terms "map-as-logo" or "logo map," by which he means that the specific shape of a state's territory comes to represent its politico-historical entity.[43] Anderson uses the simile of "a detachable piece of a jigsaw puzzle" to describe the way such maps define a territory as unitary vis-à-vis its neighbors and the rest of the globe. Thongchai Winichakul goes further, coining the term "geo-body" to refer to the construct which includes a nation's "territory, and its related values and practices" created through the confrontations and displacements of geography.[44] Both Anderson and Thongchai discuss the use of maps solely in the context of colonialism in South-East Asia, but what they have to say can be applied to maps and their relations to territory generally. One effect of such a "national" map is the unspoken but powerful way it compels its viewers to identify with the political entity therein embodied and displayed. The map insists on the importance of the shape of the territory, and this shape begins to assume tremendous political importance as emblematic for the territory in question.

Like many features of the Hamidian educational system that gradually replaced much of the inherited Tanzimat-era components, Ottoman logo maps were relatively slow to appear in the schools. In the meantime, the continental maps continued to hold sway. This situation changed in the mid-1890s. Although concerned to correct the ways the empire's borders were drawn in European maps, as late as 1894 the Ministry of Education was still requesting funds for the printing of continental maps based on European originals to be used in the provincial schools.[45] By 1896, however, the new logo maps had

---

[43] Benedict R. O'G. Anderson, *Imagined Communities: Reflections on the Origin and Spread of Nationalism* (London: Verso, 1991), 175. Anderson acknowledges the influence of the dissertation written by Thongchai Winichakul. This research, since published as *Siam Mapped: A History of the Geo-Body of a Nation*, builds on Anderson's notion of the imagined community but ultimately insists on the power of geography to shape the national construct. Several parallels between Thailand and the Ottoman Empire in this period (no direct, but decisive indirect, colonial control; selective official importation of Western culture; the long reign of a powerful king in the late nineteenth and early twentieth centuries; and the displacement of an older geography by the new) make for suggestive comparison.

[44] Thongchai Winichakul, *Siam Mapped*, p. x.

[45] ŞD 213/38. 22 Cemaziyelevvel 1312 (21 Nov. 1894). It is interesting to note that this document singles out the borders of Eastern Rumelia as a cause for concern in the maps published in Paris by Hachette. Eastern Rumelia had been annexed by Bulgaria in 1885, but the empire remained loath to admit this almost a decade later. This document shows that concern with cartographic accuracy was sufficient to warrant the formation of a

reached the provincial schools. Following a Sultanic decree, the old continental maps were withdrawn and a new map depicting all Ottoman territory was commissioned.[46] The serasker confirmed that he had complied with the decree; the offending maps had been gathered, he reported, and the new imperial map was produced by the General Staff in a six-panel format.

With the passage of time, the state placed increasing emphasis on creating school maps that expressly represented the empire. Although the education bureaucracy continued the old policy of requesting continental maps for its expanding system,[47] new maps that focused on the Ottoman Empire were also displayed in the schools from the mid-1890s onward. A prime example of the map of the empire used in state schools was produced at the turn of the century and was based on Kiepert.[48] For example, in April 1903 the Financial Bureau of the Council of State (Şura-yı Devlet) approved the requisition of 5,000 maps "combining Ottoman Europe, Asia, and Africa" to be used in the primary schools.[49] This was a continuation of the trend toward producing maps that suited Ottoman, as opposed to European, needs.

Moreover, the terms under which such imperial logo maps were to be drafted indicate that the state was becoming more actively involved in the specific details of the cartographic process. In this case, the mapmakers were required to use a previously existing map of the empire as their model. The same document stipulates that the map-makers include the names of rivers, mountains, and territories (bilâd), and show railroads, and even ordains the type of script to be used in cartographic labeling.[50] Once a sample was produced, it was to be checked against the model. Then it was to be printed according to precise terms; to be comprised of four large panels, to include a scale, divisions,

commission to determine that school maps, like textbooks, meet official scrutiny before being allowed into the schools. The commission mentioned here was chaired by Abdurrahman Şeref (1835–1925), then director of the Mekteb-i Mülkiye. Perhaps due to his influence, maps for the provincial idadî schools were selected on the basis of those in use in the Mülkiye.

[46] Y Mtv. 181/62. 16 Rebiülahir 1316 (3 Sept. 1898).

[47] See e.g. Y Mtv. 205/107, which shows that continent maps were still being procured for the walls of rüşdiye and idadî schools in August 1908.

[48] It is dated 1317 AH (1899–1900 CE). A good example of this sort of map can be seen in Fig. 9.

[49] YA Res. 120/53. 27 Muharrem 1321 (25 Apr. 1903).   [50] Ibid.

Hamidian map of the Ottoman Empire. Now the empire appears complete. (Source: The British Library)

colors, and writing, all of which were to be produced in accordance with the model. The document further stipulates that the maps be submitted within three months and even dictates the precise financial terms of the transaction, including budgetary source of the funding and the price and rate of exchange to be used.[51]

Noteworthy is the emphasis placed on providing students with geographic knowledge of the empire, even at the primary level. Conforming with the curriculum, which had been reformed only the previous year, in 1902,[52] students were to be taught an abridged version of Ottoman geography at the ibtidaî level. The depth of instruction would be increased as the students progressed to the rüşdiye and idadî levels. The state was acting to ensure that its students were geographically literate.

Maps designed for students increasingly clung to the fig-leaf of the empire's *de jure* borders. Just as official documents speak of the need for vigilance against European attempts to slight Ottoman territory, the Ottomans' own maps frequently present a more favorable logo map than actual jurisdiction would justify. For example, a pocket-sized Ottoman atlas approved by the Ministry of Education in 1906 and published the following year presents a rather fanciful view of the extent of Ottoman dominion.[53] The pink of Ottoman sovereignty is extended to include "Tunus emareti," whereas Tunis had been occupied by France since 1881. Likewise, Egypt is presented as Ottoman, even though Ottoman rule was little more than a legal fiction after the British military occupation of 1882.[54] Bulgaria is treated as an Ottoman tributary, and Eastern Rumelia, annexed by Bulgaria in 1885, is presented as a province of the empire like any other. The province of Yemen is drawn without regard for the British presence in Aden or the Hadramawt. An American who was present in Istanbul during the transition from Hamidian to Young Turk rule recorded his observations concerning the maps in use at the idadî school in the Kabataş section of the capital: "I was shown here a map of Europe, used in the geography classes, upon

[51] YA Res. 120/53. 27 Muharrem 1321 (25 Apr. 1903).   [52] BEO 178072.

[53] Tüccarzade İbrahim Hilmî, *Memâlik-i Osmaniye Cep Atlası* (Istanbul: İbrahim Hilmî, 1323 [1907]).

[54] Diplomatically, the Ottoman position in Egypt was on occasion surprisingly influential. See Deringil, "The Ottoman Response to the Egyptian Crisis of 1881–2," *Middle Eastern Studies*, 24 (1988), 3–24.

which Greece, Egypt and the Balkan states were colored as belonging
to Turkey. The Orientals do not like to face facts."[55] As we will see
below, such an exaggerated view of Ottoman dominion, while tempting for propaganda purposes, could produce unforeseen problems for
the state when students began to realize the *de facto* situation.

The Hamidian use of school maps adds to our overall understanding of the state's agenda during this period. Increasingly interested in
fostering a sense of unity among its subjects, the late Ottoman state
recognized the attractive utility and concision of the map format. In
keeping with its abiding desire for control, the government was
extremely careful about the presentation of its territory in cartographic
form. Moreover, by insisting on maps that focused attention on the
empire as a whole, as opposed to divided among separate continents,
the Hamidian state was reinforcing the notion of Ottoman territoriality in a fixed geographical space and communicating that notion to
the young generation. While the state did allow continental maps to
remain in place in the classroom after their Ottomanized analogs had
been distributed, this may be attributed in part to a practicality that
was loath to abandon costly materials. It may also be explained by the
broad notion of synthesis that informed much of Hamidian educational policy. That such maps were drawn on a European model is
perhaps also the reason for their longevity in a system that was in many
ways an attempt to beat the West at its own game, playing by its own
rules and often deferring to its standards and style. Nevertheless, it
is clear that by altering the way its own territory was framed, the
Hamidian state was aware of the need to strengthen its image and to
convey that newly sharpened image to the empire's youth. How that
image was received is the subject to which I now turn.

A MAP IN MEMORY

So far the discussion has approached the question of Hamidian school
maps from the vantage-point provided by contemporary artefacts. Due
to their limited number and to the dearth of secondary works on this
subject, the scope of the discussion was expanded so as to include references to maps in schools other than those at the idadî level. Such an

---

[55] Stanwood Cobb, *The Real Turk* (Boston: The Pilgrim Press, 1914), 136.

expansion is possible because of the single source of the Ottoman educational map, the military. Maps produced for all levels of schools, both civil and military, were created by the military establishment. All evidence points to the fact that similar maps were used at the various state school levels. Furthermore, descriptions of maps found in the documents jibe with available extant maps and those visible in the photographs of schools in the photograph collection of Abdülhamid II. As we have seen, a fair amount of information about the state's agenda can be gleaned from these sources.

What is more difficult to evince is the effect that these maps had on the students who studied them. In fact, it is one of the principle frustrations of a project such as this one that, while much can be learned about the state's agenda from an examination of archival records and teaching materials, the effect of the schooling process on the student remains largely opaque. There is one type of source which, although fraught with historiographical liability, can help to elicit an understanding of the student's perspective. This is the memoir or autobiography, a genre the use of which requires great care even in the best of conditions due to the inherent problems of memory and the passage of time. Because of the time-lag involved, any memoirs written by former students of the Hamidian state schools are perforce written in a very different political milieu.[56] There were a number of critical events that require us to treat such memoirs with caution: the break-up of the empire; the demise of the Caliphate; the emergence of full-blown nationalist sentiment; and the birth of successor states that almost invariably generated either a disparaging or a nostalgic view of the Ottoman Empire. Nevertheless, memoirs offer a variety of anecdotal information which they alone can provide.

There exists one example of this genre that bears directly on our attempt to understand the effects of late Ottoman educational cartography. This is the story of Şevket Süreyya Aydemir, who published his autobiography entitled *Suyu Arayan Adam* (The Man in Search of Water) in 1959.[57] Aydemir's life is an interesting one, the path of which

---

[56] On the problems and potential of autobiographical sources for the study of this period see my "Education and Autobiography."

[57] Şevket Süreyya Aydemir, *Suyu Arayan Adam* (Ankara: Öz Yayınları, 1959). For the details of his life and works, see Louis Mitler, *Contemporary Turkish Writers: A Critical Bio-bibliography of Leading Writers of the Turkish Republican Period up to 1980*

is suggestive of the broad transformations involved in the emergence of the nationalist out of the imperial milieu. Born in Edirne in 1897 to a recently settled migrant family from the Danube region, Şevket Süreyya attended the military rüşdiye there between 1907 and 1910. After serving in the Ottoman army during World War I in the Caucasus, he remained in Russian Azerbayjan to teach school after the war. Influenced by the Bolshevik Revolution, he became a Marxist and received a degree in economics in Moscow in 1920. After returning to the Turkish Republic, he ran afoul of the authorities and was imprisoned. He transformed himself into a nationalist and served in the Education and Finance ministries. He is perhaps best remembered for his biography of Mustafa Kemal Atatürk, entitled *Tek Adam* (One Man Alone).

Important for our discussion of cartography is his description of the way the map in his school classroom in the 1900s affected the development of his political consciousness. The fact that Şevket Süreyya attended a military and not a civil school raises the question of whether or not it can be considered germane to this discussion. The curricular difference between these parallel sets of institutions was, however, not as great as might be imagined, particularly after the movement to unify the civil and military branches of the state educational program in 1891. The most important area of distinction appears to have been one of culture. Students in the military schools performed military drill and imbibed an atmosphere rich with military tradition. Still, the similarities were remarkable. In both sets of institutions the students dressed in uniform, recited slogans such as "Long live the sultan!" (padişahım çok yaşa), and participated in an ordered daily routine best described as regimented. Generally, then, the differences between the schools were not so great as to preclude referring to the memoirs of a military student. As to the specific question of the validity of Aydemir's experience vis-à-vis school maps, there is one important qualification that must be made. Whereas in civil school classrooms the maps were the only visual material, apart from the blackboard, maps in the military

(Bloomington: Indiana University Research Institute for Inner Asian Studies, 1988), 48–9; Osman Nebioğlu, *Türkiye'de Kim Kimdir: Yaşayan Tanınmış Kimseler Ansiklopedisi* (Istanbul: Nebioğlu Yayınevi, 1961–2), 98; and Şerif Mardin, "The Ottoman Empire," in Karen Barkey and Mark von Hagen (eds.), *After Empire: Multiethnic Societies and Nation-building* (Boulder, Co.: Westview, 1997), 117–18.

schools were displayed along with pictures of military heroes drawn from both Ottoman and non-Ottoman history. In the military school context, the map of the Ottoman empire could thus have hung along-side a picture of Mehmed the Conqueror or Napoleon. The juxtaposition of visual material intended, presumably, to inspire military greatness with that intended to teach geographical familiarity with the empire ensured an altered learning atmosphere when compared with that of the civil schools. It does not require a leap into the psychology of the subconscious to guess at the effect of the powerful interplay of these visual images. The atmosphere of military success must have infused the representation of Ottoman territory and vice versa. At the very least, the milieu in which information from the map was obtained marks the military experience as distinct. That being said, there were important commonalities with the civil school experience, including the fact that maps manufactured for both the civil and military schools were produced by the Ottoman military.

In any event, Şevket Süreyya's description of the map of the Ottoman Empire prominently displayed in his classroom in Edirne confirms our understanding of the type of school maps in use in this period. He recalls that "on the maps which hung on the classroom walls, the territory of this great empire was shown with a pale pink hue."[58] The imperial maps introduced by the Hamidian state were designed, as we know, to foster identification with the empire on the part of the student. To this end they used color (pink, like the British) and a central geographic focus to create a unified image of the empire. In the case of Şevket Süreyya, the result was a strong affinity between pupil and empire, which he remembers learning to think of as "the Ottoman state, that is, our state." The thought process he describes in his memoir led him to identify himself entirely with the state and its cause, even to the point of willingness to sacrifice his own life. While the civil schools never sought to elicit such dramatic results, they were interested in fostering a sense of collective dedication to the Ottoman cause. Once Şevket Süreyya's identification with the empire was complete—"the state meant everything to me"—it was natural for him to feel the perceived slights against the Ottoman Empire as personal. He relates that at first the Ottoman territories as presented on the map

[58] Aydemir, *Suyu Arayan Adam*, 45.

seemed as wide as the world. However, they also began to seem narrow when compared with the territories that had been under Ottoman sovereignty in the past. He made the inevitable comparison between earlier and present imperial borders:

These lands even seemed few. Among the children who gathered before the maps between classes, I traced the border of the countries that had been broken off from our land (and naturally unjustly broken off): the Caucasus, the Crimea, Bessarabia, Romania, the Danubian provinces, even Algeria and the countries of the Atlas [i.e. Morocco] smoldered in all of our imaginations.[59]

Aydemir goes on to recount how such imagining kindled his desire to restore the former territories to the empire and to suppress the uprisings that were breaking out against it.

Although perhaps to a lesser degree, repeated reference to maps of the empire must have produced a similar reaction among students in the civil schools. It is the natural and perhaps necessary intent of military education to inculcate a deep sense of loyalty and sacrifice; such attempts are the *sine qua non* of military training. The similarities in the curricula of these parallel sets of institutions, however, compel us to look at the broader implications of the message that they were respectively imparting. Beyond the specific tasks that these institutions were charged with, in other words, military, civil, and bureaucratic preparedness, there were more general, and thus in some ways more important, lessons to be imparted. Some of the probable consequences were intended, but others were not. It is in helping us to theorize about the thought processes provoked by exposure to a new pedagogical tool such as the map that the memoir of Şevket Süreyya Aydemir is so helpful. Whether or not his experience can be accepted as valid for most students, either in military or civil schools, is debatable. Its chief merit is that, by allowing us to glimpse the suggestive effect of such material upon just one individual, it enables us at least to consider a wider array of potential understandings.

Here it is necessary to recall that the supply of maps to the growing number of students in state-run schools constituted an important phase in the long-term continuum of Ottoman mapping, a continuum that moved from a period when the majority of those who perceived the

[59] Ibid. 46.

physical territory of the empire did so without the aid of cartographic imagery, toward an era when maps would become routine. For most of Ottoman history the number of Ottoman subjects having recourse to maps was extremely restricted. The chief images available to those pondering imperial territory were verbal. Prime among these were the phrases "Memalik-i Mahruse-i Şahane," the divinely protected imperial possessions, and "Memalik-i Osmaniye," the Ottoman possessions. These terms left no distinct impression of what constituted Ottoman lands, other than the fact that they were plural, protected, and per- tained to the House of Osman. It made no claim for any specific piece of territory; on the contrary, this appellation could presumably be made to apply to any territory under Ottoman jurisdiction.

State-supplied cartography did not eliminate this verbal image of Ottoman territory. In fact, school map-makers labeled the empire with some variant of the traditional name, such as General Map of the Impe- rial Possessions (*Umum Memalik-i Şahane Haritası*).[60] Yet Hamidian school maps represent a turning-point in the Ottoman cartographic tradition. By supplying the technology of the map on a large scale for the first time, the state ensured that the (carto)graphic image of territory would replace the verbal; a "map consciousness" was being created.[61] This would have two main effects. First, the introduction of Ottoman logo maps allowed those who studied them to see their political and geographical milieu in two-dimensional terms. Students in, say, Salonika, Erzurum, or Baghdad could now see their own posi- tion both with respect to the capital and with respect to their fellow subjects in other provinces, most of which doubtless had been mere abstractions before the map's arrival. Secondly, observers could now be encouraged to look beyond the borders of their own locality and to perceive the relative position of their province and country in world perspective.

In their study of mental geography, Peter Gould and Rodney White demonstrate the importance of relative spatial perception on

---

[60] Tüccarzade İbrahim Hilmî, *Memalik-i Osmaniye Cep Atlası* (Istanbul: İbrahim Hilmî, 1323 [1905–6]); BL Map Library 43305 (59).

[61] For a discussion of the development of "map consciousness" in early modern Europe, see David Buisseret (ed.), *Monarchs, Ministers, and Maps: The Emergence of Cartography as a Tool of Government in Early Modern Europe* (Chicago: University of Chicago Press, 1992), 1–2.

individuals' familiarity with their own geographic and socio-political entities.[62] While we have nothing like the data they have available for their study, which draws upon contemporary surveys, it is nevertheless possible to apply their approach suggestively to the late Ottoman period. Gould and White construct maps based upon the awareness and preferences of the people they studied in a variety of locations on the globe. Their work shows that, while all people "know" the maps of the countries where they live, they tend to exhibit greatly differing awareness of regions other than their own. The "isographs" Gould and White construct for a particular country are their approximations of the mental maps of their subjects. They are therefore a scientifically derived version of Saul Steinberg's well-known and often imitated cover illustration for the *New Yorker* magazine suggesting a stereotypical New Yorker's distorted and self-centered view of the world.[63]

Consider the mental maps of Ottoman subjects in the Hamidian period. Although we can only hypothesize about them, it is fair to say that the widespread adoption of the map, chief instrument of geographic science, must have altered their composition. By providing a two-dimensional display of the empire, the map confronted its viewers with specific locations for the towns, cities, mountains, rivers, and so on that he or she had only previously seen physically or imagined with the help of verbal description. Perhaps the north-as-up orientation of the new maps also forced some readjusting of mental geographic arrangements. Moreover, the all-at-once display on which a map insists encourages its viewers to think of the simultaneous existence of others like themselves in other parts of the empire. Indeed, the curriculum for students in the rüşdiye and idadî schools called for the sixth year to cover Ottoman geography on a province-by-province basis, thereby ensuring that the students learn about other parts of the empire.[64] Wall maps covering the main continents ensured that the students learned something of the world beyond the empire's borders as well. This

---

[62] Peter Gould and Rodney White, *Mental Maps*, 2nd edn. (Boston: Allen & Unwin, 1986).

[63] "A View of the World from Ninth Avenue," *New Yorker*, 29 Mar. 1976. The cartoon represents the West Side of Manhattan in great detail, but everything west of the Hudson River is left intentionally vague; New Jersey is thus rendered as alien as China.

[64] *Salname-i Nezaret-i Maarif-i Umumiye*, 2. defa. (Istanbul: Matbaa-yı Amire, 1317 [1899–1900]), 288 ff.

inherent simultaneity of the map was being reinforced by the existence of so many similar schools in the Ottoman educational system and, more generally, by the increasing prominence of the manifold and growing instruments of the centralized bureaucratic state. The expanding networks of roadways, rail and telegraph lines, inspectors, and census workers could, with the help of a map, now be seen as parts of an overall system, and not merely as isolated instances of official initiative. In short, the map must have encouraged Ottoman students to think of themselves in new ways; it not only reordered their relationship with the capital city but also fostered a common sense of belonging to a centralized political unit.

Conversely, however, the cartographic format may have fostered mental maps less advantageous to the state's agenda. Those who harbored separatist leanings may have been emboldened by the mapping of so many distant regions containing the disparate groups that, as was increasingly apparent, were contemplating secession from the empire. At the very least, such imagining could produce a realization that the other simultaneously existing groups were different in a variety of ways. Those susceptible to ethnic, religious, or nationalist sentiment were perhaps encouraged by what the maps revealed, namely, that the empire, far from being the unified entity of central government hopes, was actually comprised of many varied parts that some might consider ripe for secession.

In a broader context the use of school maps must also have encouraged young Ottoman subjects to think of the empire of which they were subjects—and to which the state was attempting to cement their political loyalty—in the context of the other countries of the globe. As we have seen in the case of Şevket Süreyya's comparison of the former Ottoman borders with their greatly reduced current shape, this awareness did not necessarily work to the state's advantage. Although the state wanted its subjects and bureaucrats to be cognisant of the international situation and to be able to distinguish foreign virtue from vice, it was also quite wary of "losing" its subjects to the orbit of Western Europe. More germane to the subject of geography, knowledge of the Hamidian empire's contemporary borders, when coupled with even the most rudimentary knowledge of past Ottoman achievement, invited unflattering comparison.

Once the map was introduced into the classroom setting, a number of eventualities were possible. At the very least, students were encouraged to ponder the political entity of which they were subjects in new ways. As Anderson has shown, framing the territory in the map-as-logo format focuses attention on the political entity in question. This may produce a number of effects. In the case of the late Ottoman Empire, some of these were doubtless alternatives the state never intended. The students may, as intended, develop a new or a renewed sense of loyalty for the regime. They may, however, find themselves beginning to question assumptions concerning the state that had hitherto remained unacknowledged. In his memoirs written in the 1930s, Hüseyin Cahid Yalçın, a student at the idadî school situated on Divan Yolu in Istanbul in the later years of Abdülhamid's reign, and an important journalist in the Young Turk and early Republican periods, reflects back on the way Ottoman territory was presented in school. He recalled the case of Bulgaria: "We fooled ourselves by still referring to the 'Prince of Bulgaria' and the 'Governor of Eastern Rumelia.' In our schools we had our children read, 'Bulgaria is ours.' Bulgaria had been long gone . . ."[65] By using such slogans and the maps that supported their assertions establishing a fixed notion of Ottoman territoriality, the state abandoned what one theorist has termed "a universal advantage of territoriality," namely, the practice of avoiding delineation of the territory under control.[66] Furthermore, by presenting such material in conjunction with the strong dose of nostalgic admiration for the empire's past achievements that appeared in the newly commissioned history textbooks, late Ottoman education may have unwittingly invited comparisons with the heyday of Ottoman success that reflected unfavorably upon the current sultan. The grounds for such comparison were particularly ripe in the case of geography. A student like Şevket Süreyya found it natural to compare the empire's current boundaries with those that included the many former possessions that had been lost over time. It does not require a great stretch of the imagination to see that such a line of thought could easily result in questioning, if not outright undermining, of the regime.

[65] Hüseyin Cahid Yalçın, "Meşrutiyet Hatıraları, 1908–1918," in *Fikir Hareketleri*, 82 (1935), 54.
[66] Robert David Sack, *Human Territoriality*, 27.

CONCLUSION

Maps tell us more about the agenda that lies behind their creation than about how they were received. In the case of the late Ottoman Empire, they provide us with graphic evidence of the way Hamidian policy shifted away from the Tanzimat approach to education. Just as conceiving of the need to expand state education in a competitive context and bolstering the religious component of its school curriculum are signs of important changes introduced by Hamidian education policy, so too is the cartographic record symptomatic of a break with the immediate past. The state's use of cartography in the Abdülhamid II period graphically illustrates the way the state adapted the technology of instruction to meet its needs. But because these needs were themselves in flux, the technology played a role in shaping the education that the state was offering. As Thongchai Winichakul has shown, the notion of territoriality is one that is created through the discursive process occasioned by geography and its chief agent, the map. The maps we have analyzed here demonstrate their power as political symbol. While the state's use of this technology was probably not yet sophisticated enough to succeed in a calculated manipulation of its subjects' notions of territoriality, it seems clear that it was well on its way to redirecting the manner in which these proto-citizens conceived of their state. In retrospect, the interruption of this venture, brought on by the empire's dissolution following World War I, prevents us from seeing the full course of the imperial endeavor.

Maps do, however, allow us to begin to understand the ways the state's program affected its proto-citizens. The science of geography, so heartily endorsed by the late Ottoman educational system, carried with it a powerful technology. The introduction of the map to Ottoman public school students can only have altered their mental maps. As we have seen in the case of Şevket Süreyya Aydemir, the new technology carried with it unanticipated consequences. While the change to imperial logo maps was a correction that jibed with the rest of Hamidian policy, it also invited unfavorable—and perhaps unfair—comparisons with the glory days of the empire. Dangerously, the empire was attempting to render its young generation geographically literate at the very time that its borders were contracting so rapidly.

The unanticipated by-products of Hamidian education policy highlight just how new and untested a venture state-run education was. The widespread introduction of the map reflects the dramatic shift to Western-style education and culture, even when moderated by Hamidian efforts to Ottomanize the entire process. By introducing new ways of conceiving the world, and the place of the Ottoman Empire in particular, late Ottoman education proved to be more of an experiment than state officials had thought, with results that they could hardly have foreseen.

6

Morals

INTRODUCTION

Like the empire's borders, public morality was deemed to be in particular need of strengthening in the late Ottoman period. But while the geographical contractions displayed state weakness vis-à-vis external forces, the moral realm seemed to reveal the empire as coming unhinged from within. External hands could be perceived, it is true, behind the threat of religious conversion menacingly embodied in the form of foreign missionaries, yet the conversions that did take place were almost entirely at the expense of the empire's non-Muslim population. Public morality seemed to be at risk as much from the loss of Ottoman and Islamic modes—of thought, practice, and even dress—as from the arrival of harmful ideas and fashions from the West. In response, a wide range of calls for revivifying the empire were asserted on the basis of moral regeneration—and many of these did not emanate from the state. In the growing popular press, in the cartoons that accompanied it, in the burgeoning popular fiction, and in the writings of politically and socially engaged Ottomans, morally defined solutions were summoned to redress the imperial malaise.[1] Whether in the form of a heavily didactic fictional characterization, pictorial images, or straightforward pleas, the moral imperative could seem to dominate the public sphere. As Elizabeth Frierson has shown in her study of the

[1] For an overview of some of the fiction being written in this period, see, *inter alia*, Evin, *Origins and Development of the Turkish Novel*; on cartoons, see Nora Şeni, "Fashion and Women's Clothing in the Satirical Press of Istanbul at the End of the 19th Century," in Şirin Tekeli (ed.), *Women in Modern Turkish Society: A Reader* (London: Zed Books, 1995), 25–45; and Palmira Brummett, *Image and Imperialism in the Ottoman Revolutionary Press, 1908–1911* (Albany: State University of New York Press, 2000).

late Ottoman women's press, morality—or rather the loss of it—was a burning issue of the day. We need only refer to one female reader's views to capture much of the spirit of the response. A subscriber to the leading Ottoman women's newspaper *Hanımlara Mahsus Gazete* (The Ladies' Own Gazette), named Sadika, linked public morality with public education: "Real and complete implementation of the rules of chastity and morality can be achieved not by compelling all women to stay at home, not to go outside or cover themselves all up when they do go out, but by helping them to correct their thinking and enlighten themselves."[2] As we are about to see, this letter captures both the general response and the state's corrective approach to morality. Strengthening the state, this line of thinking continued, depended upon strengthening Islamic morality.

This chapter addresses the Hamidian campaign to inculcate the inherently internal construct of morality through such external devices as curricular adjustments and textbooks.[3] Like so much of the Hamidian educational agenda, the moral instruction initiative represented an attempt to inject Islamic content through modern means and modes of organization. Just as buildings and maps played a critical role in articulating Abdülhamid II's attempt at fostering imperial allegiance, the campaign to infuse moral education into the Ottoman school system used the physical elements of schooling to produce change in patterns of thought, association, and belief. The physical apparatus of learning was readjusted in an attempt to affect the metaphysical. The moralizing agenda of the educational project was, moreover, the logical extension of the Hamidian reaction to what were perceived to be the deleterious effects of foreign educational encroachment on the empire's youth. Convinced of the necessity of a centralized educational system in large part to ward off the threat of educational competition from abroad, the Hamidian state was now acting to ensure that its students would be supplied with the moral wherewithal to withstand the challenges inherent in that threat.

This chapter begins with the assumption that schools are inherently

---

[2] Frierson, "Unimagined Communities," 68.
[3] A more succinct but comparatively focused form of the argument presented in this chapter can be found in my "Islamic Morality in Late Ottoman 'Secular' Schools," *IJMES* 32/3 (2000), 369–93.

arenas of moral interaction. The work of Philip Jackson and others in the Moral Life of Schools Project has shown that, perhaps even more than we realize, moral considerations permeate the life of the modern school.[4] Their project analyzed schools in the American Midwest during the late twentieth century, but much of their findings are universal to the processes, orderings, and relationships described under the general rubric of "modern education." Their taxonomy of the areas in which "the moral" occurs offers a helpful framework for analysis. Jackson and his co-workers group moral activity into two broad categories: Moral Instruction and Moral Practice.[5]

For practical reasons, the discussion of morality in the context of late Ottoman education cannot include the same taxonomic range; the information simply does not exist, at least as far as we are currently aware. The Moral Life of Schools Project had the advantage of observing and recording classroom activity as it unfolded, an obvious impossibility for schools that operated roughly a century ago. Nevertheless, the material that is available to us allows for considerable latitude. As Jackson and colleagues emphasize, the benefit of using such a categorization is that:

If the main function of this outline is to call attention to the pervasiveness of moral considerations as they impinge upon educational affairs, a secondary function and one of hardly less importance is the subtlety of this effect. That subtlety is reflected in our two sets of categories, the first set focusing on the moral influences that are most readily observable and the second set on those that are least easily observed.[6]

In the late Ottoman case, a further amplification of this schema, or rather another level of understanding, is needed, namely, the moral dimension associated with the state's schooling project in the first place.

---

[4] Philip W. Jackson, Robert E. Boostrom, and David T. Hansen, *The Moral Life of Schools* (San Francisco: Jossey-Bass, 1993).

[5] Ibid. 42. These categories are divided further into the following schema: "*Moral Instruction*: (1) Moral Instruction as a Formal Part of the Curriculum; (2) Moral Instruction Within the Regular Curriculum; (3) Rituals and Ceremonies; (4) Visual Displays with Moral Content; (5) Spontaneous Interjection of Moral Commentary into Ongoing Activity.
Moral Practice: (6) Classroom Rules and Regulations; (7) The Morality of the Curricular Substructure; (8) Expressive Morality within the Classroom."

[6] Ibid. 43.

Unlike the case of their North American counterparts, late Ottoman state schools owed their very existence to an imperative, the contest with Western Europe, that had a large religio-moral component. This religio-moral dimension has been given short shrift, if not completely eclipsed, in the historical literature which persists in referring to the schools as "secular."[7] What follows, therefore, represents an attempt to demonstrate the extent to which religion and morality permeated the entire project. Before addressing the specific aspects of morality in late Ottoman education as practiced in the schools, I examine the moral underpinnings of the project as a whole.

The motivation for launching this moral campaign derived from the desire to ward off foreign encroachment, a threat which was critical to motivating the Hamidian educational endeavor in the first place. In keeping with overall Hamidian policy, the response to external encroachment was an indigenous one. Although the spur to activity was largely external and the organizational structure employed was heavily influenced by the Western European presence and methods, the Hamidian response had deep roots in Ottoman and Islamic tradition, and should thus be seen as part of an internal battle. In the face of a variety of challenges, the school system was meant to inculcate its students with an Islamic sense of morality. We will return to the question of what this entailed in the next section of this chapter.

Moral inculcation represented an important dividend of the entire state education system. All of the time, effort, and money that the late Ottoman state had spent, and continued to spend, on building the highly centralized school network provided Abdülhamid's government with the opportunity to redirect the content of the education it intended to deliver. The Hamidian government placed its own stamp on this content by insisting on a more overtly religious and imperial orientation.[8] The "secular" system envisioned during the preceding

---

[7] See my "Islamic Morality."

[8] The contemporary example of "morale laïque" in France shows that a moral campaign need not have been religiously based. Nevertheless, while there are some striking parallels between the French and Ottoman educational reform movements, they are ultimately two very different processes. On the French efforts to inculcate a "secular" notion of morality, see Phyllis Stock-Morton, *Moral Education for a Secular Society: The Development of Morale Laïque in Nineteenth Century France* (Albany: State University of New York Press, 1988).

Tanzimat period was now to be put to work for an altered religious, cultural, and political agenda. The government placed great faith in the power of moral instruction as a means of safeguarding the empire's future.

THE MEANING OF "MORALS"

It would be appropriate here to consider the meaning of the term "morals" in the context of late Ottoman education. We have already formed a partial explanation. Conceived as a means of combating the negative effects of the Western penetration into the Ottoman Empire, the instruction of morals was largely envisioned as a corrective measure. In order to mitigate the deleterious consequences of foreign influence, the state seemed naively to suggest, its subjects needed only to be shown a model infused with Ottoman and Islamic referents.[9] It is important to bear in mind that the Hamidian educational project was not simply, as Modernization theory would have had us believe, an attempt to import "modern" practices and modes of thinking into the imperial domains.[10] It did, of course, engage in such direct importation, but it was ultimately concerned with preserving the empire by adopting Western methods and adapting them for its own purposes. As our discussion of the curricular emphasis on "morals" has revealed, the Western-based school system proved easy to modify. The insertion of moral content into the curriculum was perhaps the defining example of the Hamidian effort to refit the Tanzimat curriculum to accord with its view of late Ottoman realities.

But what exactly was the term "morals" meant to convey? In what follows I briefly consider the philological and contextual evidence before turning first to the state's campaign to reinsert morality into the curriculum and then to a textbook specifically produced to teach morals to late Ottoman students. Philologically, the Ottoman Turkish term

---

[9] The way such an idealized view worked itself out in practice naturally depended upon a wide range of individual interpretations, on the part of the teachers, and receptions, on the part of the students.

[10] For recent critiques of modernization theory, see Talal Asad, *Genealogies of Religion: Discipline and Reasons of Power in Christianity and Islam* (Baltimore, Md.: Johns Hopkins University Press, 1993), and Messick, *The Calligraphic State*.

"ahlâk," which I have been rendering as "morals," connotes a range of meanings.[11] Here, the term "ahlâk," as it is transliterated from its Ottoman Turkish form, has been translated as "morals" because it conveys the plural sense of its Arabic derivation and, more important, because it preserves the sense of a set of collective or communal ideals. Şemseddin Sâmî's dictionary of 1900, incidentally published to commemorate the twenty-fifth anniversary of Abdülhamid's reign, is instructive in this regard. The entry under the term "hulk" defines that term as "natural disposition" or "characteristic", but goes on to dwell mostly on the plural form "ahlâk." Three definitions are provided. The first offers a neutral stance, stating that "ahlâk" are both the good and bad dispositions with which every person is endowed. The second meaning is that of a particular division of philosophy which treats the issue of human ethics. The third definition moves away from the normative neutrality of the first two meanings. No longer both good and bad, "ahlâk" are here defined solely as "good dispositions" (*iyi huylar*) and as "the virtues (*fezail*) that adorn the human being with respect to sense and truth" (*ma'nen ve hakikaten*). "In students, morals are to be looked for before all things." The term public morality (*ahlâk-i umumî*) is then introduced and defined as "the qualities that have been accepted as custom in a society." An example follows: "It is absolutely necessary to protect public morality from sedition (*fesad*)."[12] It is this last, communal sense that informs the usage of the term "morals" in the parlance of the late Ottoman educational project.

In the official memoranda, in fact, the term "morals" was given little positive definition; rather, it was the *absence* of "morals" and their being "broken" which stand out. This absence was blamed for "heedlessness," and for a general loss of Islamic identity exhibited by change in dress and the adoption of "Frankish habits." Ultimately, the sorry state of morals was deemed to have an adverse effect on the loyalty to the Ottoman state and its titular head, the sultan/caliph.

[11] Interestingly, the English word "character" was translated as *akhlāq* in an Egyptian translation of Samuel Smiles's *Self Help*. In that case, good old-fashioned British "character" was intended to cure Egyptians of their "indolence." Mitchell, *Colonising Egypt*, 80. In the Ottoman case, by contrast, the religio-moral meaning of the term warrants rendering it as "morals." That is also the preponderant sense in which it is understood in modern Arabic.

[12] Redhouse gives the phrase *fesad-i ahlâk* as "bad morals, demoralization of character." *Redhouse Yeni*, s.v. *fesad*.

Morals were declared to be "broken" (*bozuk*).[13] As we have seen, Ottoman officials advanced the notion of intensified moral instruction as the solution to reverse the disappointing trends they identified in the realm of public morality. Bolstering the main moral solution, namely, the emphasis on moral instruction, was a complementary set of actions that included increasing the teaching of Arabic, adding theological subjects to the curriculum, assigning texts devoted to the life of the Prophet Muhammad, and enforcing religious observance.

MODIFYING THE CURRICULUM

The Hamidian government exhibited a continual impulse to modify the school curriculum it had inherited. As in so many other areas, Abdülhamid II appointed a series of commissions to effect the changes he envisioned for the fledgling system.[14] These commissions appeared early and often in the Hamidian period, evidence of an almost constant inclination to modify the system's content, even as its formal structure was being articulated.

The first reference to a commission charged with the task of reforming the curriculum of the Ottoman schools in the Hamidian period appeared as early as February of 1885, less than one year after the estab-

---

[13] The charge of broken morals appears so frequently in the descriptions of late Ottoman education as to make citing examples somewhat superfluous. Apart from the official correspondence on the subject referred to above, Cevdet Paşa's account of educational change in the empire is particularly interesting, as much for his own role in the process as for his criticism of it. See e.g. YEE 18/1860, in which Cevdet states: "Meanwhile, the Education Ministry was not able to make progress on this front (*Maarif Nezaretince de iş ilerü götürülemedi*). Let alone the idadî schools, even the ibtidaî schools failed to reach a satisfactory state. The curricula were constantly being altered. It is among the matters deserving attention that the religious principles (*akideler*) of the students who previously emerged from the schools were correct (*dürüst*), but after these alterations and changes the majority of those who emerged have broken religious principles (*akideleri bozuk*). These circumstances are taking the public education (*terbiye-i umumiye*) down the wrong path. As for the Ottoman State which was founded on the basis of religiosity (*diyanet*), its future appears grave (*vahim*) . . ." See also YEE 18/553–616, YEE 11/1763, and YA Res. 105/13.

[14] For an extended treatment of this topic, see my forthcoming article, "Emphasizing the Islamic: Modifying the Curriculum of Late Ottoman State Schools", in Klaus Kreiser and François Georgeon (eds.), *Enfances et jeunesses dans l'histoire de l'islam* (Paris: Maisonneuve, 2001).

lishment of the Education Tax that ushered in a spate of idadî school construction. From that date until the end of his reign, Abdülhamid II empanelled a remarkably large number of commissions instructed to adjust the schools' curriculum. Each of these commissions had its own particular agenda but they all shared a common purpose, namely, the improvement of moral education throughout the empire.

The raft of commissions created by the sultan in this period and the correspondingly large number of reports they inevitably produced reveals the process by which Abdülhamid's bureaucracy attempted to inject moral education into what had initially been a much more secular system. As stipulated in the Education Regulation of 1869, the idadî schools were not intended to provide courses in morality or religion of any sort.[15] The first commission seems to have been instructed to adjust the schools' curriculum but not to address the subject of moral education. Its recommendations were limited to such subjects as the language of instruction. It suggested that Arabic replace Turkish as the chief language of instruction in schools in the Arab provinces, and that French be abolished completely from the rüşdiye schools and be relegated to the status of an optional language in the idadîs and the Mekteb-i Mülkiye.[16] It also recommended the removal of several scientific courses from the crowded idadî curriculum. Although these changes appear not to have been adopted,[17] they represent the first evidence of an attempt to alter the school's curriculum on an empire-wide scale.

Within a year Abdülhamid II created another curricular review commission. Starting a trend that would continue throughout his reign, the sultan charged the new commission with a more far-reaching brief. As we have already seen, the imperial decree issued by the palace on

[15] The Maarif Nizamnamesi contains no courses in morals in its idadî curriculum (p. 14). Students at the rüşdiye level were, however, to follow a course entitled the Principles of the Religious Sciences (*mebadi-yi ulûm-u diniye*) (p. 9). The copy of the Regulation referred to here is that found in YEE 37/330.

[16] ŞD 209/54. 10 Cemaziyelahır 1303 (16 Mar. 1886). As we will see subsequently, the increased attention paid to Arabic, the language of the Qur'an, was critical to the moral element in the Hamidian educational agenda.

[17] Ibid. Our information about this commission comes from a document written by Münif Paşa. It refers to this commission, which was created during the term of Münif's predecessor in the Education Ministry, Mustafa Paşa, in disparaging terms, stating that all it had to show for its work was a single protocol (*mazbata*), which he reproduces.

29 January 1887 ordained the creation of a commission to be chaired by the highest Muslim dignitary in the empire, the şeyhülislam.[18] This commission was charged with "reforming and correcting the curricula being studied in the Mekteb-i Mülkiye and the other Muslim schools" of the empire. The appointing of the şeyhülislam to head such a consultative body was just one of the signs portending the changes that Abdülhamid was to introduce into his school system. Moreover, the reference to the schools in the state system as being "Muslim schools" indicated that the phraseology of the dispatches sent to Istanbul from the provinces discussed in Chapter 2 had been adopted by the highest echelon of central government authority.

The change in education policy, however, went far beyond the level of personnel appointments and semantics. The very rationale for the changes to come spoke volumes about the new approach. The decree states that need for reform has been made clear by "signs of weakness in the religious principles (*akaid*) of graduates of the Mülkiye and other Islamic schools." Furthermore, placing this need for curricular reform in a larger context, the document explicitly referred to the enviable state of moral education as practiced in the non-Muslim schools of the empire as a goad to change. Like the documents encountered in the discussion of the educational competition which focused on the role of foreign and indigenous non-Muslim schools as a spur to the expansion of the Ottoman state system in the first place, this decree cites the non-Muslim schools, "which are in every way preferable in this regard," as a major factor in its rationale for inserting morals into the state schools.[19]

The decree focused on the example of the non-Muslim schools as a source of emulation for their Ottoman counterparts. "By reorganizing their curricula, the non-Muslim schools have striven for excellence with respect to their students' morals and have produced results," the text of the decree announced. By contrast, in the Muslim schools "the opposite situation is a source of regret to the sultan." The culprit was identified as the "irregularity of the curricula of the Muslim schools," which had "predictably resulted in the heedlessness of the Muslim students." The prescribed remedy was the reorganization of the curriculum. Not for the last time, the example of the non-Muslim schools

---

[18] İrade Dah. 80409. 4 Cemaziyelevvel 1304 (29 Jan. 1887).   [19] Ibid.

served as a spur to reforming their counterparts in the state's own system.

Since the task of "reorganizing the curriculum" was not precisely defined, the selection of the individuals charged with carrying out that objective was significant. The choice of the şeyhülislam to head the commission was a clear indication of the increased role Abdülhamid II entrusted to the ulama in shaping educational policy. To be sure, the sultan was not granting exclusive control of the process to the religious establishment; this commission, like almost all of its successors, was comprised of a roughly even balance of civil bureaucrats and ulama. From this it is clear that for the Hamidian period, the prevailing notion that education was wrested away from the ulama and handed over to the civil bureaucracy is highly problematic.

Nevertheless, the identification of certain commission members as being civil bureaucrats or ulama is not in itself satisfactory. The men described under each of these two rubrics represented a spectrum of ideological and political orientations that belies the existence of tidy compartments.[20] Moreover, there was often a good deal of overlap. A member of the ulama could frequently be found in positions generally associated with the strictly scribal ranks. This being the case, it is necessary, whenever possible, to consider the biographies of the individuals involved in an attempt to discern their educational background and political leanings.

The two men explicitly mentioned in the imperial decree ordering the curricular reform commission were the şeyhülislam and the assistant director of the Mekteb-i Mülkiye. Both men reappear frequently in the many commissions that would work to refit the schools' content in the Hamidian period. Üryanîzade Ahmed Esad Efendi (b. 1813) served in the position of şeyhülislam from 1878 until his death in 1889.[21] The son of a *kadı*, or judge administering Islamic law, Ahmed Esad was also appointed kadı, serving in Üsküdar, Eyüp, Madina, and Istanbul before being appointed kazasker of Rumeli and of Anatolia. In 1876 he

---

[20] For a discussion of several leading Ottoman ulama of the Tanzimat whose career paths traversed the boundary between civil and religious bureaucracy, see Richard L. Chambers, "The Ottoman Ulema and the Tanzimat," in Nikki R. Keddie (ed.), *Scholars, Saints, and Sufis: Muslim Religious Institutions in the Middle East Since 1500* (Berkeley: University of California Press, 1972), 33–46.

[21] Gövsa, *Türk Meşhurları*, 120.

was appointed as a member of the newly formed Meclis-i Âyân (Chamber of Notables). Two years later he was appointed şeyhülislam. İbnülemin states that he "won the extraordinary favor and confidence of the sultan."[22] This was perhaps due to Ahmed Esad's staunch defense of sultanic authority over the issue of ministerial responsibility (*mes'uliyet-i vükela meselesi*) during the negotiations over the constitution of 1876, and his opposition to Midhat Paşa during the latter's trial in 1881.[23] Ahmed Esad's previous work in heading a commission charged with modifying and reforming (*ta'dil ve ıslah*) the proposed Law of Ministerial Responsibility according to the *şeriat* (Islamic canonical law) seems likely to have favorably disposed Abdülhamid II to tap him for the analogous task awaiting the curricular reform commission.

The other man specifically mentioned in the decree embodied an intriguing mixture of influences. From the scant material available concerning Hacı Recaî Efendi, it seems that he was an individual who blurred the distinctions usually drawn between civil bureaucrats and members of the ulama. Born in Istanbul in 1840, Recaî attended a mosque school before entering the rüşdiye in Eyüp, the shrine center on the Golden Horn.[24] He graduated from that institution in 1857 and entered the Mahrec-i Aklâm school, a forerunner of the idadî, graduating with a "first" in 1861. Upon his graduation Recaî assumed a teaching position at the same school, beginning a long list of teaching assignments in various schools in the capital. According to Ahmed Cevdet, Recaî was actively involved in the work of a temporary council formed during Sultan Abdülmecid's reign to deliberate about the forms that reordering public education should take.[25] In 1881 he was appointed assistant director of the Mekteb-i Mülkiye, the position in which he served when selected for the curricular reform commission. His responsibilities increased in 1890 when he was also appointed

---

[22] İnal, *Son Sadrıazamlar*, ii. 692.

[23] Ibid. 911; Mehmed Zeki Pâkalın, *Osmanlı Tarih Deyimleri ve Terimleri Sözlüğü* (Istanbul: Millî Eğitim Basımevi, 1946), ii. 344.

[24] This and all subsequent biographical information on Hacı Recaî is taken from Mücellitoğlu Ali Çankaya *Mülkiye Târihi ve Mülkiyeliler*, 2 vols. (Ankara: Örnek Matbaası, 1954), i. 259 and *Son Asir Türk Tarihinin Önemli Olayları ile Birlikde Yeni Mülkiye Târihi ve Mülkiyeliler (Mülkiye Şeref Kitabe)*, 5 vols. (Ankara: Mars Matbaası, 1968–9), ii. 829–30.

[25] YEE 18/1860. 24 Şaban 1309 (24 Mar. 1892).

director of the Tribal School (*Aşiret Mektebi*). When Abdurrahman Şeref was appointed director of Galatasaray in 1892, Recaî was appointed to fill the vacancy created in the post of director of the Mekteb-i Mülkiye, a position that he held until the Young Turk Revolution of 1908.[26] The courses he taught included such subjects as French, Ottoman Turkish, mathematics, and geography.

While his curriculum vitae would suggest that this was an above-average civil official, Hacı Recaî Efendi appears distinctive in one respect; the titles by which he was referred suggest a degree of Islamic associations not generally affixed to a member of the civil bureaucracy. The first of these, "hacı," denotes that he had made the pilgrimage to Mecca. (But the students of the Mülkiye made light of their harsh director's title; they had a saying which maintained that while Zihnî had become a hacı in Mecca, it was only Recaî's camel which could claim that distinction.[27]) The second sobriquet, that of "efendi," had two potential meanings in this period. For non-Muslims it served as the equivalent of the Muslim title "bey." When the term "efendi" appeared following a Muslim name, as it clearly did in the case of Recaî, it generally marked the individual in question as a member of the ulama. Pakalın offers a likely explanation: those elevated to the rank of "bâlâ," as was Recaî one year after being named director of the Mülkiye, were given the title "efendi."[28] In any event there is in both Recaî's background and nomenclature a strong suggestion that he straddled the distinction between *memur* (civil official) and *'alim* (cleric).

The issue of Recaî's status becomes important when seen in light of the question of the composition of the various commissions

[26] The key to his longevity in the Hamidian bureaucracy may have been his inclination to suppress troublesome issues. For example, there was an incident at the Mülkiye in which he reacted strongly to an attempt by students to petition for a change in the law that required them to wait until they reached the age of 25 before being granted their initial bureaucratic assignment. According to this account, Recaî, referred to as the "famous Hacı Recaî Efendi," stated that "students should not interfere in such matters," and threatened those involved with prison and was on the verge of expelling them. A fellow teacher, Zihnî, came to the aid of the students. This Zihnî had accompanied Recaî on the pilgrimage to Mecca. Çankaya, *Mülkiye Târihi*, i. 393–4. See also Blake, "Training Arab-Ottoman Bureaucrats," 118 and Çankaya, *Son Asir*, ii. 829–30. The incident in question is based on the memoir of a former student named Mustafa Reşat Mimaroğlu, a 1902 graduate of the Mülkiye.

[27] Çankaya, *Mülkiye Târihi*, i. 393–4.

[28] Pâkalın, *Tarih Deyimleri ve Terimleri Sözlüğü*, art. "Efendi," i. 506.

empaneled by Abdülhamid II. In general, such bodies were comprised of a roughly even mix of civil bureaucrats and ulama. The ostensible even-handedness of these appointments would necessarily have to be called into question if one or more of the civil officials were seen to be acting as *de facto* figures of the religious establishment.

The reports produced by the 1887 curricular reform commission reflect the work of both Ahmed Esad and Hacı Recaî Efendi. Almost within one month of the date of the decree creating the commission, the body completed the report detailing the changes it intended for the empire's schools. This report is interesting for several reasons. First, because the report was produced by the şeyhülislam's office, it was penned in the Persianate Divanî script, a fact that makes it visually distinct from the normal correspondence concerning educational matters. Secondly, the physical distinctiveness is indicative of the change in outlook represented by the commission's agenda. Starting a trend that would last throughout the Hamidian era, the cover letter of the commission's report stressed the need to "strengthen the religious principles" (*takviye-i akaid*) of the students attending the state's schools.[29] The letter suggests two types of approaches aimed at accomplishing this goal. One was to "reorganize and reform" the curriculum. The other was to ensure that the students carried out their prescribed prayers. In other words, the schools were to oversee moral as well as intellectual development.

The full memorandum produced by the commission reveals the scope of the project it had undertaken. The curriculum of each type of school had been reviewed and a number of meetings had been convened at the Office of the Şeyhülislam (*Bâb-i Fetvî*) to discuss the changes to be made.[30] Interestingly, the main focus of the commission's attention was reserved for the lower levels of the schooling pyramid. As part of its report, the commission prepared revamped curricula for the ibtidaî and rüşdiye schools. The higher schools, here meaning the

---

[29] Y Mtv. 25/52, 1. lef. 6 Cemaziyelahir 1304 (2 Mar. 1887). The Turkish term *akaid* is a plural form of the Arabic *'aqidah*, meaning article of faith, tenet, doctrine, etc. In late Ottoman parlance, the term *akaid* was synonymous with the study of the principles of the Islamic faith (*akaid-i islamiye*). Şemseddin Sami, *Kamûs-i Türkî* (Dersaadet [Istanbul]: İkdam Matbaası, 1317 [1899–1900]), 944.

[30] Y Mtv. 25/52, 2. lef. 6 Cemaziyelahır 1304 (2 Mar. 1887).

idadîs and those above them, were dealt with in a separate document prepared by Hacı Recaî and also included with the report.[31]

Recaî's recommendations reveal the extent to which religion figured in the curricular reform effort. He suggested that, like French, Arabic be taught in every grade of the idadî schools and all of the higher institutions. Arabic literature and the principles of translation from Arabic to Turkish and vice versa were to be featured. Next, he recommended creating new "courses on the biographies and features of the Prophets, the historical deeds of the companions of the Prophet, and the biographies of the religious authorities (*eimme-i din*) and the famous ulama."[32] Furthermore, he proposed that the projected lessons in religious principles include "the instruction of the science of morals (*ilm-i ahlâk*) and of Islamic jurisprudence (*fıkıh*) in abridged form."

These specific changes suggested for the idadîs conform to the strategy contained in the commission's memorandum and, more generally, to the overall tenets of Hamidian education policy. This strategy consisted of several key points. First, it emphasized the importance of proper pre-adolescent education as a necessary condition for the religious basis of the entire religious community. "For a millet, the establishment of matters of belief truly depends on being led and guided on that path in the beginning stages of adolescence."[33] Secondly, it recommended augmenting the time allotted to religious instruction. "Since the instruction of both the religious sciences and the Arabic language in the ibtidaî and rüşdiye schools has been found to be insufficient," the memorandum continues, "it is necessary to expand their period of instruction and to 'balance' their curriculum." "Balancing" meant increasing the proportion of religious instruction, including "the teaching here also of treatises on belief (*resail-i itikadiye*) sufficient to fend off the danger" posed by students' "being occupied with Western works and writings that are harmful to Islamic morals and to the exalted sultanate."[34] Thirdly, these curricular efforts were to be supported by extra-curricular changes. The memorandum specifically mentions the necessity of having the students perform their prayers as a congregation. "To assure the proper functioning of the schools' instruction in this respect," the commission's memorandum

---

[31] Y Mtv. 25/52, 3. lef. ND.   [32] Ibid.   [33] Y Mtv. 25/52, 2. lef.   [34] Ibid.

goes on to suggest the appointment of the ʿalim Yahya Reşid Efendi, a madrasa instructor and a member of the Council of Şeriat Investigation (*Meclis-i Tedkikat-i Şerʿiye*), to oversee inspection, that perennial stand-by of Hamidian state control. Here is Hamidian education policy in microcosm: a moving away from the more overtly secular aspects of the Tanzimat conception of Ottoman education toward a consciously Islamic basis, and all of this being carried out against the backdrop of foreign encroachment which renders the changes all the more pressing.

Because the subject of the curricular reform commissions can perhaps only justly be assessed in a longer treatment than is possible here, it is necessary to be quite selective in approach. In what follows I proceed thematically, referring to many, but by no means all, of the documents generated by the commissions in order to evince the trends of their work across the chronological sweep of the Hamidian period.

It is almost always possible to discern the influence of Western encroachment in the work of the reform commissions. As has been stated repeatedly, the Hamidian educational program should be seen as a consciously Ottoman and Islamic venture, particularly in contrast to that of the consciously Westward-looking agenda of the preceding Tanzimat era. The growing Western presence in the empire itself lent an urgency, even a militancy, to the Hamidian efforts in the field of education.

In these documents, wariness of Western influence takes two forms. One appears in response to the physical presence of foreign educators operating in Ottoman territory. Just as foreign education operated as both a positive and negative spur to state activity, so also did it act as a double stimulus to alter what was taking place in Ottoman classrooms. On the one hand, the foreign schools were seen as potential objects of emulation. For example, the minister of education, Zühdü Paşa, wrote to the palace in 1893 begrudgingly holding up the curriculum of the missionary schools as successful.[35] Zühdü singled out the teaching of three subjects that the Protestant missionary schools have used to great advantage in furthering their own political, religious, and cultural agenda. These were: religious principles, history, and English. The education minister explicitly links each of these subjects with its

---

[35] YEE 35/232. 19 Muharrem 1311 (2 Aug. 1893).

purported aim. Thus: "The first of these three is for the purpose of spreading Protestantism; the second is to engender some political sentiments (*bir hissiyât-i siyasiye*) in the minds of the public and the Ottoman subjects in particular; and the third is for competition with France."[36] According to Zühdü, these methods were responsible for the fact that young Ottoman subjects "have become accustomed to Frankish habits and customs due to the influence of their teachers, and they remain subjects in name only, their minds having been changed." While Zühdü Paşa did not say so directly, the mention of these successful methods seems clearly intended to inspire their emulation by the Ottoman state school system.

On the other hand, as we have seen in Chapter 2, the missionary schools produced a more defensive reaction. A common theme running through the memoranda submitted by provincially based civil servants to the capital was the need to combat the "dangers" inherent in the foreign educational presence on Ottoman territory. Building state-run alternatives figured as the first line of defense in Ottoman strategy, supported, as we have seen, by complementary policies such as sending preachers throughout the countryside to warn against the dangers of foreign schooling and appointing teams of inspectors to monitor the foreign institutions. These were adjunct strategies; the main thrust of the state's response was building its own schools, institutions in which the state could have full control over how the students lived and what they learned.

As with the education endeavor generally, the European presence loomed large over the agenda of curricular modification. Lurking in the background was the unavoidable fact that Ottoman subjects increasingly opted to be educated in Europe or in foreign schools operating within the empire. This was a "situation that was a cause of regret to his Imperial Highness."[37] In the thinking of the Hamidian bureaucracy, obviating the need for Ottoman students to study abroad could

---

[36] Ibid.

[37] Y A Res. 112/59. 22 Safer 1319 (10 June 1901). It is interesting to note the involvement of the Ottoman military in the issue of curricular reform. This file includes a memorandum submitted by the "Tophane-i Amire Müşiri ve Umum Mekâtib-i Askeriye-i Şahane Nâzırı." The Hamidian government had been actively involved in efforts to unify the curricula of all of the empire's civil and military schools since 1309. See AYN 1428, 210.

be effected by decree. The students could merely be ordered to return. But, by proposing certain changes to the domestic alternatives, the Ottomans were tacitly acknowledging the importance of the quality and relevance of their own educational offerings. In order to render Ottoman schooling a more realistic, not to mention palatable, option for the individuals involved, the state proposed several changes. These included streamlining the course load of students in most schools, which were deemed to suffer from a curriculum described as "crowded."[38] In order to combat this problem, lesson schedules with a reduced number of classroom hours were produced. The other, albeit less specifically articulated, recommendation was to devote more attention to lessons relating to "Islamic principles."

The political and economic interest of the state argued in favor of repatriating students who had been sent overseas to further their education. In fiscal terms, such substitution would save the Treasury both the cost of supporting the students living abroad and the costs associated with redundancy. The memorandum of the Meclis-i Mahsus includes the estimate that the state would save 300,000 kuruş annually by having them return.[39] But the main benefit for repatriating the students in Europe, some of whom were described as not actually studying but wandering about like vagabonds, was to render them dependent upon the state's own educational control.

Western influence can also be detected in another recurring theme in the correspondence relating to the commissions, namely, the purging of European elements deemed to be detrimental to Ottoman society. This response seems to have been motivated by the growing trend toward European affectation in the empire as a whole, as evidenced by changing sartorial and literary tastes. Most visible in each of these spheres were the changes in women's and, to a lesser extent, men's fashions, in the form of such European imports as the parasol, the corset, spats, top hats, and so on, and in the genre of the novel. Often the two were fused, as when late Ottoman novelists turned their atten-

---

[38] The Ottoman attempt to streamline the crowded curriculum had parallels in Western Europe. In Germany, France, England, Scandinavia, and Russia fears abounded that students would be debilitatingly overburdened by the expanded curricula they faced. The most lively debate over the "overburdening question" raged in Wilhelmine Germany. See Albisetti, *Secondary School Reform in Imperial Germany*, 119 ff.

[39] Y A Res. 112/59. 2. lef.

tion—and frequently their scorn—on the more excessive examples of mimicry of the West in late Ottoman society.[40] More specifically, of course, the curricular refitting campaign was an attempt to temper the spate of cultural and ideological borrowing inherent in the Tanzimat era education plan.

This campaign sought to purge the detrimental elements and replace them with course content that would produce students both morally sound and politically loyal. According to a memorandum produced by the Meclis-i Mahsus in 1900, it was necessary to take action to ensure that, "those graduating from the established schools possess the attainments of science and knowledge (*müktessebât-i ilmiye ve fünûniye*) that are necessary according to the progress of modern civilization, that they obtain intellectual incisiveness and religious firmness, that they be faithful to the sublime sultanate and endowed with sound morals."[41] As this passage indicates, the Hamidian educational objective did not include a wholesale rejection of the West (a.k.a. "modern civilization"). Rather, it sought what it repeatedly referred to as a "modification" that would draw on the attainments of both the Western and Eastern traditions.[42] It aspired to take the best of the European advances while attempting to keep the attendant dangers at bay. Inculcating sound (in other words, Islamic) morality was thus intended as a prophylaxis against the contagion implicit in the encroachment of the West.

As we have seen, what exactly was entailed in such an endeavor was not fully articulated. Much in the way that the largely inchoate notion of "education" was so freely heralded as a general panacea for the empire's ills, moral instruction was advanced as the means of assuring that this new type of education conformed to official aspirations. In order to explicate precisely what was intended to be imparted under the rubric of Morals that appeared on the curricula of virtually every school in the late Ottoman system, it is necessary to examine the texts intended for classroom use. In other words, we need to move from the largely negative definition provided in the memoranda of Ottoman officials involved with the education project to the positive example of a teaching text.

---

[40] For discussion of these trends, see Frierson, "Unimagined Communities," Evin, *Origins and Development*, and Şeni, "Fashion and Women's Clothing," among others.

[41] Y A Res. 105/13. 3. lef. 13 Ramazan 1317 (15 Jan. 1900).   [42] Ibid.

TEXTBOOKS

The Hamidian government attached great weight to the role of texts in the process of education. It devoted considerable attention to the commissioning, controlling, inspection, and occasionally the banning of a variety of texts that appeared in the schools of the late Ottoman Empire. Although we know very little about the process that selected certain authors to write books for classroom use,[43] it is clear from several types of evidence both that the Hamidian state commissioned a large number of textbooks, and that it was extremely vigilant with regard to the content of such texts. The large rise in the numbers of textbooks published in the late Ottoman period is symptomatic both of the remarkable proliferation of state schooling and of the commensurate role that the written text played in the education process. As yet no comprehensive scholarly work has been done on these books. Nuri Doğan's investigation represents an important but limited start in that direction.[44] Doğan consulted eighty-six school textbooks used in the rüşdiye and idadî schools, but even his list is by no means exhaustive. His analysis is a much-needed introduction to the larger task of attempting to re-create and understand the pedagogical practices of the late Ottoman period. Left unstudied are the various issues surrounding the way these texts, once commissioned and written, were actually used both inside and outside the classroom.

What little we can know at this stage is limited to what we can deduce from the way Hamidian officialdom treated texts in the context of the state schools. Hamidian policy vis-à-vis textbooks can be summarized as follows: the state exhibited extreme wariness, perhaps even paranoia, over the presence and content of texts in the schools. The state bureaucracy expended considerable effort to keep unauthorized texts out of its students' hands and to ensure that they read works that had been properly vetted instead. The commissions created to inspect

---

[43] More is known about the state's role in fostering general literary production. In keeping with a long tradition of Ottoman state patronage, Ahmed Cevdet records the fact that his *Tarih-i Cevdet* was produced for the *Encümen-i Danış* in the 1850s. Each member of that Academy of Knowledge, as it is sometimes translated, deemed capable of doing so was encouraged to write a book. Cevdet Paşa also produced a catechism (*ilmihal*) to be used in the sıbyanî schools. YEE 18/1860. 24 Şaban 1309 (24 Mar. 1892).

[44] Nuri Doğan, *İlk ve Orta Dereceli Okul Ders Kitapları ve Sosyalleşme (1876–1918)* (Istanbul: Bağlam, 1994).

and control the state schools generally were also responsible for inspecting the texts in use there, and for rooting out any material not deemed appropriate. For example, the detection of some texts of a political nature in the book-bags of several students at the idadî in Izmir in 1903 occasioned Mehmed Kâmil Paşa to recommend that an official be dispatched from Istanbul to investigate the matter.[45] Commissions were also, at least on one occasion, charged with inspecting the actual notes that students took down from the lessons delivered by their teachers and the lithographed study sheets produced from the teachers' original drafts.[46]

Such vigilance was to be expected with regard to illegal printed material originating outside the system, yet it also extended to works that actually had been produced within it. For example, when the charge that the controversial subject of the death of Abdülhamid's predecessor Sultan Abdülaziz was inappropriately handled in an Ottoman history textbook in use in the sıbyanî schools was brought to the attention of the authorities in 1887, rapid action followed. The text in question, Selim Sâbit Efendi's *Muhtasar Tarih-i Osmanî*, contained a passage that referred to Abdülaziz's death as a suicide. The palace responded with outrage at the fact that the censorship committee had allowed the text to be published, and ordered that it be recalled and replaced with a statement to the effect that Abdülhamid's predecessor had succumbed to an illness.[47] It is interesting to note that Selim Sâbit Efendi was a member of the Grand Education Council (*Meclis-i Kebir-i Maarif*) and an important contributor to the education movement.[48]

[45] The texts were: *Üss-i inkılâb*; *Mahkeme-i kubra*; and *Mesail-i şarkiye*. MKP 86/15–1439. Gurre-i (i.e., 1) Muharrem 1320/17 Mart 1319 (30 Mar. 1903). The fact that Ahmed Midhat Efendi's *Üss-i inkılâb* is referred to as prohibited (*memnu*) is curious. The work was a defense of Abdülhamid's accession in 1876 and played a role in Ahmed Midhat Efendi's political rehabilitation: EI2, s.v. "Ahmad Midhat," by Bernard Lewis. The mention of *Üss-i inkılâb* as being prohibited may indicate either that the officials involved assumed the book to be banned on the basis that its title contained the dirty word "revolution" (*inkılâb*), or that the authorities wished there to be no political discussions among students at all, or both.

[46] Y Mtv. 114/19, 2. lef. 29 Receb 1312 (26 Jan. 1895). This inspection occurred in the Mekteb-i Mülkiye and the idadî schools of Istanbul and Üsküdar. Similar inspections of student notebooks were a feature of the imperial school for the sons of tribal leaders. See Rogan, "Aşiret Mektebi," 93–94.

[47] Blake, "Training Arab-Ottoman Bureaucrats," 78.

[48] YEE 11/1179. 8 Rebiülevvel 1305 (24 Nov. 1887).

Even more intriguing is the fact that this same text was reported
to have been illegally printed and distributed within the empire by
Iranians,[49] a situation which undoubtedly added to official concerns
surrounding both that particular book and the general conviction that
the state needed to be on guard against the dangerous nature of the
printed word.

Notwithstanding the problems that texts could pose, or precisely
because they were so troublesome, the Hamidian government devoted
considerable attention and resources to texts intended for education.
The growing state bureaucracy was, after all, an institution that functioned largely by controlling the written and, increasingly, the printed
word. Moreover, the text was precisely that medium which the coercive powers of the state were best suited to control. As Deringil has
noted, the Ottoman bureaucracy even went so far as to recommend at
one stage that lessons on Turkish grammar be read from a book on
morals.[50] Certainly, the state was attracted to the potential of what
Brinkley Messick has termed "new textual technologies."[51] Not surprisingly, the printed text was a critical element of the new schools.
This is not, of course, due to its inherent technical superiority over that
produced by hand. Aesthetics aside, the printed page offers neither
greater nor lesser benefit to the process of education at the individual
level. What it offers is rather the potential for exactness of replication,
and for mass scale.[52] The printed text represents the pedagogical
embodiment of the standardizing ideal that defines modern-style
education. Enlisting the printing press in the service of the centralized
school system allowed for a textbook to be commissioned by the center
and then to be distributed to every node in the Ottoman schooling
network.

---

[49] İrade Dah. 83089. 20 Rebiülevvel 1305 (6 Dec. 1887).

[50] Deringil, *Well-Protected Domains*, 95.

[51] Messick, *The Calligraphic State*, 115.

[52] After the publication of Benedict Anderson's *Imagined Communities*, it is almost
incumbent on an author to mention both the economic and nationalist implications of
the printing press in the service of any self-cognisant "community." Most of the textbooks
produced for the Ottoman state education system seem to have been printed by private
firms in the capital. As far as I am aware, nothing has been written on the connection
between capitalist enterprise and the growth of state-sponsored education, although the
cumulative value of all the various transactions involved in the construction and supply
of the thousands of schools founded by the Hamidian state must have been impressive.

Yet it would be incorrect to conclude that print culture inflicted a clear defeat over its handwritten equivalent. Indeed, there seems to have been no rivalry between them at all. Messick seems to lament the fact that in the Yemen the individual writing board was replaced by the communal blackboard.[53] He sees this as symptomatic of the vanishing of a pedagogical system based on the individual in favor of that which denigrates the individual vis-à-vis the group. But, it may be suggested, the writing slate was replaced not only by the blackboard but also by the textbook. There is, of course, nothing intrinsically anti-individual about a printed text. On the contrary, the relationship between solitary reader and text might be held up as being central to the definition of modern individuality. Regrettably, we have little evidence that would explain the ways in which individual students interacted with their school texts of the sort, say, that Robert DeMaria displays through an analysis of the marginal comments to be found in Samuel Johnson's library.[54] In the absence of such information, my approach is thus speculative.

Now let us add some concrete evidence to our discussions of morals and texts by turning to an example of the books that the Hamidian state produced for the purpose of teaching morality to its young charges. Such texts were the logical extension of the impetus, described above, to inject moral education into the curriculum in response to the negative effects of Western encroachment. Conceived of as part of an indigenous response to an exogenous force, and situated in the midst

---

[53] Messick, *The Calligraphic State*, 105. In general, Messick's wide-ranging and stimulating book is invaluable for its insights into the role that the written word played in Yemeni society and for providing a richly contextualized reading of textual importance. However, one aspect in which his treatment of education can be misleading is the way he contrasts the "old" versus the "new" techniques of pedagogy. In this, in my view, exaggerated assessment of educational change, he is following the lead of Timothy Mitchell, an influence he readily acknowledges. The effect of Messick's insistence on an old/new dichotomy prevents him from seeing the shared traditions between the two education systems. (For the similarities, see Ch. 4 above.) Curiously, this has the effect of eroding Messick's otherwise effective critique of colonial efforts to exaggerate the contrast between the "traditional" and the "modern" in order to justify the imposition of "orderly" Western practices (for example, in the area of legal reform).

[54] Robert DeMaria, Jr., *Samuel Johnson and the Life of Reading* (Baltimore, Md.: Johns Hopkins University Press, 1997). I have recently begun research into the subject of learning to read and the transition from Ottoman Empire to Turkish Republic, and hope to have more to say about this in the future.

of an institution that owed much to both Western and Ottoman influences, late Ottoman school textbooks were understandably heterogeneous creations.

A SCHOOL TEXT: *THE GUIDE TO MORALS*

Due to considerations of time and space, the following discussion will be confined to a single textbook.[55] The work in question, entitled *Rehber-i Ahlâk* (The Guide to Morals), was written by Ali İrfan [Eğriboz] and published in the year 1899–1900.[56] Given the variety of possible late Ottoman school texts from which to choose, the selection of one particular text requires some explanation. For obvious reasons, the text to be analyzed here needed to have been written in the Hamidian period and produced specifically for use in the state schools, preferably at the idadî level.[57] It had to treat the subject of morality and, naturally, be accessible for research purposes. The several texts that met these criteria all appear to have approached the subject of morals from a similar standpoint in terms of the selection and treatment of the concepts to be covered.[58] In the end, I chose the *Rehber* because, unlike the other texts available, it has not been analyzed elsewhere.[59]

Like the late Ottoman education project generally, the *Rehber-i Ahlâk* mixes elements inspired by Western Europe with those exhibiting a clearly Islamic and Ottoman lineage. The text owed its very existence

[55] For a study of a second text that largely confirms the findings derived from the first, see my "Islamic Morality."

[56] Ali İrfan [Eğriboz], *Rehber-i Ahlâk* (Istanbul: A. Asaduriyan, 1317 [1899–1900]). The text in question was consulted at the Rare Book Library of Istanbul University (catalogue number: 80572).

[57] In general the title pages of texts intended for use in the state schools reveal the particular level for which they were composed, the fact that they had been approved by the Education Ministry, and the date and number of the ministry's permit (*ruhsatname*).

[58] These texts included: Abdurrahman Şeref, *İlm-i Ahlâk* (Istanbul, 1316 [1898–9]); Ali Rıza, *İlm-i Ahlâk* (Istanbul, 1318 [1900–1]); and İsmail Hakkı (Manastırlı), *Mevaid el-En'am fi Berahin-i Akaid el-İslam* (Istanbul, 1309 [1891–2]). All were consulted at Istanbul University's Rare Book Library.

[59] No biographical information concerning Ali İrfan appears in the standard reference sources for late Ottoman authors, e.g. Mitler, Tahir, *Türk Dili ve Edebiyatı Ansiklopedisi*, or even Gövsa. Doğan does refer to another text written by Ali İrfan, entitled *Çocuklara Talim-i Fezail-i Ahlâk* and published in Istanbul in 1894–5. This earlier text was, like the *Rehber*, produced for both the rüşdiye- and idadî-level schools.

to having been selected to assist in the instruction of one of many courses comprising a curriculum mandated by the central government in a system inspired by the example of Western Europe. Furthermore, the fact that each student had his own copy of the work distinguishes it from the "traditional" pedagogical practice of the Islamic world.[60] Perhaps it is a result of our own late twentieth-century view of the place of religious subjects in the school curriculum that makes us think so, but there does seem to be a distinction to be drawn between the internal consistency of the core curriculum of the madrasa experience and the contrasting polyglot nature of the Hamidian curriculum. Combining morals with chemistry and French derives from a very different tradition than the one which linked grammar with logic, theology, and jurisprudence.[61]

Several of the text's formal aspects likewise call to mind the Western pedagogical tradition. The physical appearance of the pages of the bulk of the text in the *Rehber* exhibits a feature quite rare in late Ottoman literary production: glossary entries are supplied below the main text in the form of a footnote apparatus. The notes, separated from the main text by a horizontal line, serve to explicate words and phrases presumably considered difficult to the student readers. Synonyms provide the chief means of this explication. Frequently, a word of Arabic or Persian origin is parsed with a Turkish equivalent, but this is not always the case. Occasionally a non-Turkish word appears to explain a word of similarly non-Turkish origin.

Punctuation is another strikingly exogenous feature of the text in question. The script tradition of the Arabo-Islamic world typically eschews punctuation. Over the course of the nineteenth century this situation began to change. Punctuation markers, and spacing devices such as indented paragraphs, representative of the Latin-based scripts

---

[60] Some of the best accounts of "traditional" educational practices in the Islamic world may be found in Jonathan Berkey, *The Transmission of Knowledge in Medieval Cairo: A Social History of Islamic Education* (Princeton: Princeton University Press, 1992), Messick, *The Calligraphic State*, and Roy P. Mottahedeh, *The Mantle of the Prophet: Religion and Politics in Iran* (New York: Simon & Schuster, 1985).

[61] For a recent treatment of the "traditional" madrasa curriculum in the Sunni world, see Maria Eva Subtelny and Anas B. Khalidov, "The Curriculum of Islamic Higher Learning in Timurid Iran in the Light of the Sunni Revival under Shāh-Rukh," *JAOS* 115/2 (1995), 222.

crept into the printed and, less frequently, the handwritten texts produced in the Ottoman Empire.[62] The trend that rendered Ottoman
institutions increasingly similar in formal appearance to their Western
counterparts was thus reinforced by a parallel movement in the
literary and cultural spheres of the empire. The *Rehber* reflects this
trend, exhibiting many symptoms of the Western editorial tradition.
Hyphens, commas, ellipses, question-marks, exclamation-marks,
quotation-marks, and periods all appear liberally throughout the text,
as do the separation and indentation of paragraphs. In most cases such
punctuation is redundant. For example, periods almost invariably
appear in the wake of verbal forms that inherently indicate the con-
clusion of the thought being expressed.[63] Commas and periods
often unnecessarily precede the conjunctive particle "ki", which by
itself heralds the imminence of a variety of clauses.[64] Likewise, commas
appear between items in a series even when they are already separated
by the conjunction "gerek" which serves the same function.[65] These
largely superficial aspects of the *Rehber*'s formal articulation reflect the
broader pattern of adapting Western modes of organization reflected
in the state school system and in important aspects of late Ottoman
society at large.

There is, however, a more substantive aspect of the text's formal
organization that suggests the strong influence of the Ottoman and
Islamic heritage. This is the fact that approximately 90 per cent of the
text appears in the form of questions posed by a student and the
answers supplied by a teacher.[66] This didactic method recalls an important mode of theological disputation prevalent in Ottoman and Islamic

---

[62] Cf. similar trends in Meiji Japan.

[63] The verbal form *dir/dır* is the most rampant example, appearing on almost every
page of the text.

[64] e.g. Ali İrfan, *Rehber*, 53.

[65] e.g. Ibid. 51: *Kendimizden gerek ilm, gerek paye, ve gerek since büyük olanlara niçün
itaat ve ihtiram etmemiz lazımdır?* (Why must we obey and respect those greater than us
in knowledge, status [lit. share], and age?)

[66] Excluding the brief introduction, 68 of the book's 76 pages of text (i.e. 89%) employ
the question-and-answer format. Those that do not are the last two sections of the text,
which are devoted to a collection of verse and prose entries, presumably mnemonic
devices which touch on the subjects expounded upon in the bulk of the text. Parenthet-
ically, the inclusion of these poems and sayings is perhaps significant for the continuity,
albeit severely marginalized, with the Perso-Arabic textual tradition that gave great weight
to the poetic.

history.[67] Of closer provenance is the question-and-answer format to be found in the opinions (*fetva*) rendered by the Ottoman şeyhülislams since the early years of the empire and by all muftis since very early in Islamic history, and those employed by such a popular late Ottoman mode of communication as the Karagöz (shadow puppet) theater.[68] The question–response technique is a formal device which also has a direct bearing on the content of the text. Like the fetva-rendering of the şeyhülislam, the voice providing the answers assumes an unquestionably authoritative role. "The student" poses the questions, which are, of course, fully and correctly answered by "the teacher." Even the terms used to denote these two roles contribute to defining the sense of the knowledge being imparted. While the term used for questioner is the Persian-derived word "şakird," the word denoting the teacher is the Arabic "muallim." Now, in the official parlance of the state education apparatus generally, "şakird" is virtually interchangeable with the Arabic "talebe." But synonyms for "muallim," such as "ustad," rarely appear. Given the Hamidian-era trend toward re-emphasizing the religious dimension of the state education endeavor, this nomenclature adds to the religious nuance of the teacher–student relationship. For the term "muallim" has a clear association with the "ilmiye," the religious establishment responsible for "traditional" learning. Such learning, "ilm," is to be understood in contradistinction to the "new-style" education, referred to as "maarif," and usually parsed as the "learning of useful things" or as "the process of becoming acquainted with things unknown."[69] The nuance of religious authority imparted by the term "muallim" is particularly pronounced in a context where the teacher is holding forth on the subject of morality.

It is only when we move beyond the *Rehber*'s form to consider its content that we begin to see how squarely it stands in the Islamic and Ottoman traditions. Given the fact that this text was created for use in

[67] As my colleague Sean Gilsdorf kindly points out, the question-and-response format was also a key feature of European medieval scholastic discourse, which, of course, shares much with its counterpart in the Islamic world. In this case, it seems unlikely that the specifically European tradition would have influenced the creation of the *Rehber* in this fashion, but that possibility is not completely inconceivable.

[68] EI2, s.v. "Fatwā," by E. Tyan and J. R. Walsh. For specific examples of *fetva*-rendering in the sixteenth-century Ottoman Empire, see Ertuğrul Düzdağ, *Şeyhülislam Ebusuûd Efendi Fetvaları Işığında 16. Asır Türk Hayatı* (Istanbul: Enderun, 1983).

[69] Berkes, *Development*, 99.

an ostensibly interdenominational educational project, its use of strictly Muslim sources and concepts is striking. There are naturally elements of the Islamic system of morality which it shares with other religious traditions, and these appear in the *Rehber*. Nevertheless, this text relies upon unquestionably Islamic terms, sources, and concepts in expounding the moral duties incumbent upon the young subjects of the Ottoman Empire.

The Islamic identity of the text appears through both form and substance. The most obvious examples of this are the mention of the Prophet Muhammad, specifically Islamic duties and injunctions, and the citation of Hadith. The Prophet is first mentioned in the section of the text devoted to explaining "diyanet," which might be translated as "religion," "religiosity," and/or "piety." In response to the Student's question, "In what way are we to be religious?" the Teacher responds in quintessentially Islamic terms:

By always performing and implementing without hesitation all of the commands of God, the Possessor of Majesty, and our Prophet Muhammad Mustafa, may God the Exalted bless him with the best salutations; by pronouncing the Attestation of Faith; by performing prayers five times [per day] in the direction of the *kıbla* [i.e. toward Mecca] in a pure state; by fasting; by giving alms; if it is in our capacity, by performing the pilgrimage to Mecca; and, without any shortcoming or deliberation, by loving them [i.e. God and His Prophet] with the utmost capacity of our hearts and keeping them in our mind and words at all times.[70]

It would be difficult to find more explicit evidence of the text's Islamic identity than the foregoing articulation of the Five Pillars of Islam.

Other important features of Islamic discourse reinforce the *Rehber*'s sectarian nature. Most obvious is the liberal sprinkling of Hadith, the reported sayings and doings of the Prophet Muhammad, to bolster the argument. For example, the section on Cleanliness (*nezafet*) typically begins with the Student's simple query: "What is cleanliness?" To this the Teacher replies:

TEACHER: Maintaining orderliness in our clothes, our belongings, and all our limbs.
STUDENT: Why must we be orderly?

---

[70] Ali İrfan, *Rehber*, 10–11. For an expression of the need to ensure that young students learned the Muslim credo (*amentü*) in the sıbyanî schools, see Ahmed Cevdet's draft of a catechism in YEE 18/1860.

TEACHER: In the first place, in accordance with the meaning of the noble Hadith (Cleanliness stems from belief [*an-nazzāfah min al-imān*]), our maintaining orderliness is one of the divine commands; secondly . . .[71]

The Hadith stands out from the rest of the text both through the use of parentheses and its being rendered in the original Arabic.

When the *Rehber* seeks to inculcate key values deemed necessary to the maintenance of discipline in the schools, it is no coincidence that many of these values have a clearly Islamic resonance. These values include such concepts as: religiosity (*diyanet*); laudable moral qualities (*ahlâk-ı hamide*); cleanliness (*nezafet*); effort (*mesai*); ascetic discipline (*riyazet*); sound management (*hüsn-ü idare*); contentment (*kanaat*); knowledge (*ilm*); patience (*sabır*); forbearance (*hilm*); order (*intizam*); self-knowledge (*tecrübe-i nefs*); self-control (*ıslah-ı nefs*); restraining the tongue (*zabt-ı lisan*); self-restraint (*ictinab-ı heva-yı nefs*); obedience and respect (*itaat ü ihtiram*); sense of justice (*hakşinaslık*); sociability (*ünsiyet*); benevolence (*hayırhâhlık*); faithfulness (*sadakat*); kindness and gentleness (*nevaziş ü mülayemet*); sincerity (*muhâleset*); justice (*adalet*); love and brotherhood (*muhabbet ü uhuvvet*); and duty (*deyn*). The *Rehber* devotes a chapter to explaining each of these concepts through the question-and-answer format. Interestingly, and not surprisingly, the longest chapters are those on Obedience and Respect, and Faithfulness. Let us turn to the first of these to see how the author marshals Islamic principles in imparting his catechism:

STUDENT: What is obedience?

TEACHER: Submission to and reliance on the commands, according to the canonical law of Islam (*şer'-i şerif*), of those who are more intelligent and greater than we with respect to both age and station.

STUDENT: Whom must we obey?

---

[71] Ali İrfan, *Rehber*, 14. The fact that this appears to be an invented modern "Hadith," probably a calque on the proverb "Cleanliness is next to Godliness," seems of little significance; it was used as if it were a Hadith in this text. Other examples of the use of Hadith to support the moral tenets of the text can be found in passages relating to contentment (*kanaat*, p. 26) and restraining the tongue (*zabt-ı lisan*, p. 40). On other occasions, the author relies on divine authority without explicitly citing Hadith text by stating that "God has ordained us" to do such and such, or that "God has ordered us" to do such and such. Similarly, the Islamic principle of a duty incumbent upon an individual or the community (*farz*) is used to reinforce the necessity of acting in a certain way. For example, self-restraint (lit. refraining from the passions of the self) is thus said to be necessary and perhaps obligatory (*vâcib ve belki farz*, p. 43).

TEACHER: It is a necessity that we obey and respect [the following:] First, God the Exalted, the Creator and Destroyer of places, hearts, and especially, all creatures; secondly, the Prophet, the Possessor of Glory; thirdly, those greater than we, such as our father and mother, the sultan, the teacher [*ustad*, glossed as "*hoca*" in the footnote], and officers.[72]

It is clear from this passage that the implicit hierarchy is both an Islamic and an Ottoman one. God alone could, of course, refer to any religion's conception of the Deity, but when the word "Allah" is immediately followed by the Arabic formula "ta'alla," meaning "may [He] be exalted," so typical of Islamic phrasing, the specifically Islamic nature of the text is clear. This is clearly confirmed by the second object of obedience, the Prophet Muhammad. Parents are inherently universal, but in the context of the imperial school system the mention of sultan, teacher, and officers have obvious Ottoman referents.

The Islamic–Ottoman link implicit in this passage is a reprise of the tone established in the Introduction (*Mukaddeme*). This initial section begins by praising God and lauding the sultan's role in causing education to be spread throughout the empire through the establishment of schools, printing houses, and libraries, each of which is a "proof which announces the Truth."[73] The educational agenda of Abdülhamid II cements the connection between the Divine and the Imperial. The dissemination of knowledge in this context implies the spreading of religion. Precisely which religion is being referred to is clear from the Islamic basis of the Ottoman Empire in general and the specifically Islamic phrasing employed. Given the comparative evidence for religiously inspired education presented earlier, it is important to remember that "secular" education in the West saw nothing amiss in regular

---

[72] Ali İrfan, *Rehber*, 43–44. That the sultan was clearly identified as being the focus of student loyalty is nothing new. As we have seen, students in all of the state schools had frequently to repeat the phrase *padişahım çok yaşa* (long live the sultan), an utterance that was often reinforced by banners that festooned the school buildings during times of ceremony.

[73] Ali İrfan, *Rehber*, 3. The phrase is *birer bürhan-ı hakikat beyan*. This nominal compound contains three Arabic terms, *burhān*, *haqiqah*, and *bayān*. The words *burhān* and *bayān* appear in the Qur'an, and the main nominal form derived from the root Ḥ-Q-Q appears hundreds of times and is one of the attributes of God. Due to the Qur'anic association of these terms and those sharing the same Arabic root, they are rich with Islamic resonance, appearing frequently in the titles of important theological works and, in the modern era, journals throughout the Islamic world.

reference to God, in widespread recourse to overtly religious morality, and in the linking of God and country. By injecting clearly Islamic referents into the classroom, the Ottoman state was thus very much in line with its world time contemporaries.

The Islamic elements of the *Rehber* are, however, certainly not limited to formal or semantic associations. As we have seen in the examples cited above, a clearly Islamic conception of thought and action informs the content of the text. Perhaps more significant than the appearance of a variety of Islamic elements in the *Rehber* is the extent to which its author draws upon them in pursuing his pedagogical agenda.

In its explanation of morals, Ali İrfan's text emphasizes qualities that are of great importance to the patrimonial and bureaucratized nature of the late nineteenth-century Ottoman Empire. Religious justification is marshaled in support of an interrelated cluster of attributes that we will label "quietist." This brings together such complementary qualities as respect for authority, duty, loyalty, and hierarchy, all critical to the Hamidian neo-patrimonial agenda. Indeed, the *Rehber*'s approach to the related concepts of obedience, loyalty, and morality resembled those voiced by the former grand vizier Mahmud Nedim Paşa:

Loyalty is honesty in words and deeds, [it is] material and moral safekeeping. The following concepts are all derived from loyalty: blessedness, compassion, probity, and patriotism. Possessors of these qualities are called loyal and those who prefer their opposites are liars and traitors. Happiness and peace in the affairs of the state originate from loyalty.[74]

The rapid expansion of the Ottoman bureaucracy in the nineteenth century entailed qualitative as well as quantitative change. The proliferation of ministries, commissions, and the elaboration of a palace bureaucracy that paralleled that of the sublime Porte all required considerable manpower. The men taken into this expanded scribal service had not only to be capable bureaucrats but loyal servants of the sultan as well. The state school system was charged with the critical task of producing such doubly suitable candidates. The *Rehber*'s approach to inculcating the key values listed above illustrates one facet of the state's campaign to supply the state's personnel needs.

[74] Cited in M. Şükrü Hanioğlu, *The Young Turks in Opposition* (New York: Oxford University Press, 1995), 23, n. 178.

The quietism of the *Rehber* makes frequent use of patently Islamic tenets and principles, but also reaches beyond the strictly canonical domain to delineate a broader conception of normative behavior. The clearest example of the way in which the text extends beyond the realm of the shariʻa, in which Qurʼan and Hadith directly support the text, and into the sphere of less clearly religious areas of human interaction, is the way it treats the concept of duty. As we have seen above in our discussion of the text's discussion of the Five Pillars of Islam, the *Rehber* makes ample use of core Islamic notions in adumbrating one aspect of those duties incumbent upon the individual (*farz-i ayn*). A cognate of the same term (*ferize*, plural *feraiz*, meaning religious duty) appears in the text to connote duties not associated with Islamic practice *per se*, such as the universal obligation to love one's parents, siblings, friends, or whatever one holds dear,[75] and the need to work and to avoid its opposite, laziness.[76] Conversely, the text takes general notions found in the Qurʼan and Hadith and provides a practical application. Thus, the oft-repeated patience (*sabr*) of the Qurʼan assumes a more specific context in the chapter with the same name in the *Rehber*.

STUDENT: What is patience?

TEACHER: Patience means enduring every misfortune and calamity. As for this, it is such a fine and admirable moral quality that, just as when we are patient we endure without complaint every evil [that befalls us], so also do we never pay attention to the calumnies made against us by evil and corrupt men, and we are on guard against soiling our tongue with cursing and offense.[77]

This still hypothetical context of practicing patience is given further grounding in a subsequent passage by more nearly fixing its temporal and geographical locus:

STUDENT: What are the merits of patience?

TEACHER: When we are patient, it does not do to be grieved or sorry in the face of illnesses, misfortune, and grief. By always saying, (God has ordained it this way[;] it is necessary to be patient and bear it[. T]his, too, will certainly pass.), we do not allow the illnesses and troubles to increase but rather we are always hopeful that we will find health and prosperity

---

[75] Ali İrfan, *Rehber*, 7–8.   [76] Ibid. 16–17.   [77] Ibid. 29.

. . . Apart from that, if we are good, we will have performed good deeds for the state and the millet, benefited everyone, and rendered permanent our good name in this world.[78]

A similar concern for regulating daily activity appears in other attributes of the *Rehber*'s quietism. The concepts of forbearance (*hilm*), order (*intizam*), obedience and respect (*itaat ü ihtiram*), and restraining the tongue (*zabt-ı lisan*) each have their own chapter in the text. In delineating these attributes and advocating their adoption, the text mixes religious and non-religious justification. Thus, it argues for restraining the tongue both by presenting the Arabic of the Hadith "Salāmat al-insān fī hafẓ al-lisān" (i.e. man's well-being stems from restraining his tongue) and by citing the Turkish folk proverb "Ok yarası geçer ama dil yarası geçmez" (i.e. the wound of an arrow will pass but not the wound of the tongue).[79] Likewise, the *Rehber* relies upon both what it terms "religious" and "natural" reasons in advocating love and respect for one's parents. The text reinforces the dual nature of its argumentation by citing both "holy books" (*kutub-u mukaddese*) and evidence from the animal kingdom.[80] Such love and respect should also characterize the student's relationship with his teacher (*hoca*).

STUDENT: In what way should we respect their excellencies our honorable teachers (*muallimin-i kiramımız hazratını*)?

TEACHER: It is our duty to love our hocas, like our parents, more than everyone else, not to ever forget them by committing their advice and wise writings to memory, to conform to them always, and sometimes even if due to our inopportune actions they become angry, scold, or blame, not to resist them but to be quiet and obedient and never to blame or insult them, to learn by heart at once the assignments and lessons they assign, to complete our education, and, after obtaining the diploma, to treat them with extraordinary respect and obedience even if we become more knowledgeable and superior [to them in rank].[81]

The text defines the teacher's role explicitly in parental terms:

---

[78] Ibid. 31. (Parentheses supplied in the original.) [79] Ibid. 40.

[80] Ibid. 47. The passage cited is "Love your father and mother all of your life with sincerity of heart, listen to their commands, and do not engage in bad acts against them."

[81] Ibid. 49.

STUDENT: Why must we respect our teachers (*ustad*)?

TEACHER: The rights of our teachers (*muallim*) are every bit as great as those of our parents with respect to us. Because [while] our parents are the cause of our existence and our growth, our teachers rescue us from the world of ignorance by teaching us and instructing us in both upbringing (*terbiye*) and science and knowledge (*ulûm ü fünûn*). In this respect we come to be considered distinguished and respected by the people. We live with all repose, and, ultimately, we leave life with a lasting good name.[82]

As this passage demonstrates, the position of the teacher vis-à-vis the student not only equals but exceeds that of his parents. By initiating the student into the world of "terbiye" and science and knowledge, the teacher provides an *entrée* into a world of success where one can make one's mark. This is a world where, by implication, the parents do not belong. Their role in the child's life is reduced to birth and early childhood development.[83] They are thus equated with the "world of ignorance." It is a telling aspect of the state's moralizing campaign that it is the teacher, in this context clearly an extension of the Ottoman state, who can effect the student's rescue from the ignorant orbit of the family.

The removal of the family from the locus of education, its moral component in particular, cleared the way for the pre-eminence of the relationship between the state and the student. The state, acting through the local bureaucrats employed in each school, stands *in loco parentis*, a status reinforced by the fact that more and more of the schools at the idadî level were being converted to boarding institutions. The trend toward renovating the existing idadî schools to accommodate boarders began with the schools in the larger cities of the empire. Archival evidence reveals that the paperwork for such changes began within only five years of the creation of the Education Share of 1883.[84] By November 1890 there were boarding idadîs in Selânik,

---

[82] Ali İrfan, *Rehber*, 49–50.

[83] In time, of course, states everywhere would act to increase its *in loco parentis* status even more through the kindergarten. Ali İrfan's suggestion that "everyone should send their children to school while they are young" hints at the downward trend in the age of school entry that lay ahead for the Ottoman Empire and its successor states. Ibid. 29.

[84] For example, imperial decrees authorizing expenditures to convert the idadîs in Manastır and İzmir dates from 1888. For İzmir, see İrade MM 4199. 17 Zilkade 1305 (26 July 1888). For Manastır, İrade MM 4223. 3 Zilhicce 1305 (11 Aug. 1888). Schools so converted generally thereafter accepted both boarding and day students.

Yanya, Manastır, Izmir, Damascus, Beirut, and Aleppo.[85] Zühdü Paşa expanded on this trend, advocating the expansion of the schools capacity to house students overnight to all of the provincial and district centers in order that the benefits of education not be confined to those who lived in towns. By late 1892 students from the countryside could also board at the idadîs in Edirne, Tekirdağ, Kırkkilise, Bursa, Erzurum, Midilli, Konya, Trabzon, Ankara, Sivas, Kastamonu, Adana, and Diyarbekir.[86] Now the students were literally being taken out of the familial context and into the care of the state.

The incorporation of the young student into the world of the state— the world which promised success and a lasting good name—depended upon several interrelated concepts. Prime among these are loyalty and obedience, attributes that imply a clearly ordered and defined hierarchy. It is, after all, the state as embodied first in the person of the sultan, and then in the form of his servants, that the students were directed to obey.[87] By integrating the hierarchy of the schools within that of the state and, in turn, that of the cosmos, the *Rehber* emphasizes the Islamic and Ottoman elements of its educational project. Like the maps introduced into late Ottoman classrooms, books such as Ali İrfan's reinforced the Hamidian agenda aimed at creating a positive identification between the empire's official apparatus and its youth.

SUPERVISION

Having taken measures to control classroom texts, the state bureaucracy was nevertheless unwilling to leave it at that. The Hamidian bureaucracy was well aware that what transpired in a classroom could easily be made to subvert the state's original intention. Attempting to prevent such threats to the pedagogical order, the government resorted to the by-now familiar recourse of stipulating more supervision and inspection. Such supervision took several forms. One target of central government control was what its teachers were actually doing and saying in the classroom. State bureaucrats seem to have been well aware

---

[85] ŞD 210/55. 14 Rebiülahir 1308 (27 Nov. 1890).

[86] İrade M 1310 R 1. 12 Rebiülahir 1310 (3 Nov. 1892).

[87] We have referred above to the passage in the *Rehber* that spells out the ordinal hierarchy of loyalty for young Ottoman subjects to follow: first, loyalty to God; second, to the Prophet Muhammad; and third, to the sultan, teachers, and officers.

that classroom teachers could not always be counted on to deliver the idealized lessons of the *Rehber*. The selection and subsequent monitoring of the classroom teachers were obviously crucial to the success of the entire project. Although unfortunately little is known about the specific ways in which teachers were selected, various evidence points to a general tension between the imperative to fill a growing number of teaching positions and the similarly rising concern for hiring men of political and religious soundness.[88] The criteria for teachers in the state schools enumerated in the Education Regulation of 1869 were hardly exclusive. Candidates had to be subjects of the Ottoman Empire and to have attained the diploma of the normal schools (*Darülmuallimin*) or its equivalent. Preferably, teachers being hired for each level of schooling would have attained the diploma corresponding to that section of the normal school, but this was not absolutely mandatory. There is no mention of the necessity of their possessing sound moral qualities.[89] In spite of the moves taken during the Hamidian period to live up to the situation envisioned in the 1869 Regulation, there seems to have been a perpetual shortage of qualified teachers, particularly those who could live up to the new emphasis on morals. The fact that teacher salaries were quite low added to the problem.[90] Furthermore, the increased vigilance being manifested by the central government concerning moral rectitude and political allegiance among the schools' teachers ensured that filling positions with properly vetted candidates became even more difficult.

Anecdotal archival evidence suggests that the state may have had as much trouble monitoring its teachers as it had with its students. For example, in 1890 reports reached Yıldız Palace concerning the unfortunate behavior of a history teacher at the Mekteb-i Mülkiye. According to the decree promulgated to correct the situation, a certain Midhat Bey had been ignoring the previously accepted history textbook, declaring it to be abridged. He had his students writing down the history of Egypt, Greece, and Rome every day in history class, later

---

[88] For a discussion of the problem of finding teachers for the new schools, see Kodaman, *Abdülhamid*, 145–56.

[89] YEE 37/330, 53–6.

[90] For example, a decree from early 1888 refers to the resignation of a teacher at the idadî in Izmir due to the low level of remuneration. İrade Dah. 83697. 16 Cemaziyelevvel 1305 (30 Jan. 1888).

having them produce fair copies (*tebyiz*) from their draft copies (*müsvedde*). This process was apparently leaving the students with no time for their other lessons. Moreover, he was reported to have been subverting school decorum by mocking the other teachers and by wasting class time with meaningless words and exhibiting signs of levity. Worse still was the charge that Midhat Bey was deemed to be undermining the religious principles of his students. Apart from certain transgressions regarding Christianity, he was alleged to have mockingly discussed religious principles (*akaid-i diniye*), "the lofty morals of some of the Prophets," and the four orthodox schools of Islamic jurisprudence.[91] The imperial decree adopted to respond to this situation underscores the necessity of schoolteachers' not wasting time by straying from the prescribed texts. They should instead give serious attention to correcting their students' belief (*tashih-i itikad*) and to their moral education (*tehzib-i ahlâk*). Interestingly, the decree extrapolates from the case at hand to declare that "in the Islamic schools the subject requiring the utmost attention is the matter of strengthening Islamic principles."[92]

A year later, a similar case of a teacher's poisoning the environment arose in Aleppo. The Education Ministry's accountant (*muhasebeci*) for the province of Aleppo was reported to be corrupting both his students' moral beliefs and the people's obedience to the government. This teacher, whose name is Cibrail Dallâl Efendi, is deemed to have engaged in "actions and publications which run contrary to the language of obedience and allegiance."[93] His most egregious offenses were his having translated an ode (*kaside*) that was extremely critical of the Hamidian regime, entitled "The Throne and the Statue" (*Al-'arsh wal-haykal*), and his having sent a letter to the French newspaper *Le Courier du Soir*. Also potentially troublesome was the following year's report of a meeting in Izmir whose participants included a teacher at the local trade school (*mekteb-i sanayi*).[94] To make matters worse, the memorandum of the Meclis-i Mahsus referred to above calls attention to the

---

[91] İrade Dah. 91851. 24 Şaban 1307 (15 Apr. 1890).
[92] Ibid. *Mekâtib-i İslâmiyede en ziyade riayet olunmak lâzım gelen şey takviye-i akaid-i İslâmiye maddesi.*
[93] AYN 1428, 306. 27 Rebiülahir 1309 (30 Nov. 1891).
[94] MKP 86/15-1488. 10 Safer 1320 (19 May 1902).

regrettable fact that "hocas" were not being used to teach the lessons in morals that had been added to the schools by 1900.[95]

The supervision of the state educational system was not limited to teachers. Indeed, most of the attention was devoted to the students. Inspection was, once again, a preferred method. Two types of inspection were utilized. The first was the appointing of more inspectors, each of whom would be responsible for a particular geographical area. Hiring more inspectors and the bureaucratic apparatus to support them was a solution invoked in many important memoranda on the subject of curricular reform.[96] Moreover, a critical element in the composition of the inspection committees to be established was that they be largely staffed by members of the ulama.

A second means of supervision was the creation of permanent inspectorships in each idadî school and many of the higher academies in Istanbul. This took the form of an additional administrator. The position of the *müdir-i sani*, which might best be translated as "vice-principal,"[97] was in existence by the first years of the twentieth century, by which time the Hamidian government had cause to fear (with good reason, as it turned out) internal as well as external threats to the regime. Nevertheless, the creation of the position of vice-principal was in many respects a natural consequence of the concern with both moral development in the classroom and moral activity outside it. The duties of the vice-principal included overseeing lessons relating to the "religious and moral sciences."[98] He was also to devote special attention to the students' training (*terbiye*) and instruction in religious manners (*âdab-i diniye*) and proper morals (*ahlâk-i hasane*). Apart from keeping a watchful eye out for inappropriate and harmful material in the lessons the students read and the assignments they wrote, the vice-principal was to monitor their religio-moral conduct. He was charged with warning pupils who fell short in fulfilling their religious duties and whose deportment and actions ran contrary to sound morals (*hüsn-ü ahlâk*).[99] After the first such warning the students were to be reprimanded. That proving fruitless, the vice-principal was then, in consul-

---

[95] YA Res. 105/13. 3. lef. 13 Ramazan 1317 (15 Jan. 1900).

[96] See e.g. YEE 11/1763; YA Res. 105/44; BEO 178072; Yıldız Maruzat Defterleri 13947.

[97] This term at least has the virtue of capturing the disciplinary (read warden-like) function of the role played by "vice-principals" in public high schools in the USA.

[98] *Düstûr*, 1. tertib. vol. 8, p. 434.   [99] Ibid. 435.

tation with the principal, to assign the necessary punishment, a subject to be taken up below.

In classic bureaucratic fashion, the regulation attempted to quantify moral conduct. Other duties of the vice-principals included preparing examinations in the religious and moral sciences and the composing of annual reports detailing each student's attainments in those courses at the end of the year.[100] The vice-principals were similarly charged with keeping a register to record each student's affairs and morals and the degree to which he performed his religious obligations. According to the contents of this register, at year's end each student was to be assigned a score that would correspond to his religious and moral training (*terbiye-i diniye ve ahlâkiye*). As the sum of these yearly numbers was to be imprinted on the student's diploma, the aggregate effect of these yearly moral report cards could have a lasting impact on a student's career.

In tabulating the moral training and behavior of students in its civil schools, the bureaucracy was adopting the practice previously in use in the empire's military schools. This borrowing across the divide separating the civil and military schools is not surprising, given the attempts made to forge a unified curriculum.[101] As we noted in our discussion of school maps, the military and civil schools shared many common features, not least of which was the attempt to implement an ordered daily regimen. While we will return to the subject of school discipline below, it is here necessary to comment on the way the tabulation of moral activity was carried out.

Consider the case of one Arif Hikmet Efendi, a student in the idadî section of the Imperial War College. For reasons that are not clear, the secretariat of Yıldız Palace requested information from the school's director concerning the educational career of this student, who was then in his mid-twenties.[102] In his reply to the palace, dated 15 October 1895, the director includes a copy of what might be called the student's "moral report card." It provides us with detailed information about the educational career of this young man and his brushes with the disciplinary authority of the late Ottoman school system. Naturally, the

---

[100] Ibid.

[101] On the unification of the military and civil curriculum, see e.g. AYN 428, 210.

[102] Y Mtv. 129/175. 25 Rebiülahir 1313 (15 Oct. 1895).

fact that this case originated in the context of the military establish-ment limits its utility for informing a discussion of moral life in the civil schools. Nevertheless, the civil school system's subsequent adop-tion of the practice of keeping moral records of its students, the afore-mentioned similarities between at least some important aspects of the civil and military educational experiences, and the lack of any known examples of such reports in the Abdülhamid period all suggest the importance of the practice of tabulating a student's moral behavior.

Of interest here is the inclusion of ostensibly religious activity along with infractions normally associated with school discipline. Arif Hikmet was punished for missing prayers just as he was for misbehav-ing in class or skipping it altogether.[103] For example, the report indi-cates that he was docked two weeks' leave for failing to attend the *yatsı*, or nighttime, prayers on 10 July 1889. During the following year he received the same punishment and the same two demerits for applying mustache oil in class with the aid of a mirror. His many other offenses included both insulting and striking a fellow student, various cases of absenteeism, buying candy on credit, bringing a complaint against officers present during examinations, failing to salute officers he encountered while traveling during vacation, and others. His two most imaginative feats involved using forged documents to commandeer state animals for a trip to the countryside, and tricking doctors who examined him while he was let out of prison to go to the hospital into allowing him to take a trip to the countryside for rest.

The disciplinary system with which Arif Hikmet was frequently at odds involved two methods of punishment. One was corporal in the broad sense of the term, that is, it constrained the student's movement by denying him leave-time or by confining him to barracks or to prison. The system could also inflict corporal punishment in the more narrow sense: he could be beaten. The other mode of punishment provided for a consequence of longer duration, presumably, than the physical effects of controlled violence inflicted on the student's body. It main-tained a written record of the incidents of his disobedience. According to the schema at work in the military idadî schools attended by Arif

---

[103] Y Mtv. 129/175. 25 Rebiülahir 1313 (15 Oct. 1895). This suggests parallels with nominally secular schools in other countries, such as preparatory schools in England and the USA.

Hikmet between 1886 and 1894, each student was assigned an initial "moral score" (*ahlâk numarası*) of fifty points. Each instance of disobedience received a numerical value, ranging in the case of Arif Hikmet Efendi from one to twelve points. A running total that decreased in size with every transgression but reflected the annual addition of the fifty-point allotment was kept in the margin of the *defter*. This allowed both for administrators to make comparisons between students and for the student's behavior to remain associated with him throughout his school career and, since the total appeared on his diploma, in future years as well. Arif Hikmet, presumably one of the more penalized students, had by the end of his third year compiled a score of 102 out of a possible 150 points. Lapses in religious observance were counted toward this "moral" total just like any other demerit. Always pragmatic, the system for inducing moral belief and action included both incentives and disincentives.

CONCLUSION: SAFEGUARDING THE EMPIRE'S FUTURE

The emphasis the Hamidian state placed on inculcating morals was perhaps the defining characteristic of its educational agenda. Whereas the educational policy of the preceding Tanzimat period had frequently been more concerned with adopting Western methods for their own sake, the Hamidian endeavor exhibited a marked difference in spirit and in substance. Although it shared many of the practical objectives of the previous period, for example, the imperative of filling the posts of a rapidly expanding bureaucracy and the broader notion of attempting to educate as much of the population as possible, Abdülhamid II's policy sought selectively to borrow Western pedagogical techniques in order to stave off the challenge that the West represented. The moral component of Hamidian educational policy was critical, in that it marked a desire to repulse the challenge of the West by drawing on the Islamic and Ottoman basis of the state. To carry out its moral agenda the bureaucrats of Abdülhamid II adopted certain practical measures from what they saw to be the successful examples of centralized state expansion in Western Europe. Thus, such features of Western education as boarding schools, centralized curricular planning, and textbook distribution became standard fare in late Ottoman education. The fact that it incorporated these elements of the Western approach, however, does not diminish the project's overall intention. The aim of Abdülhamid II's educational policy was to train a young generation that would have the academic skills and the political loyalty to serve its state in troubled times.

But the state's intent went beyond the mere fostering of positive associations among its young charges. By expanding the capacity to board its young subjects and by emphasizing the religio-moral aspects of their development, the Hamidian state exhibited an unprecedented degree of involvement in their daily lives. The history of late Ottoman education underscores the fact that the expansion of the state in the modern period was not merely an abstract concept, but rather one which had critical ramifications on the group and individual level. All across the empire students left their homes and were entrusted into the hands of the state and its representatives. While it remains difficult to discern the effect of this relationship with any precision, it is clear that the dynamic between state and individual was dramatically changed. Gone were the days in which the state remained a distant abstraction for most of its subjects. The modern state would no longer rely on intermediaries, generally communal in organization, in its relationship with the governed. Now the state apparatus reached out into provinces, sub-provinces, and smaller and smaller hamlets to educate, tax, conscript, count, and inoculate its people. Many of the young men who attended the state schools founded in the reign of Abdülhamid II would spend the rest of their lives in one or another form of state service. The state in question would have changed over the course of their lives, in many cases several times. But the fundamental mission of the state as arbiter of many facets of their lives would remain a remarkably constant influence.

In this and the preceding chapters I have approached the educational mission of the Hamidian state from a number of different and, it is hoped, complementary perspectives. I began by placing the Hamidian effort in an international and imperial context. Faced with the alarming inroads of educators from overseas, neighboring states, and indigenous minority groups, the government of Abdülhamid II countered by expanding the fledgling state school system it had inherited from his predecessors. As the views of a variety of Ottoman officials in Istanbul and the far-flung provinces reveal, the servants of the state conceived of the need to expand state educational options in direct relationship to the competition. While a considerable literature has been devoted to the spread of non-Muslim schools in this period, the connection between them, the foreign missionary institutions in particular, and the late Ottoman commitment to state education had never been properly understood. By addressing the views of Ottoman officials stationed in various provinces, we have seen, both individually and cumulatively, the effect of the pleas they addressed to the capital. For officials serving in almost any given province, the struggle being waged over education was tantamount to a battle for the hearts and minds of the empire's youth and, hence, its very future.

In order to understand the competing tendencies in the complex relationship between Eastern and Western influences affecting the world of Hamidian education, it was necessary to turn our attention back to the preceding Tanzimat period. The history of the Galatasaray lycée, exemplar for the idadî schools, epitomizes the Hamidian departure from the prevailing educational policy. What was begun as a joint Ottoman–French venture in the Tanzimat era was thoroughly modified to reflect the strong Islamic emphasis of the Hamidian period. As the idadî schools appeared across the breadth of the empire to complete the system envisioned in the Tanzimat agenda, they embodied the changed official attitude toward state education. Schools originally conceived, under considerable European pressure, to educate Muslim and non-Muslim children together in a "mixed" environment were now referred to routinely as "Muslim schools."

Seen from the perspective of a struggle to ward off foreign encroachment, many heretofore curious aspects of the Hamidian educational effort make sense. The increasingly adversarial Hamidian approach to schooling helps to explain, for example, the tremendous financial and political commitment directed to the school-building effort in a time of a straitened Treasury and dwindling diplomatic resources, and the fact that money earmarked for the construction of ostensibly secular schools was spent to send itinerant ulama through some provinces to inveigh against the dangers of the competing forms of education being supplied by the foreigners. An understanding of the competitive context also elucidates the Hamidian campaign to modify the schools' curriculum almost as soon as they were built. Schools commonly labelled "secular" and "Western" reveal themselves to have provided courses in the Islamic sciences and morality along with French and chemistry, a juxtaposition for which the prevailing historical literature leaves us unprepared.

Our discussions of the architecture and disciplinary agenda of the schools made it clear that these institutions, far from acting as agents of cultural bifurcation, actually assimilated Western and Ottoman influences. Although patterned after French lycées in both plan and section, the idadî schools incorporated a number of modifications that squared them with Ottoman and Islamic tradition. Such symbolically rich ornaments as the sultan's monogram, the fluid lines of poetry dedicating the building, and the star-and-crescent motif mediated their otherwise classicizing façades and meshed with the more obvious physical signs of Islam such as the area reserved for the school's mosque. Similarly, the school calendar and disciplinary stance were organized on overtly Islamic principles. The schools created an environment of patriotism and religious observance while educating their charges in those subjects deemed necessary to help the Ottoman Empire catch up with the West.

Teaching materials likewise squared modern necessity with Ottoman objectives. The Hamidian educational establishment modified classroom maps, symbols of up-to-date technology, to reflect a more organic and politically useful conception of Ottoman territory. Slavish imitations of European maps composed to display each continent in isolated fashion gave way to cartographic renditions that maintained the integrity of the Ottoman Empire. Like the maps, school textbooks devoted to moral instruction reflected another aspect of the synthesis created in late Ottoman schools. Ottoman educators used the Western-derived technological efficiency inherent in both centralized curricular planning and the textbook format to disseminate an overtly Islamic notion of morality, thus revealing the ease with which the modern and the traditional, the old and the new, could be fused together in an educational system that forces us to rethink the widely held view of cultural dualism in the late Ottoman Empire.

The Ottoman educational effort during the reign of Sultan Abdül-hamid was nothing less than an attempt to safeguard the empire's future. Confronted with what it deemed a hostile array of educational competition, the Hamidian state fought back. By building a school system that incorporated much of Western organizational methods and some of its educational content, the late Ottoman state endeavored to stave off the encroachment that it saw as threatening the thinking and behavior of its youth, and hence its very future. Through such efforts as reshaping the ways the young generation of Ottoman subjects would envision their empire and inculcating moral values drawn from Islamic tradition, the Hamidian education project was attempting to inoculate its charges from the worst of Western influence while taking advantage of the "secret wisdom" that Western learning had to offer.

In spite of this effort to use the schools to inculcate Islamic religiosity and Ottoman loyalty, they are frequently cited as hastening the end of the Hamidian era. Students educated in Abdülhamid II's educational institutions played an active role in the Young Turk Revolution of 1908, and eventually in helping to create the national states that succeeded the Ottoman Empire in the Balkans and the Middle East. This paradox might be taken to demonstrate that the Hamidian schooling effort ended in failure. To be concerned with the issue of whether it succeeded or failed is, however, to fall into the binary trap that is symptomatic of much of this period's historiography. The Hamidian educational endeavor is, to my way of thinking, more important as an attempt. By incorporating the variety of influences we have observed in the foregoing chapters, the late Ottoman schools reveal much about the state's perception of its current predicament and the measures necessary to improve the empire in the future. More than being either a success or a failure, the schools are important in that they represent a range of possibilities and tendencies that made sense in their chronological and geographical context. If judged from the standpoint of the nationalist era, in other words, across a wrenching mental barrier, these schools naturally appear to have been working at variance with the flow of history. Absent such an ahistorical teleology, however, the Hamidian schools represent an earnest and entirely logical response to the "demands of the present."

This brings us back to the point raised in Chapter 1 about the importance of seeing the Ottoman educational endeavor as an integral part of a global phenomenon. Throughout this book I have stressed the importance of the indigenous context in shaping Ottoman educational change, insisting on it, in fact, because of the prevailing historiographical tendency to see education as a Western implant. Yet this indigenization of modern education is precisely what makes the Ottoman case of a piece with trends elsewhere in the world in this period. Ottoman educators were, like their global counterparts, working to bring foreign educational elements into the service of the state, which in turn re-created some of the dynamics surrounding the imported construct, as Arjun Appadurai has noted.[104] The simultaneity of this dynamic of indigenization is what makes the Ottoman, or any other educational narrative, both unique and part of a broader global trend. The unique features of the late Ottoman case—the reworking of the Tanzimat model in the face of stiff educational and cultural competition; the pervasive recourse to Islamic content, symbolism, and daily patterning; and the insistence on public morality, to name only a few— are of course only properly intelligible in the broader context of Ottoman history, and the period of "reforms" in particular. Yet the triumph of the indigenous over against the presumptive onslaught of Western influence is ultimately what makes the Ottoman case understandable to any observer of educational change in the modern period. Through the reworking of the Western model, the insistence on Ottoman and Islamic referents, however reified in their new context, the articulation of the spatial and disciplinary patterns of the schools, the reformulation of Ottoman and world geography, and the repeated recourse to Islamic morality, the late Ottoman educational project responded to the "demands of the present" in ways that both underscored its indigenous emphasis and reaffirmed its place along its partners in "world time."

I began this book by calling attention to the controversy surrounding the so-called return of Islam to the educational environment. Fiercely opposed by secularists determined to hold on to the presumption of a rigid separation of religion and state-supplied education, and supported by those bent on restoring what they consider to be religion's proper place in the schools, Islam's place in education in contemporary society is one of the most hotly contested issues in Turkey today. If this study can lend any historical perspective to the current impasse, it is that we need to understand the complex interplay between "religion" and "secularism" not as sharply defined entities, but

---

[104] "Disjuncture and Difference in the Global Cultural Economy," in Patrick Williams and Laura Crisman (eds.), *Cultural Discourse and Post-Colonial Theory: A Reader* (New York: Columbia University Press, 1994).

rather as ones whose edges are continually being blurred, redefined, and nuanced according to changing conceptions of what constitutes the "demands of the present." Instead of a historical trajectory that juxtaposes wild swings between secular and religious periods in the late Ottoman and Republican eras—for example, from Tanzimat to Hamidian to Kemalist—it is more accurate to envision recombinations of largely the same elements reflecting changes in emphasis over time. Just as more recent research on the Tanzimat period has revealed the strong dose of Islamic rationale that coincided with the presumed secular approach inherent in plans to revivify the empire for its own sake and according to its own principles,[105] so also is new research on the early Republican period beginning to reveal a more synthetic approach to education.[106] It seems clear that future research into the field of education in the late Ottoman and Republican periods will further demonstrate the need to take a critical look at such old labels as "Western," "secular," or "modern" as obstacles to understanding the complex interrelationship between different types of curricular content and between contrasting approaches to the overall purpose of education and the environment in which it was, and continues to be, carried out. Only such a nuanced approach to the ways in which education was conceived and implemented by the state will allow us then to contemplate in sufficient depth the various ways in which it was received by the great variety of students for whom it was intended. But that is another story.

[105] See Abu Manneh, "Islamic Roots;" Bülent Özdemir, "Ottoman Reforms and Social Life: Reflections from Salonica, 1830–1850", Ph.D. diss., Birmingham University (2000); and the promising research being carried out by Vehbi Baysan for his dissertation entitled "Ottoman Education Policy During the Tanzimat Period," at the University of Manchester.

[106] See e.g. Barak Salmoni, "Islam in Turkish Educational Materials, 1923–1950," paper presented at the Annual Meeting of the Middle East Studies Association, Washington, DC, 21 Nov. 1999.

BIBLIOGRAPHY

I. ARCHIVAL SOURCES

A. Başbakanlık Osmanlı Arşivi, Istanbul (BOA)

Bab-ı Âli Evrak Odası (BEO)
  Ayniyât (AYN)
  Maarif Gelen-Giden
  Meclis-i Vükelâ Mazbataları (MV)
  Şura-yı Devlet Gelen-Giden (ŞD)
  Vilayât Gelen-Giden

İradeler
  Dahiliye (İrade Dah.)
  Husûsiye (İrade Hus.)
  Maarif (İrade M)
  Meclis-i Mahsus (İrade MM)
  Şura-yı Devlet (İrade ŞD)

Dahiliye Nezâreti Belgeleri
  Dahiliye Nezâreti Siyasî Kısım Belgeleri (DH. SYS)

Haritalar

Rumeli Müfettişliği Evrâkı
  Rumeli Müfettişliği Arzuhalleri (TFR.ı.ŞKT)

Yıldız Esas Evrâkı (YEE)
  Mütenevvi Mârûzat Evrâkı (Y Mtv.)
  Sadâret Resmî Mârûzat Evrâkı (YA Res.)
  Sadâret Husûsî Mârûzat Evrâkı (YA Hus.)
  Sadrazam M. Kâmil Paşa Evrâkı (Yıldız Esas Evrâkına Ek) (MKP)
  Yıldız Perâkende Evrâkı (Y Prk.)

B. İstanbul Üniversitesi Nâdir Eserler Kütüphanesi, Istanbul (IU)

Albümler
Eski Harflı Türkçe Kitapları
Haritalar

C. Library of Congress, Washington, DC (LC)

Photograph Collection of Sultan Abdülhamid II.

D. *The British Library, London, UK (BL)*
India and Oriental Office Library
Map Library

II. PUBLISHED PRIMARY SOURCES

ABBOTT, G. F., *Turkey in Transition* (London: Edward Arnold, 1909).

AYDEMİR, ŞEVKET SÜREYYA, *Suyu Arayan Adam* (Ankara: Öz Yayınları, 1959).

BLISS, DANIEL, *The Reminiscences of Daniel Bliss* (New York: Fleming H. Revell, 1920).

AL-BUSTĀNĪ, SULAYMĀN,*'Ibrāh wa Dhikrā, aw al-Dawlah al-'Uthmāniyya qabla al-Dustūr wa ba'dahu*, ed. Khālid Ziyādah (Beirut: Dār al-Ṭalī'ah, 1978).

CEVAD, MAHMUD İBN EL-ŞEYH NÂFI', *Maarif-i Umumiye Nezareti Tarihçe-i Teşkilat ve İcraati* ([Istanbul]: Matbaa-ı Amire, 1338 [1919–20]).

COBB, STANWOOD, *The Real Turk* (Boston: The Pilgrim Press, 1914).

CORTAMBERT, EUGÈNE, *Petit cours de géographie moderne*, 26th edn. (Paris: Hachette, 1873; repr. 1889).

CORTAMBERT, RICHARD, *Aventures d'un artiste dans le Liban: anecdotes— moeurs—paysages* (Paris: Librairie française E. Maillet, 1864).

CUINET, VITAL, *La Turquie d'Asie: Geographie administrative, statistique, descriptive et raisonée de chaque province de l'Asie-Mineure*, 4 vols. (Paris: Ernest Leroux, 1890).

Düstûr. Birinci Tertib. vols. 5–8 (1884–1908). (Ankara: Başvekâlet Devlet Matbaası, 1937–43).

[EĞRİBOZ], ALİ İRFAN, *Rehber-i Ahlâk* (Istanbul: A. Asaduriyan, 1317 [1899–1900]).

ENGELHARDT, ED. *La Turquie et le Tanzimat, ou histoire des réformes dans l'empire ottoman depuis 1826 jusqu'a nos jours* (Paris: A. Cotillon, 1882).

HAKKI, İSMAİL (MANASTIRLI), *Mevaid el-En'am fi Berahin-i Akaid el-İslam* (Istanbul, 1309 [1891–2]).

HİLMÎ, TÜCCARZÂDE İBRAHİM, *Memâlik-i Osmaniye Cep Atlası* (Istanbul: İbrahim Hilmî, 1323 [1907]).

LEÏLA HANOUM, *Le Harem imperial et les sultanes aux XIXᵉ siècle* ([Paris]: Editions Complexe, 1991).

LEYLA HANIMEFENDİ, *The Imperial Harem of the Sultans: Daily Life at the Çırağan Palace During the 19th Century* (Istanbul: Peva, 1994).

[Maarif-i umumiye nezaret-i celilesi], *Leylî ve neharî umum mekâtib-i idadiye-*

i mülkiye'ye mahsus olarak maarif-i umumiye nezaret-i celilesince mukadema tanzim ve bu defa tadil ve tashih edilen ders programları ile talimât dir (Dersaadet [Istanbul]: Asır Matbaası, 1318 [1900–1]).

Mekteb-i Sultani (Istanbul: Matbaa-yi Amire, 1918).

MURAD, MEHMED, *Turfanda mi yoksa Turfa mi* (Millî roman) (Istanbul: Mahmud Bey Matbaası, 1308 [1890–1]).

RAMSAY, W. M., *The Revolution in Constantinople and Turkey* (London: 1908).

RIZA, ALİ, *İlm-i Ahlâk* (Istanbul: Karabet Matbaası, 1318 [1900–1]).

SABRÎ, EYYUB, *Mir'at ül-Haremeyn* (Kostaniniye [Istanbul]: Bahriye, 1306 [1888–9]).

SAİD, MEHMED, *Said Paşa'nın Hatıratı*, 3 vols. (Istanbul: Sabah Matbaası, 1910).

Salname-i Devlet-i Aliye-i Osmaniye (Istanbul: Matbaa-yı Amire, 1300 [1883]).

Salname-i Nezaret-i Maarif-i Umumiye, 5 vols. (Istanbul: Matbaa-yı Amire, 1316 [1898], 1317 [1899], 1318 [1900], 1319 [1901]; Istanbul: Asır Matbası 1321 [1903]).

SALVE, [LOUIS] DE, "L'Enseignement en Turquie: Le lycée impérial de Galata-Séraï," *Revue des deux mondes*, 5 (1874), 836–53.

SÂMÎ, ŞEMSEDDİN, *Kamûs-i Türkî* (Dersaadet [Istanbul]: İkdam Matbaası, 1317 [1899–1900]).

ŞEREF, ABDURRAHMAN, *İlm-i Ahlâk* (Istanbul, 1316 [1898–9]).

TESTA, LE BARON I. DE, *Recueil de Traités de la Porte Ottomane avec les puissances étrangères depuis le premier traité conclu, en 1536, entre Suléyman 1ᵉʳ et François 1ᵉʳ jusqu'a nos jours* (Paris: Ernest Leroux, 1892).

UBICINI, ABDOLONYME and PAVET DE COURTEILLE, *État présent de l'Empire ottoman* (Paris: Librairie Militaire de J. Dumaine, 1876).

[YALÇIN], HÜSEYİN CAHİD, *Kavgalarım* ([Istanbul]: Tanin Matbaası, 1326 [1908–9]).

—— "Meşrutiyet Hatıraları, 1908–1918," *Fikir Hareketleri* 82 (1935).

YALÇIN, HÜSEYİN CAHİT, *Siyasal Anılar* (Istanbul: Türkiye İş Bankası Kültür Yayınları, 1976).

III. SECONDARY SOURCES

ABOU-EL-HAJ, RIFAAT ALI, "The Social Uses of the Past: Recent Arab Historiography of Ottoman Rule," *IJMES* 14 (1982), 185–201.

ABU-MANNEH, BUTRUS, "Jerusalem in the Tanzimat Period: The New Ottoman Administration and the Notables," *Die Welt des Islams*, 30 (1990), 1–44.

—— "The Islamic Roots of Gülhane," *Die Welt des Islams*, 34 (1994), 173–203.

ADAS, MICHAEL, *Machines as the Measure of Men: Science, Technology, and Ideologies of Western Dominance* (Ithaca, NY: Cornell University Press, 1989).

[ADIVAR], ABDÜLHAK ADNAN, *La Science chez les Turcs Ottomans* (Paris: Librairie Orientale et Américaine, 1939).

ADIVAR, ABDÜLHAK ADNAN, *Osmanlı Türklerinde İlim* (Istanbul: Maarif Matbaası, 1943).

AHMAD, FEROZ, *The Young Turks: The Committee of Union and Progress in Turkish Politics, 1908–1914* (Oxford: Oxford University Press, 1969).

AKARLI, ENGİN DENİZ, "The Problems of External Pressures, Power Struggles, and Budgetary Deficits in Ottoman Politics under Abdulhamid II (1876–1909)," Ph.D. diss., Princeton University (1976).

—— "Friction and Discord Within the Ottoman Government Under Abdulhamid II," *Boğaziçi Univeristy Journal—Humanities*, 7 (1979), 3–26.

—— "Abdülhamid II's Attempt to Integrate Arabs into the Ottoman System," in David Kushner (ed.), *Palestine in the Late Ottoman Period: Political, Social, and Economic Transformation* (Jerusalem: Yad Izhak Ben Zvi, 1986).

—— "Ottoman Documents Concerning the Governorate of Mount Lebanon (1861–1918)," *Studies on Turkish–Arab Relations*, 1 (1986), 13–19.

—— *The Long Peace: Ottoman Lebanon, 1861–1920* (Berkeley: University of California Press, 1993).

—— "Modernity and State–Society Relations in Late Ottoman History and Historiography," paper presented at the University of Chicago, May 1998.

AKKUTAY, ÜLKER, *Enderûn Mektebi* (Ankara: Gazi Üniversitesi Basın-Yayın Yüksekokulu Basımevi, 1984).

AKYOL, İBRAHİM HAKKI, "Tanzimat Devrinde Bizde Coğrafya ve Jeoloji," in *Tanzimat; Yüzüncü yıldönümü münasebetile*, vol. 1 (Istanbul: Maarif Matbaası, 1940).

ALBISETTI, JAMES C., *Secondary School Reform in Imperial Germany* (Princeton: Princeton University Press, 1983).

ALKAN, MEHMET Ö., "Osmanlı İmparatorluğu'nda Eğitim ve Eğitim İstatistikleri, 1839–1924," in Halil İnalcık and Şevket Pamuk (eds.), *Osmanlı Devleti'nde Bilgi ve İstatistik/Data and Statistics in the Ottoman Empire* (Ankara: T. C. Başbakanlık İstatistik Enstitüsü, 2000).

ALLEN, ANN TAYLOR, "Feminism, Social Science, and the Meanings of Modernity: The Debate on the Origin of the Family in Europe and the United States, 1860–1914," *The American Historical Review*, 104/4 (1999), 1085–113.

ALLEN, WILLIAM, "The Abdul Hamid Photograph Collection," *History of Photography*, 8 (1984), 119–45.

ALSTON, PATRICK L., *Education and the State in Tsarist Russia* (Stanford, Cal.: Stanford University Press, 1969).

AMIN, CAMRON MICHAEL, "The Attentions of the Great Father: Reżā Shāh, 'the Woman Question,' and the Iranian Press, 1890–1946," Ph.D. diss., University of Chicago (1996).

AMIR-MOKRI, CYRUS, "Redefining Iran's Constitutional Revolution," Ph.D. diss., University of Chicago (1992).

ANDERSON, BENEDICT R. O'G., *Imagined Communities: Reflections on the Origin and Spread of Nationalism*, 2nd edn. (London: Verso, 1991).

ANTEL, SADRETTİN CELÂL, "Tanzimat Maarifi," in *Tanzimat; Yüzüncü yıldönümü münasebetile*, vol. 1 (Istanbul: Maarif Matbaası, 1940).

APPADURAI, ARJUN, "Disjuncture and Difference in the Global Cultural Economy," in Patrick Williams and Laura Crisman (eds.), *Cultural Discourse and Post-Colonial Theory: A Reader* (New York: Columbia University Press, 1994).

ASAD, TALAL, *Genealogies of Religion: Discipline and Reasons of Power in Christianity and Islam* (Baltimore: Johns Hopkins University Press, 1993).

AYDIN, MAHİR, *Şarkî Rumeli Vilâyeti*, Türk Tarih Kurumu Yayınları, 14/12. (Ankara: Türk Tarih Kurumu, 1992).

—— "Filibe Sergisi," *Belleten* 58/223 (1994), 659–84.

BAILEY, PAUL, "Translator's Introduction," in Marianne Bastid, *Educational Reform in Early Twentieth-Century China* (Ann Arbor: Center for Chinese Studies, University of Michigan, 1988), pp. vii–xi.

—— *Reform the People: Changing Attitudes Towards Popular Education in Early 20th Century China* (Edinburgh: Edinburgh University Press, 1990).

BAYKAL, KÂZIM, *Bursa ve Anıtları* (Bursa: Aysan Matbaası, 1950).

BELYEA, BARBARA, Review Article, Denis Wood's *The Power of Maps*, *Cartographica*, 29/3–4 (1992), 94–7.

BERKES, NİYAZİ, *The Development of Secularism in Turkey* (Montreal: McGill University Press, 1964).

—— *Türkiye'de Çağdaşlaşma* (Ankara: Bilgi Basımevi, 1973).

—— "Osmanlı Eğitiminden Laik Eğitimine Doğru," in Niyazi Berkes, *Felsefe ve Toplumbilim Yazıları* (Istanbul: Adam Yayınları, 1985).

BERKEY, JONATHAN, *The Transmission of Knowledge in Medieval Cairo: A Social History of Islamic Education* (Princeton: Princeton University Press, 1992).

BİLİCİ, FARUK, "Révolution française, révolution turque et fait religieux," *Revue du monde musulman et de la Méditerranée*, 52–3 (1989), 173–85.

BİNARK, İSMET et al., *Başbakanlık Osmanlı Arşivi Rehberi* (Ankara: T. C. Başbakanlık Devlet Arşivleri Genel Müdürlüğü, 1992).

BLACK, JEREMY, "Historical Atlases Reconsidered," *The Historian: The Magazine of the Historical Association*, 39 (1993), 16–20.

BLAKE, CORINNE, "Training Arab-Ottoman Bureaucrats: Syrian Graduates of the *Mülkiye Mektebi*, 1890–1920," Ph.D. diss., Princeton University (1991).

BLAKEMORE, J. B. and J. B. HARTLEY, "Concepts in the History of Cartography: A Review and Perspective," *Cartographica*, 17/4 (1980), 1–120.

BOURDIEU, PIERRE, *The State Nobility: Elite Schools in the Field of Power*, trans. Lauretta C. Clough (Cambridge: Polity Press, 1996).

BOZDOĞAN, SİBEL, "Architecture, Modernism and Nation-Building in Kemalist Turkey," *New Perspectives on Turkey*, 10 (Spring, 1994), 37–55.

BRAUDE, BENJAMIN, "Foundation Myths of the *Millet* System," in Braude and Lewis (eds.), *Christians and Jews in the Ottoman Empire* (1982).

—— and BERNARD LEWIS (eds.), *Christians and Jews in the Ottoman Empire: The Functioning of a Plural Society*, vol. I, *The Central Lands* (New York: Holmes & Meier, 1982).

BROOKS, JEFFREY, *When Russia Learned to Read: Literacy and Popular Literature, 1861–1917* (Princeton: Princeton University Press, 1985).

BROWN, L. CARL (ed.), *Imperial Legacy: The Ottoman Imprint on the Balkans and the Middle East* (New York: Columbia University Press, 1996).

BRUMMETT, PALMIRA, *Image and Imperialism in the Ottoman Revolutionary Press, 1908–1911* (Albany, NY: State University of New York Press, 2000).

BUISSERET, DAVID (ed.), *Monarchs, Ministers, and Maps: The Emergence of Cartography as a Tool of Government in Early Modern Europe*, The Kenneth Nebenzahl, Jr. Lectures in the History of Cartography (Chicago: University of Chicago Press, 1992).

BULLIET, RICHARD W., *Islam: The View from the Edge* (New York: Columbia University Press, 1994).

BUZPINAR, TUFAN, "Opposition to the Ottoman Caliphate in the Early Years of Abdülhamid II: 1877–1882," *Die Welt des Islams*, 36/1 (1996), 59–89.

ÇANKAYA, MÜCELLİDOĞLU ALİ, *Mülkiye Târihi ve Mülkiyeliler*, 2 vols. (Ankara: Örnek Matbaası, 1954).

—— *Son Asır Türk Tarihinin Önemli Olayları ile Birlikde Yeni Mülkiye Târihi ve Mülkiyeliler (Mülkiye Şeref Kitabı)*, 5 vols. (Ankara: Mars Matbaası, 1968–9).

ÇELİK, HÜSEYİN, *Ali Suavî ve Dönemi* (Istanbul: İletişim, 1994).

ÇELİK, ZEYNEP, *The Remaking of Istanbul: Portrait of an Ottoman City in the Nineteenth Century* (Seattle: University of Washington Press, 1986.)

CERTEAU, MICHEL DE, *The Practice of Everyday Life*, trans. Steven Rendall (Berkeley: University of California Press, 1984).

ÇETİN, ATİLLÂ, "Maarif Nâzırı Ahmed Zühdü Paşa'nın Osmanlı İmparatorluğundaki Yabancı Okullar Hakkında Raporu", *Güney-Doğu Avrupa Araştırmaları Dergisi*, 10–11 (1981–2), 189–219.

ÇETİN, ATILLÂ, "II. Abdülhamid'e Sunulmuş Beyrut Vilâyetindeki Yabancı Okullara dâir bir Rapor," *Türk Kültürü*, 253 (1984), 316–24.

ÇETİNSAYA, GÖKHAN, "Ottoman Administration of Iraq, 1890–1908," Ph.D. diss., University of Manchester (1994).

CHAMBERS, RICHARD L., "Notes on the *Mekteb-i Osmanî* in Paris, 1857–1874," in William R. Polk and Richard L. Chambers (eds.), *Beginnings of Modernization in the Middle East: The Nineteenth Century* (Chicago: University of Chicago Press, 1968).

—— "The Ottoman Ulema and the Tanzimat," in Nikki R. Keddie (ed.), *Scholars, Saints, and Sufis: Muslim Religious Institutions in the Middle East Since 1500* (Berkeley: University of California Press, 1972).

CHÂTELET, ANNE-MARIE, *Paris à l'école: "qui a eu cette idée folle . . ."* (Paris: Picard, 1993).

CHEHABI, HOUCHANG E., "Staging the Emperor's New Clothes: Dress Codes of Nation-Building Under Reza Shah," *Iranian Studies*, 26/3–4 (1993), 230–3.

CIOETA, DONALD J., "Ottoman Censorship in Lebanon and Syria, 1876–1908," *IJMES* 10 (1979), 167–86.

—— "Islamic Benevolent Societies and Public Education in Ottoman Syria, 1875–1882," *The Islamic Quarterly*, 26/1 (1982), 40–55.

CLANCY-SMITH, JULIA A., *Rebel and Saint: Muslim Notables, Populist Protest, Colonial Encounters (Algeria and Tunisia, 1800–1904)* (Berkeley: University of California Press, 1994).

CLARK, KATERINA and MICHAEL HOLQUIST, *Mikhail Bakhtin* (Cambridge, Mass.: Belknap, 1984).

CLEVELAND, WILLIAM L., *The Making of an Arab Nationalist* (Princeton: Princeton University Press, 1971).

COMMINS, DAVID DEAN, *Islamic Reform: Politics and Social Change in Late Ottoman Syria* (Oxford: Oxford University Press, 1990).

CRAIG, JOHN E., *Scholarship and Nation Building: The Universities of Strasbourg and Alsatian Society, 1870–1939* (Chicago: University of Chicago Press, 1984).

CURTIS, SARAH A., "Supply and Demand: Religious Schooling in Nineteenth-Century France," *History of Education Quarterly*, 39/1 (1999), 51–72.

DAKIN, DOUGLAS, *The Greek Struggle in Macedonia, 1897–1913* (Thessaloniki: Museum of the Macedonian Struggle, 1993).

DAVISON, RODERIC H., "Westernized Education in Ottoman Turkey," *MEJ* 15 (1961), 289–300.

—— *Reform in the Ottoman Empire, 1856–1876* (Princeton: Princeton University Press, 1963).

—— "The *Millet*s as Agents of Change in the Nineteenth-Century Ottoman Empire," in Braude and Lewis (eds.), *Christians and Jews in the Ottoman Empire* (1982).

—— *Essays in Ottoman and Turkish History, 1774–1923: The Impact of the West* (Austin: University of Texas Press, 1990).

DEGUILHEM, RANDI, "Government Centralization of Waqf Administration and its Opposition: The Syrian Example," in *BRISMES Proceedings of the 1991 International Conference on Middle East Studies* (Exeter: British Society for Middle Eastern Studies, 1991).

—— "State Civil Education in Late Ottoman Damascus: A Unifying or a Separating Force," in Thomas Philipp and Birgit Schaebler (eds.), *The Syrian Land: Processes of Integration and Fragmentation, Berliner Islamstudien*, 6 (Stuttgart: Franz Steiner Verlag, 1998).

DEGUILHEM-SCHOEM, RANDI CAROLYN, "History of Waqf and Case Studies from Damascus in Late Ottoman and French Mandatory Times," Ph.D. diss., New York University (1986).

—— "The Significance of the Awqāf Documents of 19th–20th Century Damascus to Current Research," in Abdeljelil Temimi (ed.), *Actes du VIᵉ Congrès du C.I.E.P.O. tenu a Cambridge sur: Les provinces arabes à l'époque ottomane* (Zaghouan, Tunisia: Centre d'Études et de Recherches Ottomanes et Morisco-Andalouses, 1987).

—— "Idées françaises et enseignement ottoman; l'école secondaire Maktab 'Anbar à Damas," *Revue du monde musulman et de la Méditerranée*, 52–3 (1989), 198–206.

DEMARIA, ROBERT, JR., *Samuel Johnson and the Life of Reading* (Baltimore: Johns Hopkins University Press, 1997).

DENY, J., *Grammaire de la langue turque (dialecte osmanli)*, Bibliothèque des langues orientales vivantes, 5 (Paris: Presses universitaires de France, 1921; repr., Niederwalluf bei Wiesbaden: Martin Sändig, 1971).

DERINGIL, SELIM, "The 'Residual Imperial Mentality' and the 'Urabi Paşa Uprising in Egypt: Ottoman Reactions to Arab Nationalism," in Abdeljelil Temimi (ed.), *Actes du VIᵉ Congrès du C.I.E.P.O. tenu a Cambridge sur: Les provinces arabes à l'époque ottomane* (Zaghouan, Tunisia: Centre d'Études et de Recherches Ottomanes et Morisco-Andalouses, 1987).

—— "The Ottoman Response to the Egyptian Crisis of 1881–82," *Middle Eastern Studies*, 24 (1988), 3–24.

—— "The Struggle Against Shiism in Hamidian Iraq: A Study in Ottoman Counter-Propaganda," *Die Welt des Islams*, 30 (1990), 45–62.

—— "Legitimacy Structures in the Ottoman State," *IJMES* 23 (1991), 345–59.

—— "The Invention of Tradition as Public Image in the Late Ottoman Empire, 1808–1908," *Comparative Studies in Society and History*, 35/1 (1993), 3–29.

DERİNGİL, SELİM, "The Ottoman Empire and Russian Muslims: Brothers or Rivals?", *Central Asian Survey*, 13/3 (1994), 409–16.

—— "II. Abdülhamid Döneminde Osmanlı Dış İlişkilerinde, 'İmaj' Saplantısı," in *Sultan II. Abdülhamid ve Devri Semineri, 27–29 Mayıs 1992*, Tarih Araştırma Merkezi, İstanbul Üniversitesi Edebiyat Fakültesi (Istanbul: Edebiyat Fakültesi Basımevi, 1994).

—— *The Well-Protected Domains: Ideology and the Legitimation of Power in the Ottoman Empire, 1876–1909* (London: I. B. Tauris, 1998).

DIAB, HENRY and LARS WÅHLIN, "The Geography of Education in Syria in 1882, with a Translation of 'Education in Syria' by Shahin Makarius, 1883," *Geografiska Annaler*, 65 B/2 (1983), 105–28.

DOĞAN, İSMAIL, *Tanzimatın İki Ucu: Münif Paşa ve Ali Suavi (Sosyo-pedagojik bir Karşılaştırma)* (Istanbul: İz Yayıncılık, 1991).

DOĞAN, NURİ, *İlk ve Orta Dereceli Okul Ders Kitapları ve Sosyalleşme (1876–1918)* (Istanbul: Bağlam, 1994).

DRESSEN, WOLFGANG, *Die pädagogische Maschine: Zur Geschichte des industrielisierten Bewusstseins in Preussen/Deutschland* (Frankfurt: Ullstein Materialien, 1982).

DUARA, PRASENJIT, "Review of *Siam Mapped: A History of the Geo-Body of a Nation* by Thongchai Winichakul," *The American Historical Review*, 100/2 (1995), 477–9.

DUGUID, STEPHEN, "The Politics of Unity: Hamidian Policy in Eastern Anatolia," *Middle Eastern Studies*, 9/2 (1973), 139–55.

DUMONT, PAUL, "Les Provinces arabes de l'Empire ottoman sous le règne d'Abdulhamid II, vues par les attachés militaires français," *Revue d'Histoire Maghrébine*, 39–49 (1985), 177–202.

—— "Les Transformations sociales dans l'empire ottoman (fin du XIXe–début du XXe siècle): Bilan des recherches en cours," *Turcica*, 19 (1987), 75–94.

—— "Said Bey—The Everyday Life of an Istanbul Townsman at the Beginning of the Twentieth Century," in Albert Hourani, Philip S. Khoury, and Mary C. Wilson (eds.), *The Modern Middle East: A Reader* (Berkeley: University of California Press, 1993).

DÜZDAĞ, ERTUĞRUL, *Şeyhülislam Ebusuûd Efendi Fetvaları Işığında 16. Asır Türk Hayatı* (Istanbul: Enderun, 1983).

EICKELMAN, DALE F. and JAMES PISCATORI, *Muslim Politics* (Princeton: Princeton University Press, 1996).

EKLOF, ARTHUR BENOÎT, "Spreading the Word: Primary Education and the Zemstvo in Moscow Province, 1864–1910," Ph.D. diss., Princeton University (1976).

ELDEM, EDHEM, "Istanbul: From Imperial to Peripheralized Capital," in

Edhem Eldem, Daniel Goffman, and Bruce Masters (eds.), *The Ottoman City Between East and West* (Cambridge: Cambridge University Press, 1999), 135–206.

ELDEM, VEDAT, *Osmanlı İmparatorluğunun İktisadi Şartları hakkında bir Tetkik* (Ankara: Türkiye İş Bankası Kültür Yayınları, 1970).

EMİL, BİROL, *Mizancı Murad Bey: Hayatı ve Eserleri* (Istanbul: Edebiyat Fakültesi Basımevi, 1979).

Encyclopaedia Britannica, 11th edn.

Encyclopaedia of Islam, 1st and 2nd edns.

ERASLAN, CEZMİ, "II. Abdülhamid'in Hilâfet Anlayışı," in *Sultan II. Abdülhamid ve Devri Semineri, 27–29 Mayıs 1992*, Tarih Araştırma Merkezi İstanbul Üniversitesi Edebiyat Fakültesi (Istanbul: Edebiyat Fakültesi Basımevi, 1994).

ERGİN, OSMAN NURİ, *İstanbul Meketpleri ve İlim, Terbiye ve San'at Müesseseleri Dolayısıyla Türkiye Maarif Tarihi*, 5 vols. (Istanbul: Osmanbey Matbaası, 1939–43).

EVİN, AHMET Ö., *Origins and Development of the Turkish Novel* (Minneapolis: Bibliotheca Islamica, 1983).

FARAH, CAESAR E., "Arabs and Turks: Common Heritage, Common Destiny," *Studies on Turkish–Arab Relations*, 1 (1986), 61–75.

—— "The Islamic Caliphate and the Great Powers: 1904–1914," *Studies on Turkish–Arab Relations*, 2 (1987), 37–48.

—— "Protestantism and British Diplomacy in Syria," *IJMES* 7 (1976), 321–44.

—— "A Tale of Two Missions," in *Arabic and Islamic Garland: Historical, Educational and Literary Papers Presented to Abdul-Latif Tibawi* (London: Islamic Cultural Centre, 1977).

FINDLEY, CARTER VAUGHN, *Bureaucratic Reform in the Ottoman Empire: The Sublime Porte, 1789–1922* (Princeton: Princeton University Press, 1980).

—— "The Acid Test of Ottomanism: The Acceptance of Non-Muslims in the Late Ottoman Bureaucracy," in Braude and Lewis (eds.), *Christians and Jews in the Ottoman Empire* (1982).

—— "The Advent of Ideology in the Islamic Middle East," *Studia Islamica*, 55 (1982), 143–69.

—— *Ottoman Civil Officialdom: A Social History* (Princeton: Princeton University Press, 1989).

FINN, ROBERT P., *The Early Turkish Novel, 1872–1900* (Istanbul: Isis Press, 1984).

FLEISCHER, CORNELL HUGH, *Bureaucrat and Intellectual in the Ottoman Empire: The Historian Mustafa Âli (1541–1600)* (Princeton: Princeton University Press, 1986).

FORTNA, BENJAMIN C., "Education for the Empire: Ottoman State Secondary Schools During the Reign of Sultan Abdülhamid II (1876–1909)," Ph.D. diss., University of Chicago (1997).

—— "Islamic Morality in Late Ottoman 'Secular' Schools," *IJMES* 32/3 (2000), 369–93.

—— "The Kindergarten in the Ottoman Empire and the Turkish Republic," in Roberta Wollons (ed.), *Kindergartens and Cultures: The Global Diffusion of an Idea* (New Haven: Yale University Press, 2000).

—— "Education and Autobiography at the End of Empire," *Die Welt des Islams*, 41/1 (2001), 1–31.

—— "Emphasizing the Islamic: Modifying the Curriculum of Late Ottoman State Schools," in Klaus Kreiser and François Georgeon (eds.), *Enfances et jeunesses dans l'histoire de l'islam* (Paris: Maisonneuve, 2001) (forthcoming).

FOUCAULT, MICHEL, *Discipline and Punish: The Birth of the Prison*, trans. Alan Sheridan (New York: Vintage Books, 1979).

FREITAG, ULRIKE, *Geschichtsschreibung in Syrien 1920–1990: zwischen Wissenschaft und Ideologie* (Hamburg: Deutsches Orient-Institut, 1991).

FRIERSON, CATHY A., *Peasant Icons: Representations of Rural People in Late Nineteenth-Century Russia* (New York: Oxford University Press, 1993).

FRIERSON, ELIZABETH BROWN, "Unimagined Communities: Women and Education in the Late-Ottoman Empire, 1876–1909," *Critical Matrix*, 9/2 (1995), 55–90.

—— "Unimagined Communities: State, Press, and Gender in the Hamidian Era," Ph.D. diss., Princeton University (1996).

—— "Mirrors Out, Mirrors In: Domestication and rejection of the Foreign in Late-Ottoman Women's Magazines (1875–1908)," in D. Fairchild Ruggles (ed.), *Women, Patronage, and Self-Representation in Islamic Societies* (Albany, NY: State University of New York Press, 2000).

—— "Cheap and Easy: The Creation of Consumer Culture in Late Ottoman Society," in Donald Quataert (ed.), *Consumption Studies and the History of the Ottoman Empire, 1550–1922: An Introduction* (Albany, NY: State University of New York Press, 2000).

FURET, FRANÇOIS and JACQUES OZOUF, *Reading and Writing: Literacy in France from Calvin to Jules Ferry* (Cambridge: Cambridge University Press, 1982).

GAVIN, CARNEY E. S. (ed.), *Imperial Self-Portrait: The Sultan Abdul-Hamid II's Photographic Albums* (Cambridge, Mass.: The Harvard Semitic Museum, 1989).

GELLNER, ERNEST, *Nations and Nationalism* (Ithaca, NY: Cornell University Press, 1983).

GEMIE, SHARIF, "'A Danger to Society'?—Teachers and Authority in France, 1833–1850," *French History*, 2/3 (1988), 264–87.

GEORGEON, FRANÇOIS, "La Formation des élites à la fin de l'Empire ottoman: le cas de Galatasaray," *Revue du monde musulman et de la Méditerranée*, 2/72 (1994), 15–25.

GHARAYBAH, 'ABD AL-KARĪM, *Sūrīyah fī al-qarn al-tāsiʿ ashar, 1840–1876* (Cairo: Dār al-Jīl, 1962).

GHAZZAL, ZOUHAIR, *L'Économie politique de Damas durant le XIXᵉ siècle: structures traditionelles et capitalisme* (Damascus: Institut Français de Damas, 1993).

GILDEA, ROBERT, *Education in Provincial France, 1800–1914* (Oxford: Clarendon Press, 1983).

GLASSIE, HENRY, *Turkish Traditional Art Today* (Bloomington: Indiana University Press, 1993).

GÖÇEK, FATMA MÜGE, *Rise of the Bourgeoisie, Demise of Empire: Ottoman Westernization and Social Change* (New York: Oxford University Press, 1996).

GÖKAY, BÜLENT, "Turkish Settlement and the Caucasus, 1918–1920," *Middle Eastern Studies*, 32/2 (1996), 45–76.

GOLDEN, PETER B., *An Introduction to the History of the Turkic Peoples*, *Turcologica*, 9 (Wiesbaden: Otto Harrasowitz, 1992).

GÖLE, NİLÜFER, *The Forbidden Modern: Civilization and Veiling* (Ann Arbor: University of Michigan Press, 1997).

—— "The Quest for the Islamic Self within the Context of Modernity," in Sibel Bozdoğan and Reşat Kasaba (eds.), *Rethinking Modernity and National Identity in Turkey* (Seattle: University of Washington Press, 1997).

GOODY, JACK, *Literacy in Traditional Societies* (London: Weidenfeld & Nicolson, 1964).

GOULD, PETER and RODNEY WHITE, *Mental Maps*, 2nd edn. (Boston: Allen & Unwin, 1986).

GÖVSA, İBRAHİM ALÂETTİN, *Türk Meşhurları Ansiklopedisi, Edibiyatta, Sanatta, İlimde, Harpte, Politikada ve her sahada şöhret kazanmış olan Türklerin Hayatları Eserleri* ([Istanbul]: Yedigün, n.d.).

GÖYÜNÇ, NEJAT, "Ottoman Central Administration and Arab Countries," *Studies on Turkish–Arab Relations*, 1 (1986), 76–84.

GRABILL, JOSEPH L., *Protestant Diplomacy and the Near East: Missionary Influence on American Policy, 1810–1927* (Minneapolis: University of Minnesota Press, 1971).

GROISS, ARNON, "Minorities in a Modernizing Society: Secular vs. Religious Identitites in Ottoman Syria, 1840–1914," *Princeton Papers in Near Eastern Studies*, 3 (1994), 39–70.

GÜRAN, TEVFİK, *Tanzimat Döneminde Osmanlı Maliyesi: Bütçeler ve Hazine Hesapları (1841–1861)* (Ankara: Türk Tarih Kurumu Basımevi, 1989).

HALLS, W. D., *Education, Culture and Politics in Modern France* (Oxford: Pergamon, 1976).

HANİOĞLU, M. ŞÜKRÜ, *Bir Siyasal Örgüt Olarak Osmanlı İttihad ve Terakki Cemiyeti ve Jön Türklük: Cilt I (1889–1902)* (Istanbul: İletişim, 1985).

—— *The Young Turks in Opposition* (New York: Oxford University Press, 1995).

HARLEY, J. B. and DAVID WOODWARD, *The History of Cartography*, Vol. 2, Book 1, *Cartography in the Traditional Islamic and South Asian Societies* (Chicago: The University of Chicago Press, 1992).

HARRIGAN, PATRICK J., *Mobility, Elites and Education in French Society of the Second Empire* (Waterloo, Can.: Wilfrid Laurier University Press, 1980).

HAYDAROĞLU, İLKNUR POLAT, *Osmanlı İmparatorluğu'nda Yabancı Okullar* (Ankara: Kültür Bakanlığı, 1990).

HEIDBORN, A., *Droit public et administratif de l'empire ottoman*, 2 vols. (Vienna: C. W. Stern, 1912).

HERSHLAG, ZVI YEHUDA, "The Late Ottoman Finances: A Case Study in Guilt and Punishment," in Osman Okyar and Halil İnalcık (eds.), *Türkiye'nin Sosyal ve Ekonomik Tarihi (1071–1920)/Social and Economic History of Turkey (1071–1920)* (Ankara: Meteksan, 1980).

HEYD, URIEL, *Foundations of Turkish Nationalism: The Life and Teachings of Ziya Gökalp* (London: Luzac, 1950).

HOBSBAWM, ERIC JOHN, *Nations and Nationalism Since 1780: Programme, Myth, Reality* (Cambridge: Cambridge University Press, 1990).

HODGSON, MARSHALL GOODWIN SIMMS, *The Venture of Islam: Conscience and History in a World Civilization*, 3 vols. (Chicago: University of Chicago Press, 1974).

HOLOD, RENATA and AHMET EVİN (eds.), *Modern Turkish Architecture* (Philadelphia: University of Pennsylvania Press, 1984).

HOPWOOD, DEREK, *The Russian Presence in Syria and Palestine, 1834–1914: Church and Politics in the Near East* (Oxford: Clarendon Press, 1969).

HOURANI, ALBERT, "Ottoman Reform and the Politics of the Notables," in William R. Polk and Richard L. Chambers (eds.), *Beginnings of Modernization in the Middle East: The Nineteenth Century* (Chicago: University of Chicago Press, 1968).

HUREWITZ, J. C. (ed.), *The Middle East and North Africa in World Politics: A Documentary Record*, 2nd edn., vol. 1, *European Expansion, 1535–1914* (New Haven: Yale University Press, 1975).

İHSANOĞLU, EKMELEDDİN, "Qirā'ah li-tarīkh al-dawlah al-'uthmāniyyah wa 'alāqātihā bil-'ālam al-'arabiyyah min khilāl kutub al-tarīkh al-madrasiyyah al-muqarrarah fī Miṣr bayn 'āmī 1913–1980 m.," *Studies on Turkish–Arab Relations*, 1 (1986), 118–85.

"Imperial Self-Portrait: The Ottoman Empire as Revealed in Sultan Abdul-Hamid II's Photographic Albums," Special Edition of the *Journal of Turkish Studies*, 12 (1988).

İNAL, İBNÜLEMİN MAHMUD KEMAL, *Osmanlı Devrinde Son Sadrıazamlar*, 4 vols. (Istanbul: Maarif Basımevi, 1955).

İNALCIK, HALİL, "Application of the Tanzimat and its Social Effects," *Archivum Ottomanicum*, 5 (1973), 97–127.

—— "Arab–Turkish Relations in Historical Perspective (1260–1914)," *Studies on Turkish–Arab Relations*, 1 (1986), 148–57.

—— "Biases in Studying Ottoman History," *Studies on Turkish–Arab Relations*, 2 (1987), 7–10.

—— *The Ottoman Empire: The Classical Age 1300–1600* (New Rochelle, NY: Caratzas, 1989).

İNALCIK, HALİL with DONALD QUATAERT (eds.), *An Economic and Social History of the Ottoman Empire, 1300–1916* (Cambridge: Cambridge University Press, 1994).

ISSAWI, CHARLES, *The Economic History of the Middle East, 1800–1914: A Book of Readings* (Chicago: University of Chicago Press, 1966).

—— *The Economic History of Turkey, 1800–1914* (Chicago: University of Chicago Press, 1980).

—— "The Transformation of the Economic Position of the *Millet*s in the Nineteenth Century," in Braude and Lewis (eds.), *Christians and Jews in the Ottoman Empire* (1982).

İslâm Ansiklopedisi.

İZZET, MEHMED, MEHMED ESAD, OSMAN NURİ, and ALİ KAMİ, *Darüşşafaka, Türkiye'de İlk Halk Mektebi: Darüşşafaka nasıl doğdu, ne hizmetler etti, nasıl yaşiyor?* (Istanbul: Evkaf-ı İslamiye Matbaası, 1927).

JACKSON, PHILIP W., ROBERT E. BOOSTROM, and DAVID T. HANSEN, *The Moral Life of Schools* (San Francisco: Jossey-Bass, 1993).

JACOB, CHRISTIAN, "Review Article of *Cartography in The Traditional Islamic and South Asian Societies*," *Cartographica*, 30/4 (1993), 78–82.

JELAVICH, CHARLES and BARBARA, *The Establishment of the Balkan National States, 1804–1920*, A History of East Central Europe, vol. 8 (Seattle: University of Washington Press, 1977).

JOHANSEN, BABER, *Islam und Staat: Abhängige Entwicklung, Verwaltung des Elends und religiöser Antiimperialismus* (Berlin: Argument Verlag, 1982).

KAFADAR, CEMAL, *Between Two Worlds: The Construction of the Ottoman State* (Berkeley: University of California Press, 1995).

KARACA, ALİ, *Anadolu Islahâtı ve Ahmet Şâkir Paşa (1838–1899)* (Istanbul: Eren, 1993).

KARAMUSTAFA, AHMET T., "Introduction to Islamic Maps," in Harley and Woodward (eds.), *The History of Cartography*, Vol. 2, Book 1 (1992).

—— "Introduction to Ottoman Cartography," in Harley and Woodward (eds.), *The History of Cartography*, vol. 2, Book 1 (1992).

—— "Military, Administrative, and Scholarly Maps and Plans," in Harley and Woodward (eds.), *The History of Cartography*, Vol. 2, Book 1 (1992).

KARK, RUTH and SHIMON LANDMAN, "The Establishment of Muslim Neighborhoods in Jerusalem, Outside the Old City, during the Late Ottoman Period," *Palestine Exploration Quarterly*, 112 (1980), 113–35.

KARPAT, KEMAL, "The Land Regime, Social Structure, and Modernization in the Ottoman Empire," in William R. Polk and Richard L. Chambers (eds.), *Beginnings of Modernization in the Middle East: The Nineteenth Century* (Chicago: University of Chicago Press, 1968).

—— *An Inquiry into the Social Foundations of Nationalism in the Ottoman State: From Social Estates to Classes, From Millets to Nations* (Princeton: Center of International Studies, Princeton University, 1973).

—— *Ottoman Population, 1830–1914: Demographic and Social Characteristics* (Madison: University of Wisconsin Press, 1985).

—— "Images of Turks and Arabs in School Books," *Studies on Turkish–Arab Relations*, 2 (1987), 17–19.

—— "The Ottoman Ethnic and Confessional Legacy in the Middle East," in Milton J. Esman and Itamar Rabinovich (eds.), *Ethnicity, Pluralism, and the State in the Middle East* (Ithaca, NY: Cornell University Press, 1988).

—— "The Civil Rights of the Muslims of the Balkans," *Asian and African Studies*, 27/1–2 (1993), 25–45.

KASABA, REŞAT, "Treaties and Friendships: British Imperialism, the Ottoman Empire, and China in the Nineteenth Century," *Journal of World History*, 4/2 (1993), 215–41.

—— "Kemalist Certainties and Modern Ambiguities," in Sibel Bozdoğan and Reşat Kasaba (eds.), *Rethinking Modernity and National Identity in Turkey* (Seattle: University of Washington Press, 1997).

KASSIS, HANNA E., *A Concordance of the Qur'an* (Berkeley: University of California Press, 1983).

KAYALI, HASAN, *Arabs and Young Turks: Ottomanism, Arabism, and Islamism in the Ottoman Empire, 1908–1918* (Berkeley: University of California Press, 1997.)

KAYRA, CAHİT (ed.), *İstanbul Haritaları; Ortaçağdan Günümüze* (Istanbul: Türkiye Sınaî Kalkınma Bankası, 1990).

KAZAMIAS, ANDREAS M., *Education and the Quest for Modernity in Turkey* (Chicago: University of Chicago Press, 1966).

—— *Politics, Society and Secondary Education in England* (Philadelphia: University of Pennsylvania Press, 1966).

—— and BYRON G. MASSIALIS, *Tradition and Change in Education: A Comparitive Study* (Englewood Cliffs, NJ: Prentice-Hall, 1965).

KEDDIE, NIKKI R., "Secularism and the State: Toward Clarity and Global Comaprison," *New Left Review*, 226 (1997), 21–40.

KEYDER, ÇAĞLAR, "Ottoman Economy and Finances (1881–1918)," in Osman Okyar and Halil İnalcık (eds.), *Türkiye'nin Sosyal ve Ekonomik Tarihi (1071–1920)/Social and Economic History of Turkey (1071–1920)* (Ankara: Meteksan, 1980).

—— "Whither the Project of Modernity?: Turkey in the 1990s," in Sibel Bozdoğan and Reşat Kasaba (eds.), *Rethinking Modernity and National Identity in Turkey* (Seattle: University of Washington Press, 1997).

KHALID, ADEEB, *The Politics of Muslim Cultural Reform: Jadidism in Central Asia* (Berkeley: University of Calfornia Press, 1998).

KHALIDI, RASHID ISMAIL, "Social Factors in the Rise of the Arab Movement in Syria," in Said Amir Arjomand (ed.), *From Nationalism to Revolutionary Islam* (Albany, NY: State University of New York Press, 1984).

—— "Ottomanism and Arabism in Syria before 1914: A Reassessment," in Rashid Khalidi *et al.* (eds.), *The Origins of Arab Nationalism* (New York: Columbia University Press, 1991).

—— "Society and Ideology in Late Ottoman Syria: Class, Education, Profession and Confessionalism," in John Spagnolo (ed.), *Taking the Long View on the Modern Middle East: Essays in Honor of Albert Hourani* (Oxford: St Antony's College Middle East Monograph Series, 1991).

KHOURY, PHILIP S., *Syria and the French Mandate: The Politics of Arab Nationalism, 1920–1945* (Princeton: Princeton University Press, 1987).

KLEINERT, CLAUDIA, *Die Revision der Historiographie des Osmanischen Reiches am Beispiel von Abdülhamid II: Das späte Osmanische Reich im Urteil türkischer Autoren der Gegenwart (1930–1990)*, *Islamkundliche Untersuchungen*, 188 (Berlin: Klaus Schwarz Verlag, 1995).

KOCABAŞOĞLU, UYGUR, *Kendi Belgeleriyle Anadolu'daki Amerika; 19. Yüzyılda Osmanlı İmparatorluğu'ndaki Amerikan Misyoner Okulları* (Istanbul: Arba, 1989).

KOÇER, HASAN ALİ, *Türkiye'de Modern Eğitimin Doğuşu ve Gelişimi (1773–1923)* (Istanbul: Millî Eğitim Basımevi, 1970).

KODAMAN, BAYRAM, *Abdülhamid Devri Eğitim Sistemi* (Ankara: Türk Tarih Kurumu, 1988).

KREISER, KLAUS, "Public Monuments in Turkey and Egypt, 1840–1916," *Muqarnas*, 14 (1997), 103–17.

KUNTAY, MİDHAT CEMAL, *Sarıklı İhtilalci Ali Suavi* (Istanbul: Ahmet Halit Kitabevi, 1946).

KURAN, ERCÜMEND, "The Impact of Nationalism on the Turkish Elite in the Nineteenth Century," in William R. Polk and Richard L. Chambers (eds.), *Beginnings of Modernization in the Middle East: The Nineteenth Century* (Chicago: University of Chicago Press, 1968).

KUSHNER, DAVID, *The Rise of Turkish Nationalism* (London: Frank Cass, 1977).

—— "The Place of the Ulema in the Ottoman Empire During the Age of Reform (1839–1918)," *Turcica*, 19 (1987), 51–74.

KÜTÜKOĞLU, MÜBAHAT S., *Osmanlı Belgelerinin Dili (Diplomatik)* (Istanbul: Kubbealtı Akademisi Kültür ve San'at Vakfı, 1994).

KYRRIS, KOSTAS, "Turkish–Cypriot Education 1850–1905 With Reference to the Greek Community: A Case-Study of Transmission from Dominance to Non-Dominance," *Études balkaniques*, 26/4 (1990), 50–69.

LAMBTON, ANN K. S., *Qajar Persia: Eleven Studies* (London: I. B. Tauris, 1987).

LANDAU, JACOB M., "The Beginnings of Modernization in Education: The Jewish Community in Egypt as a Case Study," in William R. Polk and Richard L. Chambers (eds.), *Beginnings of Modernization in the Middle East: The Nineteenth Century* (Chicago: University of Chicago Press, 1968).

—— *The Politics of Pan-Islam: Ideology and Organization* (Oxford: Clarendon Press, 1990).

LAUWERYS, JOSEPH A., "Politics and Education," in *Arabic and Islamic Garland: Historical, Educational and Literary Papers Presented to Abdul-Latif Tibawi* (London: Islamic Cultural Centre, 1977).

LEWIS, BERNARD, *The Emergence of Modern Turkey*, 2nd edn. (London: Oxford University Press, 1968).

—— *The Political Language of Islam* (Chicago: University of Chicago Press, 1988).

LORY, BERNARD and ALEXANDRE POPOVIC, "Au carrefour des Balkans, Bitola 1816–1918," in Paul Dumont and François Georgeon (eds.), *Villes Ottomanes à la fin de l'Empire* (Paris: L'Harmattan, 1992).

MCCARTHY, JUSTIN, *Muslims and Minorities: The Population of Ottoman Anatolia and the End of the Empire* (New York: New York University Press, 1983).

MACINTYRE, ALASDAIR, *After Virtue: A Study in Moral Theory* (Notre Dame, Ind.: University of Notre Dame Press, 1981).

MANDAVILLE, JON, "Memduh Pasha and Aziz Bey: Ottoman Experience in Yemen," in B. R. Pridham (ed.), *Contemporary Yemen: Politics and Historical Background* (New York: St Martin's, 1984).

Ma'oz, Moshe, "The Impact of Modernization on Syrian Politics and Society During the Early *Tanzimat* Period," in William R. Polk and Richard L. Chambers (eds.), *Beginnings of Modernization in the Middle East: The Nineteenth Century* (Chicago: University of Chicago Press, 1968).

—— *Ottoman Reform in Syria and Palestine, 1840–1861: The Impact of the Tanzimat on Politics and Society* (Oxford: Clarendon Press, 1968).

—— (ed.), *Studies on Palestine During the Ottoman Period* (Jerusalem: Magnes Press, 1975).

Mardin, Şerif, *The Genesis of Young Ottoman Thought: A Study in the Modernization of Turkish Political Ideas* (Princeton: Princeton University Press, 1962).

—— "Power, Civil Society and Culture in the Ottoman Empire," *Comparative Studies in Society and History*, 11/3 (1969), 258–81.

—— "Super Westernization in Urban Life in the Ottoman Empire in the Last Quarter of the Nineteenth Century," in Peter Benedict, Erol Tümertekin, and Fatma Mansur (eds.), *Turkey: Geographic and Social Perspectives* (Leiden: E. J. Brill, 1974).

—— *Religion and Social Change in Modern Turkey: The Case of Bediüzzaman Said Nursi* (Albany, NY: State University of New York Press, 1989).

—— "The Nakşibendi Order in Turkish History," in Richard Tapper (ed.), *Islam in Modern Turkey: Religion, Politics and Literature in a Secular State* (London: I. B. Tauris, 1991).

—— "The Ottoman Empire," in Karen Barkey and Mark von Hagen (eds.), *After Empire: Multiethnic Societies and Nationbuilding* (Boulder, Col.: Westview Press, 1997).

—— "Projects as Methodology: Some Thoughts on Modern Turkish Social Science," in Sibel Bozdoğan and Reşat Kasaba (eds.), *Rethinking Modernity and National Identity in Turkey (*Seattle: University of Washington Press, 1997).

Markova, Zina, *Bulgarian Exarchate 1870–1879* (Sofia: Bulgarian Academy of Sciences, 1989).

Marshall, Byron K., *Learning To Be Modern: Japanese Political Discourse on Education* (Boulder, Col.: Westview Press, 1994).

Masters, Bruce, "The View from the Province: Syrian Chronicles of the Eighteenth Century," *JAOS* 114/3 (1994), 353–62.

Matthee, Rudi, "Transforming Dangerous Nomads into Useful Artisans, Technicians, Agriculturalists: Education in the Reza Shah Period," *Iranian Studies*, 26/3–4 (1993), 313–36.

Matthews, Roderic D. and Matta Akrawi, *Education in Arab Countries of the Near East* (Washington, DC: American Council on Education, 1949).

MAYNARD, RICHARD E., "The Lise and its Curriculum in the Turkish Educational System," Ph.D. diss., University of Chicago (1961).

MENASHRI, DAVID, *Education and the Making of Modern Iran* (Ithaca, NY: Cornell University Press, 1992).

MESSICK, BRINKLEY, *The Calligraphic State: Textual Domination and History in a Muslim Society* (Berkeley: University of California Press, 1993).

MEYER, JOHN W. and W. RICHARD SCOTT, *Organizational Environments: Ritual and Rationality* (Beverly Hills, Cal.: Sage Publications, 1983).

MIROIU, MIHAI, "Changing Attitudes towards the Ottomans in Romanian Historiography," *New Perspectives on Turkey*, 12 (1995), 119–28.

MITCHELL, TIMOTHY, *Colonising Egypt* (Cambridge: Cambridge University Press, 1988; repr. Berkeley: University of California Press, 1991).

MITLER, LOUIS, *Contemporary Turkish Writers: A Critical Bio-Bibliography of Leading Writers in The Turkish Republican Period up to 1980*, *Ural and Altaic Series*, 146 (Bloomington: Indiana University Research Institute for Inner Asian Studies, 1988).

MOGHADAM, VALENTINE R., "Rhetorics and Rights of Identity in Islamist Movements," *Journal of World History*, 4/2 (1993), 243–64.

MONMONIER, MARK, *How To Lie With Maps* (Chicago: University of Chicago Press, 1991).

——*Mapping It Out: Expository Cartography for the Humanities and Social Sciences* (Chicago: University of Chicago Press, 1993).

——*Drawing the Line: Tales of Maps and Cartocontroversy* (New York: Henry Holt, 1994).

MOTTAHEDEH, ROY P., *The Mantle of the Prophet: Religion and Politics in Iran* (New York: Simon and Schuster, 1985).

MUGHEID, TURKI, *Sultan Abdulhamid II. im Spiegel der arabischen Dichtung: Eine Studie zu Literatur und Politik in der Spätperiode des Osmanischen Reiches*, *Islamkundliche Untersuchungen*, 112 (Berlin: Klaus Schwarz Verlag, 1987).

MÜLLER, DETLEF, FRITZ RINGER, and BRIAN SIMON (eds.), *The Rise of the Modern Educational System: Structural Change and Social Reproduction, 1870–1920* (Cambridge: Cambridge University Press, 1987).

——"The Process of Systematization: The Case of German Secondary Education," in Müller, Ringer, and Simon (eds.), *The Rise of the Modern Educational System* (1987).

NAKASH, YITZHAK, "The Conversion of Iraq's Tribes to Shi'ism," *IJMES* 26/3 (1994), 443–63.

NALBANTOĞLU, GÜLSÜM BAYDAR, "The Professionalization of the Ottoman-Turkish Architect," Ph.D. diss., University of California (1989).

NEBİOĞLU, OSMAN, *Türkiye'de Kim Kimdir: Yaşayan Tanınmış Kimseler Ansiklopedisi* (Istanbul: Nebioğlu Yayınevi, 1961–2).

O'BOYLE, LENORE, "A Possible Model for the Study of Nineteenth-Century Secondary Education in Europe," *Journal of Social History*, 12/2 (1978), 236–47.

OKAY, ORHAN, *Batı Medeniyeti karşısında Ahmed Midhat Efendi* (Ankara: Baylan Matbaası, 1975).

ÖKE, MİM KEMAL, *İngiliz casusu Prof. Arminius Vambery'nin gizli raporlarında II. Abdülhamid ve Dönemi* (Istanbul: Üçdal Neşriyat, 1983).

Organization of Islamic Conference, *Ottoman Year-Books (Salname and Nevsal): A Bibliography and Union Catalogue with Reference to Istanbul Libraries* (Istanbul: Research Centre for Islamic History, Art and Culture (IRCICA), 1982).

ORTAYLI, İLBER, *İkinci Abdülhamit Döneminde Osmanlı İmparatorluğunda Alman Nüfuzu*, Ankara Üniversitesi Siyasal Bilgiler Fakültesi Yayınları, 479 (Ankara: Ankara Üniversitesi Basımevi, 1981).

—— "Some Observations on American Schools in the Ottoman Empire," *Turkish Public Administration Annual*, 8 (1981), 93–110.

—— "Ideological Structure of Syria and Lebanon in the 19th Century and Ottoman Counter-measures," *Revue d'Histoire Maghrébine*, 37–8 (1985), 149–55.

—— "Nineteenth Century Ottoman Administration and the Arabic Language," *Studies on Turkish–Arab Relations*, 1 (1986), 193–7.

—— *İmparatorluğun En Uzun Yüzyılı* (Istanbul: Hil Yayın, 1987).

—— *Studies on Ottoman Transformation, Analecta Isisiana*, 10 (Istanbul: The Isis Press, 1994).

OWEN, ROGER, *The Middle East in the World Economy, 1800–1914* (London: Methuen, 1981).

—— "Defining Traditional: Some Implications of the Use of Ottoman Law in Mandatory Palestine," *Harvard Middle East and Islamic Review*, 1/2 (1994), 115–31.

ÖZDALGA, ELISABETH, "Education in the Name of Order and Progress: Problems Related to the Recent Eight Year Obligatory School Reform in Turkey," paper presented at the Annual Meetings of the Middle East Studies Association, 6 Dec. 1998, Chicago.

—— *The Veiling Issue, Official Secularism and Popular Islam in Modern Turkey* Nordic Institute of Asian Studies Report Series, 33 (London: Curzon, 1998).

ÖZDEMİR, BÜLENT, "Ottoman Reforms and Social Life: Reflections from Salonica, 1830–1850," PhD. diss., University of Birmingham (2000).

ÖZDEMİR, KEMAL, *Osmanlı Deniz Haritaları Ali Macar Reis Atlası* (Istanbul: Marmara Bankası, 1992).

ÖZER, BÜLENT, *Rejonyalizm, Üniversalizm ve Çağdaş Mimarimiz üzerine bir Deneme* (Istanbul: İstanbul Teknik Üniversitesi Mimarlık Fakültesi, 1964).

ÖZGÜVEN, BURCU, "İdadî binaları," *Tarih ve Toplum*, 14/82 (1990), 44–7.

ÖZÖN, MUSTAFA NİHAT, *Türkçede Roman*, 2nd edn. (Istanbul: İletişim, 1985).

OZOUF, MONA, *L'École, l'église et la république, 1871–1914* (Paris: Editions Cana, 1982).

ÖZTUNCAY, BAHATTİN, *James Robertson, Pioneer of Photography in the Ottoman Empire* (Istanbul: Eren, 1992).

PÂKALIN, MEHMED ZEKİ, *Son Sadrâzamlar ve Başvekiller* (Istanbul: Ahmet Sait Matbaası, 1942).

—— *Osmanlı Tarih Deyimleri ve Terimleri Sözlüğü* (Istanbul: Millî Eğitim Basımevi, 1946).

PARLA, TAHA, *The Social and Political Thought of Ziya Gökalp, 1876–1924* (Leiden: E. J. Brill, 1985).

PFEIFFER, BALDUR ED., *The European Seventh-day Adventist Mission in the Middle East, 1879–1939* (Frankfurt: Peter Lang, 1981).

Piri Reis Haritası (Istanbul: T. C. B. Seyir ve Hidrografi Dairesi, 1966).

PITCHER, DONALD EDGAR, *An Historical Geography of the Ottoman Empire From Earliest Times to the End of the Sixteenth Century, with Detailed Maps to Illustrate the Expansion of the Sultanate* (Leiden: E. J. Brill, 1972).

QUATAERT, DONALD, "Part IV: The Age of Reforms," in Halil İnalcık with Donald Quataert, *An Economic and Social History of the Ottoman Empire, 1300–1914* (Cambridge: Cambridge University Press, 1994).

RAHME, YOUSSEF G., "Religious Alterity in the Thought of Islamic Reformers in the Ottoman Empire, 1856–1905," Ph.D. diss., University of Chicago (1994).

RAMSAUR, ERNEST EDMONDSON, *The Young Turks: Prelude to the Revolution of 1908* (Princeton: Princeton University Press, 1957).

REESE, WILLIAM J., *The Origins of the American High School* (New Haven: Yale University Press, 1995).

RINGER, FRITZ, "On Segmentation in Modern European Educational Systems: The Case of French Secondary Education, 1865–1920," in Müller, Ringer, and Simon (eds.), *The Rise of the Modern Educational System* (1987).

RODED, RUTH, "Social Patterns Among the Urban Elite of Syria During the Late Ottoman Period (1876–1918)," in David Kushner (ed.), *Palestine in the Late Ottoman Period: Political, Social, and Economic Transformation* (Jerusalem: Yad Izhak Ben-Zvi, 1986).

RODRIGUE, ARON, *French Jews, Turkish Jews: The Alliance Israélite Universelle and the Politics of Jewish Schooling in Turkey, 1860–1925* (Bloomington: Indiana University Press, 1990).

ROGAN, EUGENE L. "Aşiret Mektebi: Abdülhamid II's School for Tribes (1892–1907)," *IJMES* 28/1 (1996), 83–107.

—— *Frontiers of the State in the Late Ottoman Empire: Transjordan, 1850–1921*, Cambridge Middle East Studies, 12 (Cambridge: Cambridge University Press, 1999).

—— "The Political Significance of an Ottoman Education: Maktab 'Anbar Revisited," paper presented for the Syria III Conference, Bilad al-Sham: Processes of Identities and Ideologies from the 18th Century to the End of the Mandatory Period, Erlangen, 28 July–2 Aug. 2000.

RUNDSTROM, ROBERT A., "Mapping, Postmodernism, Indigenous People and the Changing Direction of North American Cartography," *Cartographica*, 28/2 (1991), 1–12.

SACK, ROBERT DAVID, *Human Territoriality: Its Theory and History* (Cambridge: Cambridge University Press, 1986).

SAKAOĞLU, NECDET, *Osmanlı Eğitim Tarihi* (Istanbul: İletişim, 1991).

SALIBI, KAMAL, *A House of Many Mansions: The History of Lebanon Reconsidered* (Berkeley: University of California Press, 1988).

SALMONI, BARAK, "Islam in Turkish Educational Materials, 1923–1950," paper presented at the Annual Meeting of the Middle East Studies Association, Washington, DC, 21 Nov. 1999.

SALT, JEREMY, *Imperialism, Evangelism and the Ottoman Armenians, 1878–1896* (London: Frank Cass, 1993).

SAQIB, GHULAM NABI, *Modernization of Muslim Education in Egypt, Pakistan, and Turkey: A Comparative Study* (Lahore: Islamic Book Service, 1983).

SCHILCHER, LINDA SCHATKOWSKI, *Families in Politics: Damascene Factions and Estates of the 18th and 19th Centuries*, Berliner Islamstudien, Band 2. (Stuttgart: Franz Steiner Verlag, 1985).

SCHLEUNES, KARL A., *Schooling and Society: The Politics of Education in Prussia and Bavaria, 1750–1900* (Oxford: Berg, 1989).

SCHÖLCH, ALEXANDER, *Palästina im Umbruch, 1856–1882: Untersuchungen zur wirtschaftlichen und sozio-politischen Entwicklung*, Berliner Islamstudien, Band 4. (Stuttgart: Franz Steiner Verlag, 1986).

SCHULZE, REINHARD, *Geschichte der Islamischen Welt im 20. Jahrhundert* (Munich: Verlag C. H. Beck, 1994).

—— "Was ist die Islamische Aufklärung?" *Die Welt des Islams*, 36/3 (1996), 317–25.

SCOTT, W. RICHARD, JOHN W. MEYER *et al.*, *Institutional Environments and*

Organizations: Structural Complexity and Individualism (Thousand Oaks, Cal.: Sage Publications, 1994).

SEIKALY, SAMIR M., "As Seen from Damascus: Kurd 'Ali's View of the Ottoman Empire," in Abeljelil Temimi (ed.), *Actes du VIe Congrès du CIEPO tenu a Cambridge sur: Les Provinces arabes à l'époque ottomane* (Zaghouan, Tunisia: Centre d'Études et de Recherches Ottomanes et Morisco-Andalouses, 1987).

ŞENİ, NORA, "Fashion and Women's Clothing in the Satirical Press of Istanbul at the End of the 19th Century," in Şirin Tekeli (ed.), *Women in Turkish Society: A Reader* (London: Zed Books, 1995).

SHAMIR, SHIMON, "The Modernization of Syria: Problems and Solutions in the Early Period of Abdülhamid," in William R. Polk and Richard L. Chambers (eds.), *Beginnings of Modernization in the Middle East: The Nineteenth Century* (Chicago: University of Chicago Press, 1968).

SHAW, EZEL KURAL, "Midhat Pasha, Reformer or Revolutionary; His Administrative Career and Contributions to the Constitution of 1876," Ph.D. diss., Harvard University (1975).

SHAW, STANFORD JAY, "Some Aspects of the Aims and Achievements of the Nineteenth-Century Ottoman Reformers," in William R. Polk and Richard L. Chambers (eds.), *Beginnings of Modernization in the Middle East: The Nineteenth Century* (Chicago: University of Chicago Press, 1968).

—— "The Yıldız Palace Archives of Abdülhamit II," *Archivum Ottomanicum*, 3 (1971), 211–37.

—— "A Promise of Reform: Two Complimentary Documents," *IJMES* 4 (1973), 359–65.

—— and EZEL KURAL SHAW, *History of the Ottoman Empire and Modern Turkey*, Vol. II, *Reform, Revolution, and Republic; The Rise of Modern Turkey* (Cambridge: Cambridge University Press, 1977).

ŞİŞMAN, ADNAN, *Galatasaray Mekteb-i Sultânîsî'nin Kuruluşu ve İlk Eğitim Yılları, 1868–1871* (Istanbul: Edebiyat Fakültesi Basımevi, 1989).

SMITH, ANTHONY D., *The Ethnic Origins of Nations* (Oxford: Blackwell, 1987).

SOMEL, AKŞİN, "Das Grundschulwesen in den Provinzen des Osmanischen Reiches während der Herrschaftsperiode Abdülhamid II. (1876–1909)," Ph.D. diss., Universität Bamberg, (1993).

SONYEL, SALÂHİ R., *Minorities and the Destruction of the Ottoman Empire, Publications of Turkish Historical Society*, 7/129 (Ankara: Turkish Historical Society Printing House, 1993).

SÖZEN, METİN, *Anadolu Medreseleri; Selçuklu ve Beylikler Devri*, 2 vols. (Istanbul: İstanbul Teknik Üniversitesi Matbaası, 1970).

SPAGNOLO, J. P., "French Influence in Syria Prior to World War I: The Functional Weakness of Imperialism," *MEJ* 23/1 (1969), 45–62.

SPULER, BERTOLD, "Das Schulwesen im Rahmen der Kulturentwicklung der südeuropäischen Völker im 19. Jh.," in *Arabic and Islamic Garland: Historical, Educational and Literary Papers Presented to Abdul-Latif Tibawi* (London: Islamic Cultural Centre, 1977).

ST LAURENT, BEATRICE, "Ottomanization and Modernization: The Architectural and Urban Development of Bursa and the Genesis of Tradition, 1839–1914," Ph.D. diss., Harvard University (1989).

—— "Ottoman Power and Westernization: The Architecture and Urban Development of Nineteenth and Early Twentieth Century Bursa," *Anatolia Moderna/Yeni Anadolu*, 5 (1994), 199–232.

STARRETT, GREGORY, *Putting Islam to Work: Education, Politics, and Religious Transformation in Egypt* (Berkeley: University of California Press, 1998).

STAVRIANOS, L. S., *The Balkans Since 1453* (New York: Holt, Rinehart, and Winston, 1965).

STEPPAT, FRITZ, "National Education Projects in Egypt Before the British Occupation," in William R. Polk and Richard L. Chambers (eds.), *Beginnings of Modernization in the Middle East: The Nineteenth Century* (Chicago: University of Chicago Press, 1968).

—— "Eine Bewegung unter den Notabeln syriens: Neues Licht auf die Entstehung des arabischen Nationalismus," in Wolfgang Voigt (ed.), *XVII. Deutscher Orientalistentag, Würzburg* (Wiesbaden: Franz Steiner Verlag, 1969).

STOCK-MORTON, PHYLLIS, *Moral Education For a Secular Society: The Development of Moral Laïque in Nineteenth Century France* (Albany, NY: State University of New York Press, 1988).

STONE, FRANK ANDREWS, *Academies for Anatolia; A Study of the Rationale, Program and Impact of the Educational Institutions Sponsored by the American Board in Turkey: 1830–1980* (Lanham, Md.: University Press of America, 1984).

STROHMEIER, MARTIN, "Muslim Education in the Vilayet of Beirut, 1880–1918," in Caesar E. Farah (ed.), *Decision Making and Change in the Ottoman Empire* (Kirksville, Miss.: Thomas Jefferson University Press, 1993).

—— *Seldschukische Geschichte und türkische Geschichtswissenschaft: Die Seldschuken im Urteil moderner türkischer Historiker, Islamkundliche Untersuchungen*, 97 (Berlin: Klaus Schwarz Verlag, 1984).

SUBTELNY, EVA MARIA and ANAS B. KHALIDOV, "The Curriculum of Islamic Higher Learning in Timurid Iran in the Light of the Sunni Revival under Shāh-Rukh," *JAOS* 115/2 (1995), 210–36.

SUNGU, İHSAN, "Galatasary Lisesinin Kuruluşu," *Belleten*, 7/28 (1943), 315–47.

SZYLIOWICZ, JOSEPH, *Education and Modernization in the Middle East* (Ithaca, NY: Cornell University Press, 1973).

TAESCHNER, FRANZ, "Djughrafiya: The Ottoman Geographers," *EI2* 2 (Leiden: E. J. Brill, 1963), 587–90.

—— "Osmanlılarda Coğrafya," *Türkiyât Mecmuası*, 2 (1926), 271–314.

Tanzimat devrine ait bir kısım Resimler ve Vesikalar (Istanbul: Maarif Matbaası, 1940).

TEKELİ, İLHAN, "Tanzimat'tan Cumhuriyet'e Eğitim Sistemindeki Değişmeler," in *Tanzimat'tan Cumhuriyet'e Türkiye Ansiklopedisi*, ii. 456–75.

TEMIMI, ABDELJELIL, "Modern Historiography as Applied to the History of the Arab Provinces in the Ottoman Period and the Problem of History Schoolbooks," *Studies on Turkish–Arab Relations*, 2 (1987), 21–5.

THOBIE, JACQUES, *Intérêts et imperialisme français dans l'Empire Ottoman (1895–1914)* (Paris: Imprimerie nationale, 1977).

TIBAWI, ABDUL LATIF, *British Interests in Palestine, 1800–1901: A Study of Religious and Educational Enterprise* (Oxford: Oxford University Press, 1961).

—— *American Interests in Syria, 1800–1901: A Study of Educational, Literary and Religious Work* (Oxford: Clarendon Press, 1966).

—— "Greater Syria 1876–1890; Divided Loyalties: Ottoman, Muslim, or Arab," *The Islamic Quarterly*, 11 (1967), 8–33.

—— *A Modern History of Syria, Including Lebanon and Palestine* (London: Macmillan, 1969).

—— *Islamic Education: Its Traditions and Modernization into the Arab National Systems* (London: Luzac, 1972).

—— *Arabic and Islamic Themes: Historical, Educational and Literary Studies* (London: Luzac, 1976).

TODOROVA, MARIA, "Bulgarian Historical Writing on the Ottoman Empire," *New Perspectives on Turkey*, 12 (1995), 97–118.

TRIMBERGER, ELLEN KAY, *Revolution From Above: Military Bureaucrats and Development in Japan, Turkey, Egypt, and Peru* (New Brunswick, NJ: Transaction Books, 1978).

TRIPP, CHARLES, "Islam and the Secular Logic of the State in the Middle East," in Abdel Salam Sidahmed and Anoushirvan Ehteshami (eds.), *Islamic Fundamentalism* (Boulder, Col.: Westview Press, 1996).

—— *A History of Iraq* (Cambridge: Cambridge University Press, 2000).

Tübinger Atlas des Vorderen Orients (TAVO) der Universität Tübingen (Wiesbaden: Dr Ludwig Reichert Verlag, 1990).

TUĞLACI, PARS, *Osmanlı Mimarlığında Batılılaşma Dönemi ve Balyan Ailesi* (Istanbul: İnkilâp ve Aka, 1981).

Türk Dili ve Edebiyatı Ansiklopedisi.

TÜRKAY, CEVDET, *Osmanlı Türlkerinde Coğrafya* (Istanbul: Maarif Basımevi, 1959).

TURNBULL, DAVID, *Maps are Territories; Science is an Atlas: A Portfolio of Exhibits* (Chicago: University of Chicago Press, 1993).

ÜNAL, HASAN, "Young Turk Assessments of International Politics, 1906–1909," *Middle Eastern Studies*, 32/ 2 (1996), 30–44.

UNAT, FAİK REŞİT, *Türkiye Egitim Sisteminin Gelişmesine Târihi bir Bakış* (Ankara: Millî Eğitim Basımevi, 1964).

VICKERS, MIRANDA, *The Albanians: A Modern History* (London: I. B. Tauris, 1995).

VIKØR, KNUT S., "Muhammadan Piety and Islamic Enlightenment: Survey of a Historiographical Debate," paper presented at the ISMM, Istanbul Workshop, July 1998.

WASTI, S. TANVIR, "The Last Chroniclers of the Mabeyn," *Middle Eastern Studies*, 32/2 (1996), 1–29.

WEBER, EUGEN, *Peasants into Frenchmen: The Modernization of Rural France, 1870–1914* (Stanford: Stanford University Press, 1976).

WILLIAMSON, BILL, *Education, Social Structure and Development: A Comparative Analysis* (New York: Homes & Meier, 1979).

—— *Education and Social Change in Egypt and Turkey: A Study in Historical Sociology* (London: Macmillan, 1987).

WINICHAKUL, THONGCHAI, *Siam Mapped: A History of the Geo-Body of a Nation* (Honolulu: University of Hawaii Press, 1994).

WOLF, ARMIN, "What Can the History of Historical Atlases Teach? Some Lessons from a Century of Putzger's 'Historischer Schul-Atlas,'" *Cartographica*, 28/2 (1991), 21–37.

WOLLONS, ROBERTA, "The Black Forest in a Bamboo Garden: Missionary Kindergartens in Japan, 1868–1912," *History of Education Quarterly*, 33/1 (1993), 1–35.

YAZICI, NESİMİ, "Son Dönemde Karahisar-ı Sahib Medreseleri ve Islah-ı Medâris Uygulaması," *Belleten*, 58/223 (1994), 635–57.

YÜCEL, HASAN ALİ, *Türkiyede Orta Öğretim* (Istanbul: Devlet Basımevi, 1938).

ZELDIN, THEODORE, "Introduction: Were there Two Frances?" in Theodore Zeldin (ed.), *Conflicts in French Society: Anticlericalism, Education and Morals in the Nineteenth Century* (London: Allen & Unwin, 1970).

—— *France 1848–1945*, Vol. 2, *Intellect, Taste, and Anxiety* (Oxford: Clarendon Press, 1977).

ZILFI, MADELINE C., *The Politics of Piety: The Ottoman Ulema in the Post-classical Age (1600–1800)*, *Studies in Middle Eastern History*, 8 (Minneapolis: Bibliotheca Islamica, 1988).

ZIRINSKY, MICHAEL P., "A Panacea for the Ills of the Country: American Presbyterian Education in Inter-War Iran," *Iranian Studies*, 26/1–2 (1993 [–4]), 119–37.

ZÜRCHER, ERIK J., *Turkey: A Modern History* (London: I. B. Tauris, 1993).

INDEX